Journal of the Early Book Society
for the study of manuscripts and printing history

Edited by Martha W. Driver
Volume 10, 2007

Copyright © 2007
Pace University Press
41 Park Row, Rm. 1510
New York, NY 10038

ISBN: 0-944473-84-9 (pbk: alk.ppr.)
ISSN: 1525-6790

Member

(CELJ)

Council of Editors of Learned Journals

™ The paper used in this publication meets the minimum require-
ments of American National Standard for information Sciences—
Permanence of Paper for printed Library Materials,
ANSI Z39.48—1984.

The *Journal of the Early Book Society* is published annually. JEBS invites longer articles on manuscripts and/or printed books produced between 1350 and 1550. Special consideration will be given to essays exploring the period of transition from manuscript to print. Articles should not exceed 8000 words or thirty typed pages. Authors are asked to follow *The Chicago Manual of Style*. A Works Cited list at the end of the text should include city, publisher, and date. Manuscripts are to be sent, in triplicate, along with an abstract of up to 150 words, to Martha Driver, Early Book Society, Department of English, Pace University, 41 Park Row, New York, New York 10038. Only materials accompanied by a self-addressed, stamped envelope (or international reply coupon) will be returned. Members of the Early Book Society who are recent authors may send review books for consideration to Susan Powell, Reviews Editor, School of English, Sociology, Politics and Contemporary History (ESPaCH), University of Salford, Salford M5 4WT UK. Brief notes on recent discoveries, highlighting little-known or recently uncovered texts and/or images, may be sent to Linne R. Mooney, Centre for Medieval Studies, King's Manor, University of York, York YO1 2EP UK. Subscription information may be obtained from Martha Driver or from Pace University Press.

Those interested in joining the Early Book Society or with editorial inquiries may contact Martha Driver by post or e-mail (MDriver@Pace.edu). Information may also be found at <www.nyu.edu/projects/EBS>. For ordering information, call Pace University Press at 212-346-1405 or visit http://www.pace.edu/press. Institutions and libraries may purchase copies directly from Ingram Library Services (1-800-937-5300).

The editor wishes to thank Gill Kent, as well as Justin Colby, Graduate Assistant, and Mark Hussey of Pace University Press, for their help and advice on this issue.

Journal of the Early Book Society
For the Study of Manuscript and Printing History

Editor:
Martha W. Driver, *Pace University*

Associate Editors:
Linne R. Mooney, *University of York*
Susan Powell, *University of Salford*

Editorial Board
Norman F. Blake, *University of Sheffield*
Julia Boffey, *University of London, Queen Mary and Westfield College*
Cynthia J. Brown, *University of California, Santa Barbara*
Richard F. M. Byrn, *University of Leeds*
James Carley, *York University*
Joyce Coleman, *University of North Dakota*
Susanna Fein, *Kent State University*
Vincent Gillespie, *Lady Margaret Hall, Oxford University*
Stanley S. Hussey, *Lancaster University*
Ann M. Hutchison, *Pontifical Institute of Mediaeval Studies and York University*
Charlotte C. Morse, *Virginia Commonwealth University*
Daniel W. Mosser, *Virginia Polytechnic Institute and State University*
Ann Eljenholm Nichols, *Winona State University*
Judy Oliver, *Colgate University*
Michael Orr, *Lawrence University*
Steven Partridge, *University of British Columbia*
Derek Pearsall, *Harvard University*
Robert Raymo, *New York University*
Pamela Sheingorn, *Baruch College and The City University of New York Graduate School and University Center*
Toshiyuki Takamiya, *Keio University*
John Thompson, *Queen's University, Belfast*
Ronald Waldron, *King's College, University of London*
Edward Wheatley, *Hamilton College*
Mary Beth Winn, *SUNY Albany*

Contents

Anne Bulkeley and Her Book in Early Tudor England

ALEXANDRA BARRATT

The importance of the study of private prayer books to our knowl-edge of late medieval literate culture, particularly that of women, and its rel-ative neglect have been recently brought to our attention by Mary C. Erler. In *The Cambridge History of the Book in Britain*, she writes:

> Closely allied to books of hours are the *preces privatae*, books of prayers collected by an owner for private use and hence individual in their choice of material. Though these books have not been given much attention, they offer a rich conspectus of popular devotion. In addi-tion, study of their hands and their choice of texts might provide additional insights on literacy, since the conjunction of Latin and English prayers is frequent. How, for instance, were these two lan-guages employed in private prayer by owners who would convention-ally be considered unlikely to be fully Latinate? . . . Prayer books, whether *horae* or personal compilations, are located at the intersec-tion of the emotive, the aesthetic, the personal and the religious, and thus must always have sustained an uneasy balance amongst these conflicting elements.[1]

My forthcoming study *Anne Bulkeley and Her Book in Early Tudor England*, of which this article will form the first chapter, seeks to redress this imbalance and to pursue some of the lines of inquiry that Erler suggests. It concerns itself with British Library MS Harley 494, a volume that has many of the features of a *preces privatae* volume but also contains a number of brief prose treatises: it might be conventionally described as a devotional miscellany, but that would understate the extent to which it was probably planned as a whole. MS Harley 494 has two further features of interest: it belonged to a woman, Dame (or Lady) Anne Bulkeley, and regardless of the precise identity of the owner, it clearly emerged from a Bridgettine "textual community" in that it contains a number of Latin and English devotional texts that were particularly associated with Saint Bridget of Sweden and the male and female English Bridgettines of Syon Abbey. Although women's book ownership was becoming much less uncommon in the later Middle Ages, any book that has a well-documented association with a woman–particularly with a member of the gentry rather than the aristocracy–is worth careful scrutiny. As Erler has written:

> evidence of women's book ownership is scarce. . . .Attention to non-aristocratic women readers . . . may offer both broader evidence of women's literacy and more complex ways of viewing this evidence in relation to cultural patterns. [2]

As for the Bridgettines, their role in late medieval English religious culture can hardly be overestimated and is indeed becoming subject to more and more intensive study.[3]

The concept of "textual community" was originally developed and popularized by Brian Stock in the context of heretical groups and their activities during the High Middle Ages, at a time when literacy and direct access to texts were severely limited. Stock regards a textual community as a form of "literacy influenced group organization," marked by "a use of texts, both to structure the internal behavior of the groups' members and to provide solidarity against the outside world."[4] The formation of such a community depended upon at least one individual "who, having mastered [the unifying text], then utilized it for reforming a group's thought and action." Clearly, the later Middle Ages was a very different environment, characterized by varying degrees of literacy far more widely diffused, but Felicity Riddy and others have developed and used the concept of the textual community in the sense of a subculture, united by an interest in particular texts, as an analytic tool in discussing women's literate practice.[5] Riddy shows how women, both "nuns and pious gentlewomen," constructed such communities by giving each other books and reading them together in small groups or *familiae*.[6] It is in this sense that the term is used here.

The manuscript in question, MS Harley 494, is a modest little book of English and Latin prayers and English devotional treatises, written on paper. It consists of:

> 113 paper leaves numbered from 1-110 (the first leaf is unnumbered, and there are two leaves numbered 4 and two numbered 90. The duplicated leaves are marked with a star*, and 90* is blank). Pages measure 144mm x 113mm; written space varies but the ruled space measures 109mm x 70mm, with between 17 and 20 lines to the page.[7]

The collation is difficult to assess, as the volume is very tightly bound (it was rebound in the 1990s). It appears to be as follows: 1^4; 2^{12}; 3^6; 4^4; 5-6^{16}; 7^{20} (or possibly $7a$-b^{10}); 8-9^{16}; 10^4. This is supported by catchwords, which are found on folios 15v, 21v, 25v, 41v, 57v, 77v, and 90*v. From the watermarks it seems that folios 4 or 5 to 106 are all of one paper stock: the watermark "is a glove with star/flower on stem protruding from one finger." There is no exact match in Briquet, but the closest examples are from the 1520s and 1530s.[8] The manuscript is plain and lacks decoration; it contains a large number of hands, discussed further below.

On the flyleaf a sixteenth-century hand has written, "Domine Anne BVLKELEY/ Attinet Liber iste" ("this book belongs to Lady, or Dame, Anne Bulkeley"), and this name appears again on the first folio. The inscription, in the form of a crudely rhyming couplet, is an unequivocal claim to ownership, unlike a name simply written in a book, as Rebecca Krug rightly points out.[9] But the concept of "ownership" can be problematic and has to be distinguished (sometimes) from those of "patron" and "donor," as Kathleen Scott explains:

> The term 'original ownership' may need brief clarification. I take the patron of a book (not its text) to be the person who – as far as one can tell today – first started its production by a scribe or scribes and by decorators, whether or not through an intermediary. If the patron kept the book for him– or herself, then the patron subsequently became the 'original owner'. . . .If the patron had a book prepared with the intention of making a gift of it . . . then the patron subsequently became a donor. . . .all patrons are not donors, nor are all donors . . . patrons of books (though they might be considered as patronizing the church or institution to which they gave books). Nor indeed are all original owners patrons, if they purchased a ready-made book.[10]

"Anne Bulkeley" was definitely the owner of Harley 494 at some time in its history; whether she was also the "patron" and whether in due course she became its "donor" are fascinating questions.

The contents of Harley 494 are of considerable interest and inevitably bear on the identity, character, and predilections of the owner and/or compiler(s), as it is quite likely the book was compiled if not at Anne Bulkeley's direct request, then at the very least with her specific spiritual needs and devotional preferences in mind. The constituent texts are extremely diverse and drawn from a surprising number of sources. They demand detailed individual attention, but for our present purposes they are here listed in summary, with very brief descriptions, incipits, and brief notes on the scribal hands. (The numeration of this list is somewhat arbitrary: some of the individual "items" in fact consist of several discrete parts, sometimes drawn from quite different sources.)

1. fol. 1r-v (Hand A) English elevation prayer. Incipit: "I do salute the moste holy body."

2. fols 2-4 (Hand B) Five Latin prayers on the Five Joys of the Resurrection. Incipit: "Laudo amo adoro."

3. fols 4r-4#r (Hand B) Eight Latin prayers for the Gifts of the Holy Spirit. Incipit: "Veni sancte spiritus."

4. fol. 4#r (Hand C) Latin prayer invoking Saint Onuphrius. Incipit: "Omnipotens se|m|piterne deus."

5. fol. 4#v (Hand D) Latin prayer to the Virgin. Incipit: "|O| gloriosa Domina."

6. fols 6-19v (Hand E) English treatise on daily living. Incipit: "The gret cause as I do thynke" (Jolliffe H.8, O.14). Includes some Latin prayers.

7. fol. 20 (Hand F) Latin office of the Virgin. Incipit: "Ave iesu cui mater uirgo sit et filia."

8. fols 20v-21v (Hand G) Eight English prayers structured around the days of the week (from Sunday to Saturday). Incipit: "O good Jhesu I beseche the."

9. fols 22-25 (Hand E) English treatise on preparation for communion. Incipit: "Intierly belouyde in god."

10. fols 26-30 (Hand E) "A short meditacion and informacyon of oure lorde Jhu schewyd to seynt Mawde by reuelacion," English treatise on morning devotions. Incipit: "In the nyght or in the mornyng." Includes some Latin prayers.

11. fols 30-31 (Hand E) English devotional exercise in self-examination. Incipit: "In the mornynge. Take good heed how þou hast gouernede the." Includes a Latin prayer.

12. fols 31-33v (Hand E) Instructions on intercessory prayer. Incipit: "Because we here haue ordured you to pray."

13. fols 33v-35 (Hand E) Four English intercessory prayers. Incipit: "The forme of prayer after an oþer maner. Vse wheþer ye like best."

14. fols 35v-61 (Hand E) "For þe receiuing of þe sacrament," English treatise. Incipit: "When ye purpose to receiue oure lorde." Followed by a series of English prayers and a final prayer in Latin.

15. fols 61v-62 (Hand H), "Certane prayers schewyd vnto a devote person callyd Mary Ostrewyk," English devotional exercise. Incipit: "Fyrst in remembraunce of the Wounde."

16. fols 62r-v (Hand I) English prayers for Gifts of the Holy Spirit. Incipit: "Lorde god ffather allmyghty."

17. fols 63-75 (Hand E) "Meditacions for tyme of the Masse," English treatise. Incipit: "The preste goynge to masse."

18. fols 75-82v (Hand E) "a deuoute meditacion and a thankefull orison to owre Lorde for his mannyfold giftes and benefettes," English prayer or set of prayers. Incipit: "O my lord god Jhesu Christ."

19. fols 82v-84v (Hand E) English translation of the O *intemerata*. Incipit: "O pure & blessid."

20. fols 84v-85 (Hand E) Set of English prayers to the Virgin. Incipit: "Thes be þe x vertues of oure lady."

21. fols 85v-89v (Hand E) "Contemplacion for the ffeste of þe Assumpcion," English enumeration of the Virgin's two sets of Seven Joys. Incipit: "The first singulere joye." Followed by a prayer, "O glorious lady quene & empresse of heuen."

22. fols 88v-89v (Hand E) English translation of chapter from Saint Bridget, *Revelationes*. Incipit: "Our lady apperid to seynt Brigitt & seyde I am the quene of heuen."

23. fols 89v-90 (Hand J) English devotion. Incipit: "A thousand tymys aue marie ye schall sey." Includes a Latin prayer with Incipit: "Adonay domine deus magnus et mirabilis."

24. fols 91-96 (Hand E) "a schorte confessionall for religious persons," English confessional formula. Incipit: "Confiteor … I knolege to almighti god." (Jolliffe C.25, O.25; E.1 (b); O.1. (b))

25. fols 96v-98v (Hand E) "An exclamacion of a penytent synner," English prayer. Incipit: "A synfulle wreche a miserable synnere."

26. fols 98v-100v (Hand E) Latin prayer to the Virgin. Incipit: "O intemerata."

27. fols 101-104 (Hand K) "Here after folowith the vij sorowes of our blessid lady," set of seven English prayers. Incipit: "O lady Mary temple of the trinite."

28. (i) fols 105r-v (Hand L) "Here folow þe bedis of pardon in englyshe of saynt gregorys pyte," English prayers. Incipit: "O swete blessyd Jhu"; (ii) fols 105v-106v set of three Latin prayers, each followed by a similar but not identical prayer in English. Incipit: "Aue maria eterni patris sponsa."

29. fol. 106v (Hand M) Latin prayer. Incipit: "Gracias ago tibi omnipotens deus."

30. fol. 107 (Hand N) Two short English prayers. Incipit: "Cast þi selff downe before oure lorde prostrate & say this. My synnys o lord."

31. fol. 107 (Hand O) Very short English note. Incipit: " Sorow for sin."

32. fols 107v-110 (Hand P) Series of three Latin prayers followed by English paraphrases, the Latin written in one script, the English in another. Incipit: "Marci peto de te des mihi dormire quiete. . . Domine ihu xpe qui illuminasti."

33. f. 110v (Hand Q) Short English prayer. Incipit: "All hayle moste benigne Jesu."

A surprisingly large number of scribes – at least seventeen – have contributed to the body of the manuscript. The principal scribe, Hand E, has written sixteen items, including all the longer devotional texts: Ian Doyle has identified him as Robert Taylor, Clerk of the Works at Syon Abbey during the early sixteenth century.[11] The Clerk of the Works was in control of Syon's extensive building operations, which were ongoing: Taylor held the position by 1501 and was still there in 1509 or even later.[12] He wrote out and signed the only manuscript of the Bridgettine *Myroure of Oure Ladye* (now split between Aberdeen University Library MS 134 and Oxford, Bodley MS Rawlinson C. 941).[13] He also wrote out British Library MS Harley 554, a translation of Savonarola's book on the life of widows. In addition, throughout the manuscript between the more substantial items many other hands (sixteen is my current reckoning) have copied out various short prayers and devotions. None of these hands has written more than a couple of pieces, and none recurs.[14] Could it be that the sixteen hands other than Robert Taylor's belong to the Bridgettine nuns of Syon? The Syon Additions for the Sisters decreed, "Silence after some convenience is to be kepte in the lybrary, whyls any suster is there alone in recordynge of her redynge," and Mary Erler has suggested that this unusual phrase "recordynge of her redynge" "is perhaps identical with the making of *florilegia* which Johannes Trithemius, among other authorities, urged on monastics."[15] Indeed, in the early sixteenth century, Syon Abbey regularly purchased paper, from 1518/19 onwards in quite large quantities. In 1528/9 the abbey spent four shillings and sixpence on one ream (twenty quires) and ten quires. Thirty quires of paper are equivalent to 720 sheets, which would make 5,760 pages. This evidence suggests "the production of a large number of books." [16]

As there are several possible owners, the precise dating of Harley 494 becomes very important. We can in fact do this with some confidence. Harley 494 contains adaptations of several early printed texts written by the Bridgettine fathers Richard Whitford and William Bonde, the printed versions of which cluster around 1530, but far more important is the presence of item 15, found on folios 61v-62. This is a spiritual exercise structured around the Five Wounds of Christ and identified by the scribe as "schewyd vnto a devote person callyd Mary Ostrewyk."

Marie d'Oisterwijk (also known as Maria van Hout) was probably born about 1470. She initially lived a devout life at home in Oisterwijk, which is now in the Netherlands but at that time was in Brabant, and later became a beguine. In 1530, while head of her small community, she met Gerhard Kalckbrenner, a Carthusian monk at the Charterhouse of Cologne. She began a correspondence with him and came to regard him as her spiritual son. In 1545, she moved to Cologne with two of her sisters in order to live near Kalckbrenner's charterhouse, a quite unprecedented arrangement as Carthusians in general went to extreme lengths to avoid contact with living women, however holy. She died on September 30, 1547.

The English text found in Harley 494 derives, by some route or other, from a spiritual exercise composed by Marie on "The Five Wounds of Christ." In 1531 Kalckbrenner had published some of Marie's writings and correspondence, including this exercise, written in Ripuarian (the dialect of Cologne and the Rhine River) rather than in Marie's native Brabant dialect.[17] The book, printed by Johann von Kempen, was entitled *Der rechte wech zo der evangelischer volkonenheit* (*The Right Path to Evangelical Perfection*), and we find the relevant exercise on signatures M6r-N5r. In his introduction Kalckbrenner gives no details about the author, not even her name, merely attributing the text to "a simple and pious person, whose name is known to God."[18] In the following year a Latin translation of part of the exercise was printed in Cologne: there is a copy of this in the Basel Universitätsbibliothek, DA VI 19 no. 13. Once again the text, found on signatures A4r-v, which is introduced by "Brother Gerard of Hamon, procurator of the Carthusians in Cologne" (that is, Kalckbrenner, who was procurator before becoming prior in 1536), is not attributed to Marie by name but to "a certain virgin, on close terms with God and most devout" ("virgo quaedam . . . deo intima ac deuotissima," sig. A1r). Kalckbrenner goes on to give some considerable detail about her spiritual history but still does not include her name, though she may well have been readily identifiable by some of his readers. In contrast, a manuscript version of another Latin translation of some of Marie's writings, including the Five Wounds exercise, found in Darmstadt MS 1204, does attribute the text to Marie. It heads the passage "Exercitium Mariae Osterwijk revelatum" (fol. 13v) but offers no further information on the author, though later in the manuscript the compiler refers to her several times as "Mater."

Probably, therefore, Harley 494 cannot be earlier than 1531 or, more likely, 1532. As we demonstrate here on codicological grounds, it is unlikely that this passage is a late addition, and although the hand in which this particular text is written (Hand H) does not otherwise appear in the manuscript, we argue further that the manuscript was conceived and written as a whole. However, neither the German nor the Latin printed editions of 1531 and 1532 identify the author of the exercise, while Harley 494 is in no doubt that the prayers were revealed to "a devote person callyd Mary Ostrewyk." The compiler(s) must either have had access to privileged information or have come into contact with the exemplar or cognates of Darmstadt 1204. (They cannot have known the latter manuscript itself as it was compiled no earlier than 1536.[19])

A final complication is that as Kirsten M. Christensen states: "Maria wrote originally . . . for the edification of her own sisters. Then when Kalckbrenner met her, he took these extant devotional writings with him to Cologne for publication."[20] And the vernacular version tells us that it was originally addressed to or composed for a community of religious women.[21] It begins:

> Hie nae volget ein geistlige oeffunge de der vurß persoenen van got geoffenbaert is tzo behoef aller goder menschen . . . *wie sy selver schrift tzo eynem convent alsoe* [emphasis mine] (fol. M6r)

> (Here now follows a spiritual exercise which to the aforementioned person was revealed by God to assist all good people . . . *which she herself wrote to a convent as follows.*)

The Five Wounds exercise, therefore, clearly existed in manuscript in its original Brabant dialogue before it was printed. Christensen discusses the likelihood that Kalckbrenner "altered the language slightly," effectively translating Marie's writings into Ripuarian for publication purposes, but concludes that otherwise "the published version . . . likely does not diverge much from Maria's original."[22] But whether it circulated widely — or at all — is a different matter. It still seems unlikely that it could have been known in England before the early 1530s: it was only then that Marie came to the notice of the Cologne Carthusians, who made a real effort to introduce her writings to a wider world and who had the international connections to disseminate her writings.

But it is still a puzzle how this obscure contemporary beguine (who must have been still alive when Harley 494 was compiled, although there is no indication of this in the text) comes to surface in this English book of prayers and devotions. The English manuscript, although well informed about Marie's name, either conceals or at least occludes her status as a beguine (as indeed did her German editor, Kalckbrenner, though possibly for different reasons).[23] There were of course no beguines as such in England, and so she is merely described as a "devout person"; this would seem to imply that she was not a religious. And as far as we know at present, there was no English translation available of Marie d'Oisterwijk's writings, whether of the vernacular or Latin versions. But the explanation for her presence in Harley 494 is probably quite simple. Marie was very much under Carthusian sponsorship and patronage, and the Charterhouse of Cologne in particular was active in making available in print the writings of male and female mystics, both living and dead. (For instance, they printed the *editiones principes* of both Gertrud of Helfta and Mechtild of Hackeborn.) There were strong links between the continental and the English Carthusians, and also between the Sheen Charterhouse and Syon, just across the Thames.

Having established a *terminus a quo* of 1531, we can also deduce the latest date by which the manuscript could have been written. Item 10, which occupies folios 26-35 and is entitled "A short meditacion and informacyon of oure lorde Jhu schewyd to seynt Mawde by reuelacion," can be shown to consist of at least four texts from different sources, although the manuscript includes no indication of this. Of these, the third is a series of intercessory prayers derived from Richard Whitford's *Golden Pystle* and begins on folio 31v. On this leaf a reference to the pope has been erased in the following passage:

> Ffurst after the ordre of charite pray for your selff, I trust ye will
> not forget. Seconde for your parentz, þat is your fathers & moders
> spirituall, as the |pope *erased*|, the bysshope, your curatz, person,
> wykare, or eny prest þat hath hard your confession.

It was precisely on June 3, 1535, that Thomas Cromwell wrote to all the diocesan bishops, instructing them "to ensure the removal of the pope from all religious services, by having the name (*papa*) erased wherever it occurred in any 'mass books and other books used in the churches.'"[24] We can be sure, therefore, that the original text in the hand of Robert Taylor was written before 1535. We can also deduce that the book continued to be in use during and after that date.

This dating of Harley 494 as written between 1531 or 1532 and 1535, in other words immediately before the unforeseen catastrophe of the Dissolution of the Monasteries, is highly suggestive. The period was crucial for the future of Catholicism and the Reformation in England, and saw the execution of Sir Thomas More and Bishop John Fisher as well as the rise and fall of the Kentish nun Elizabeth Barton, a visionary who was much encouraged by Syon Abbey and its abbess.

Having established a fairly precise dating for the manuscript, we are in a better position to address the question: who was the Anne Bulkeley who owned this book? Humfrey Wanley, the original cataloguer of the Harley manuscripts, described Harley 494 as *"formerly belonging to the Lady Anne Bulkeley; who (as I suppose) was Abbess of* (Syon?) (Berkynge?)."[25] Certainly she was neither, though unfortunately we do not know the reasons for what may have been only an educated guess on Wanley's part. (Harley 494 was presumably acquired as part of Robert Harley's block purchase of the collection of Sir Simonds D'Ewes, who died in 1650; those manuscripts became MSS Harley 1 to Harley 600 approximately.[26] There is, however, no "certain indication" that D'Ewes ever owned this manuscript.[27])

There are several possible candidates for the orginal ownership of Harley 494. A Mistress Anne Bulkeley gave a copy of a late-fifteenth-century version of the *Somme le Roi*, translated by one of the knights of King Henry V (possibly Sir Robert Shottesbrook) and by him entitled "Aventure and Grace,"[28] now Oxford, Bodley MS e Museo 23, to a Thomas Ringwood. The donation is recorded on folio 161v in the form, "Ex dono magistre Anne Bulkeley," and the catalogue dates the hand as "about 1500." The Latin title *magistra* bestowed on the donor is presumably a translation of the English term "mistress," which could indicate a married or unmarried secular woman but would not be used of a nun, though the *Somme le roi* was an immensely popular work of religious instruction.

An Alicia (also known as Anne) Bukley was a nun at Syon Abbey at the end of the fifteenth century. She died on November 6, 1495, and her name is recorded in the Syon Martirloge (BL MS Add. 22285, fol. 62v).[29] Whether or not "Bukley" is a possible spelling of "Bulkeley" is hard to gauge: in any case, Alicia Bukley died too early to be the owner of Harley 494. A second Bukley, Joan ("Joanna Bukley soror"), was also a nun there: she is recorded as early as 1513 and died, according to the Martirloge, on 29 September 1532 (fol. 57v).[30] The dates are possible, but "Joanna" seems an unlikely though not totally impossible variant of "Anna." A third Anne Bulkeley (also known as Agnes), the widow of Sir Thomas Grey, was a pious laywoman who died in 1523, making a bequest to the Charterhouse at Sheen.[31] Again, she died too early to be the owner of our book.

More promising is a fourth woman of the same name, who was a nun at the Fontevraud house of Amesbury at the time of its supression in 1539. She was awarded a pension of 100 shillings.[32] The compliant prioress received £100, but £5 per annum was not a bad pension for a woman: in the diocese of Lincoln, only 6 percent of women received pensions in the £5 to £6 13s 4d range.[33] This Anne Bulkeley appears in two pension lists, in 1540 and in 1554/5, during the reign of Mary Tudor.

A Katherine Bulkeley was abbess of Godstow Abbey near Oxford at the time of the Dissolution in 1539 (and behaved rather badly, Abbot Gasquet thought).[34] She was the sister of the first Sir Richard Bulkeley (d. 1547), servant of Cardinal Wolsey, friend of Thomas Cromwell, and a leading member of the powerful and prolific Bulkeley family of Cheadle, Cheshire, and Beaumaris, Anglesey. Unfortunately, studies of that family[35] (with which the Bishop of Bangor, Arthur Bulkeley, was connected) throw up no Anne, Agnes, or Alice Bulkeleys whose dates fit the dates of Harley 494.

Dame Anne Bulkeley, the nun of Amesbury, is probably not to be identified with the Mistress Anne Bulkeley who donated Bodleian MS e Museo 23, though it may be significant that the village of Ringwood, Hampshire, from which Thomas Ringwood may have derived his name, is fairly near Amesbury. We also know precious little about Amesbury Priory immediately before the Dissolution of the Monasteries, apart from the twin facts that it was the second largest women's religious house (a prioress and thirty-three nuns were eventually pensioned) and the fifth richest.[36] It must also have been fervent, as it initially refused in 1539 to surrender: the prioress had to be replaced by one more cooperative. We do have an interesting manuscript, Oxford Bodley MS Add. A. 42, addressed to "my dear susterys Mary and Anne wyth all the other devo3th dyscyples of the scole of cryste in youre monastery of Amysbury," which is concerned with their vocation and profession as nuns. The manuscript is dated as "first half of the 16th century," and it must of course have been written before 1539; on folio 27v there is a reference to "the honorable lady cristyane your prioresse," presumably Dame Christine Fauntleroy. It has been discussed but never printed in full, and throws some light on the piety of the community to which the owner of Harley 494 may well have belonged.[37]

But it is hard to tell from internal evidence whether Harley 494 was compiled for a lay or religious woman. The ambiguity is already there in the ownership inscription, "Domina Anna Bulkeley," as "[t]he title of 'domina' could refer to a woman who was either a secular or a religious."[38] In addition, some of the texts are ambiguous or even contradictory about the status of their reader. This is particularly significant when the evidence is to be found in passages that we have reason to believe have been specially adapted for Harley 494. For instance, Item 6 (fols 6-19v), the first text written out by Taylor and the first substantial prose text, is an adaptation of the anonymous printed *Diurnal for Devout Souls* (STC 6928). This is a rule of daily living, but adapted in our manuscript for a woman leading a devout and retired life but clearly in a secular household. Item 9, an as yet unidentified treatise on preparation for communion, recommends the reception of the sacrament once a week or once a fortnight – on the low side for a late-medieval religious, perhaps, but on the high side for a layperson. Elsewhere a prayer, adapted from William Bonde's *Pilgrimage of Perfection* (STC 3278), includes an ambiguous reference to "this present houshold" (changed from "congregation" in the printed text), which suggests a secular rather than religious environment. On the other hand, in Item 14, a version of Richard Whitford's *Due preparacion unto houselynge* (STC 25412), the reader is encouraged to make an unequivocal reference to "my holy vowe of religione that I haue . . . enterprised" (fol. 41), where the parallel passage in the printed version simply refers in general terms to "this state and degree," and there is another reference in the same text to "my degre, religion and callynge" (fol. 44v). Item 24 is "a schorte confessionall for religious persons" and the sins it enumerates include the mis-saying of liturgical services and failure to obey "oure rewle or statutes" (fol. 91v). All these hints suggest the owner/reader's religious status. Finally, there is a Latin prayer to Saint Onuphrius, a somewhat obscure saint who was, perhaps significantly, a hermit. Though devout and usually set apart from the world, hermits were often not "religious" in the technical sense of having taken vows.

However, both the identity of the principal scribe of Harley 494 and its contents strongly suggest a Bridgettine, as well as Amesbury, connection. The manuscript contains several texts associated with the Syon brother Richard Whitford, author of many printed works of humanist religious instruction aimed at a general audience, of which, up to now, no manuscript versions have been known to exist; extracts from *The Pilgrimage of Perfection* (STC 3278, printed in 1526 and 1531) by William Bonde, another Syon brother, who died in 1530 (BL MS Add. 22285, fol. 47); a chapter from Saint Bridget of Sweden's *Revelationes*, Bk 1 cap. 8; a version of the so-called Pardon Beads of Syon (here called "the beads of pardon of Saint Gregory"); and several extracts in English and Latin from the *Liber specialis gratiae* of Mechthild of Hackeborn.

The latter is particularly convincing evidence of a Syon connection, as it is a text that in both Latin and English translation seems to have enjoyed combined Carthusian and Bridgettine patronage in England. There are at least three sets of extracts from the *Liber specialis gratiae* in Harley 494: Item 2, which is entirely in Latin; Item 10, largely in English, but including some Latin prayers; and Item 28, which pairs Latin and English prayers that are complementary rather than translations of each other. Texts from Mechthild, written in three different hands, are therefore found at the very beginning of the book, near the end, and in the middle. Moreover, there is a clear and consistent pattern in the way in which the compiler(s) of Harley 494 use Mechthild's visions on each occasion: originally narrative and visionary material is mined for prayers and devotional practices that are presumed to enjoy special divine authentication and validation through the association with the saint. The extensive use of a common source, adapted on each occasion in a similar way, suggests that in spite of the numerous hands involved in its production, Anne Bulkeley's book was conceived as a whole, either by or for a particular individual.

As we have seen, we know of no Syon nun called Anne Bulkeley whose dates fit those of the manuscript. However, it is possible that she was connected with Syon in some other capacity. Although no trace of a Dame Anne Bulkeley has so far come to light in the "foreign accounts" of Syon Abbey, the owner of Harley 494 could have been one of the widows attached to Syon who lived in the "women's house." According to Caroline Barron and Mary Erler, "Syon cellaress accounts show that the women's house was used for boarding novices during their 'year of proof', as well as for female visitors."[39] But whether or not Anne Bulkeley was a Syon nun or a vowess resident at Syon, it is undeniable, on the evidence of her book alone, that she was part of a Syon "textual community." In other words, even if not directly linked in a formal institutional sense with the community, she must have been under its influence and have had access, either directly or through friends, to texts that were valued at Syon and circulated or promoted under Syon's patronage.

The concept of a literary subculture or "textual community" naturally presumes regular and constant oral and personal contact, and if Dame Anne Bulkeley was a nun at Amesbury, and theoretically at least, subject to monastic enclosure, it might seem unlikely that she could have enjoyed that kind of easy intercourse with Syon. But, in the early sixteenth century, written communication between the two institutions, possibly mediated by more mobile laymen and women, was entirely feasible. Anne Bulkeley could also have had relatives at Syon: of the four Fettyplace sisters so well documented by Erler, one was an Amesbury nun, another a Syon nun, while a third lived at Syon as a vowess.[40]

Given the large number of scribes and the initial impression that what we have in Harley 494 is merely a conglomeration of religious texts or a commonplace book — a miscellany in the true sense of the word — an argument from design has to be made. It is my contention that Anne Bulkeley's book is more appropriately to be regarded as an anthology, or possibly a compendium, and that this becomes clear if we attempt to relate simultaneously the quires or signatures, the individual texts and their themes, and the scribes. In the discussion that follows the manuscript is analyzed quire by quire in order to allow due weight to all these factors. (It should be noted that the quire numbers and signature letters are editorial conveniences, as none is actually present in the manuscript, although there are catchwords.)

Quire 1 (sig. A) consists of four leaves. Although there are no watermarks, it must have been written at the same time as Quire 2, as Item 2 crosses both quires. Item 1, the elevation prayer, could well have been added later: it is untidily written, and no frame or guide lines appear on that folio. (If any of the minor hands in Harley 494 actually belong to the owner, this seems the most likely candidate.) Scribe B writes both Item 2, prayers from the *Liber specialis gratiae*, and Item 3, an unidentified Latin devotion structured on the Seven Gifts of the Holy Spirit. This item continues onto the top of the first leaf of Quire 2 (sig. B). Beneath this, Hand C has written Item 4, a Latin prayer invoking Saint Onuphrius. The hand, script, and ink of this item are quite distinct: it could have been added later but presumably not after Item 6, which is the first item written by Robert Taylor (Hand E), starting on the third leaf of Quire 2 (sig. B3). On signature B1v appears Item 5, also in Latin, *O gloriosa*, a prayer to the Virgin written in Hand D. The rest of the leaf is blank, then on signature B2 appear some pen trials in a later hand: presumably this leaf was blank (as its verso still is) when Taylor began his first text, Item 6, an adaptation of the anonymous early printed *Diurnal for Devout Souls*. This begins on signature B3 and occupies the rest of Quire 2 (sig. B) and leaves 3 to 4v of Quire 3 (sig. C). The remainder of signature C4v is blank.

There is no obvious reason why Item 6, the first substantial text and the first text written by the main hand of the manuscript, does not appear until signature B3. Was the collection begun as a book of Latin devotions, put aside, and then re-imagined as a predominantly vernacular book of treatises and devotions? That seems to be one possible explanation. Against this, Item 2, the opening Latin prayer taken from the *Liber specialis gratiae*, is consonant with the later use of Mechthild in both English and Latin items.

The next two items could well be "fillers," as they occupy the last two leaves of Quire 3 (sig. C). Item 7 is in Latin. It is apparently an office of the Virgin, but unidentified and more or less incomprehensible. (The Latin is alarmingly corrupt.) The leaf is headed by the sacred monogram, *Jhu*: possibly a Syon characteristic. On the verso and on the subsequent leaf, Hand G has written Item 8, a series of English prayers structured on the days of the week.

On the opening leaf of Quire 4 (sig. D), Hand E reappears and begins its second text, Item 9, an unidentified treatise on preparation for Holy Communion. This leaf is headed *Jhc*. The item occupies all of Quire 4 except for the verso of the last leaf (sig. D4v), which is blank.

The same hand writes in Quire 5 (sigs E1-10) what appears to be a single continuous text, the "information" revealed to "Seynt Mawde," but which is actually at least three discrete texts, identified as Items 10 to 13. On the verso of signature E10, Hand E begins Item 14, "When ye purpose to receiue Oure Lorde," adapted from Richard Whitford's *Due Preparation unto Houseling*.[41] This occupies the rest of Quire 5, the whole of Quire 6, and Quire 7, sigs G1-4r. The lower half of signature G4r is blank; on the verso, Hand H has written Item 15, the Marie d'Oisterwijk text, which continues on to the next leaf, followed immediately by Hand I, which writes Item 16, a series of English prayers for the Gifts of the Holy Spirit, on signature G5r-v. The bottom third of this folio is torn away. On the next leaf, Hand E starts another text, Item 17. The items written by Hands H and I therefore occupy the middle of a sixteen-leaf quire, so they are unlikely to be "fillers."

Hand E then writes Item 17, "The preste goynge to masse," adapted from William Bonde's *The Pilgrimage of Perfection*: this occupies the rest of Quire 7 as far as signature G13 and is immediately followed by the same hand writing Item 18, "a devout meditation . . . to Our Lord," to signature H5v; Item 19, an English translation of the O *intemerata*; and Items 20 to 22, which consist of a set of prayers based on the Ten Virtues of the Virgin, a Contemplation for the Feast of the Assumption, and a prayer, "O glorious lady," with a chapter from the *Revelationes* of Saint Bridget, which goes through to signature H11v. The lower half of that page is occupied by Hand J's writing Item 23, a devotion of One Thousand Aves. The rest of the quire, signatures H13r (lower half) and verso, and H14, is blank, so Hand J's item could be another filler.

Quire 9 (sig. I) opens with Hand E writing Item 24, "a short confessionall for religious persons," on signatures J1-6r, lower part of the leaf blank; on signature J6v the same hand writes Item 25, "An exclamation of a penitent sinner," followed by Item 26, a Latin version of the O *intemerata*, which ends on signature J10v. It should be noted that this is the last contribution from Hand E. On signature J11r, Hand K starts to write the Seven Sorrows of Our Blessed Lady up to signature J14r; the verso is blank. The last two leaves of Quire 9 are occupied by Hand L, which writes the Beads of Pardon of Saint Gregory and the triple Ave devotion (in English and Latin). On the verso of the last leaf, at the bottom, and possibly a "filler," Hand M writes Item 30, a Latin prayer of thanks for one's guardian angel.

Quire 10 (sig. K) is of different paper stock and written in what may be somewhat later hands: Hand N writes two short English prayers; Hand O (very rough and scrawly) writes an edifying sentiment in English ("Sorow for sin"), and Hand P writes in italic three Latin prayers, each followed by an English version, with *Jhs* at the top of each page. On the final verso there is another English prayer by Hand Q (a late-medieval hand).

It seems therefore that only the following texts might be regarded as "fillers" that could have been added at different times after the manuscript was substantially complete: Item 1 (the elevation prayer); Item 4 (prayer to Saint Onuphrius); Item 5 (O *gloriosa*); Item 7 (Latin office of the Virgin); Item 8 (prayers for the days of the week); Item 32 (the final item). The final quire of the existing book, signature K, containing Items 30 to 33, might also be a later addition as a whole.

If we try to make sense of the volume from the point of view of the nature of the texts, it becomes clear that there is some degree of overall control, a master plan, so to speak. The first item, as we have seen, was probably not part of the original conception but added later, perhaps by Anne Bulkeley herself. It is an elevation prayer in English and is interesting evidence that the owner probably took this book with her to Mass. In addition, the prayer is in keeping with one of the leading preoccupations of the volume: eucharistic devotion.

The first planned text, the prayers of Mechthild from the L*iber specialis gratiae*, is a devotion taken from the revelations of a visionary woman that focuses on the Five Joys of the Resurrection. It therefore fits in with a number of other visionary women's texts and devotions and also with the frequent appearance of "numbered" devotions: prayers for the Seven Gifts of the Holy Spirit, the enumeration of the Ten Virtues and Seven Sorrows of the Virgin, the devotion of the one thousand Aves, and so on.

This is followed by a prayer invoking the Holy Spirit and requesting the Seven Gifts and then by the Saint Onuphrius prayer. One wonders what the personal significance of this prayer was for the owner: did she have connections with the weaving trade (Onuphrius, who lived naked except for a garment woven from palm leaves, was patron saint of weavers), or did she have a father, husband, or son whose Christian name was Humphrey, the English form of the name? This opening group of frankly miscellaneous devotions, however, does seem to lack any particular rationale or theme, although the items individually foreshadow several later preoccupations. It ends with a Latin prayer to the Virgin, O *gloriosa domina*, the first of many Marian devotions in both English and Latin.

The first major prose text written in English is a rule of living for a secular woman adapted from the anonymous early printed *Diurnal for Devout Souls*, which prescribes spiritual exercises for morning, at mealtimes, and at night. This is followed by two "fillers," one in Latin and the other in English. The English prayers are focused on mystical love and on the Name of Jesus, another unifying preoccupation in Harley 494.

The next item, 9, a prose treatise offering advice to someone who wishes to receive communion once a week, or once a fortnight, has not been identified. It is, however, similar in tone to Item 6 (the *Diurnal* derivative), being eminently sane and humane, though much shorter (only about a thousand words long). Like Item 6, it purports to be written in response to a request; it is not clear whether the author is addressing one or more than one person, and the implied audience does not seem to be women but rather laymen, who are expected to have ample leisure and opportunities for solitude. The writer is an advocate of frequent communion and opposed to excessive scrupulosity; he favors experience over reason and thinks it better, if in doubt, that "love overcome dread" rather than the contrary. In spite of a mildly anti-clerical remark in the beginning, he advises trust in one's confessor. He is opposed to formalism and favors a truly inward religion, so he could well be an "evangelical" Erasmian Catholic.

Item 10 begins a new quire, but as the paper stock is the same as Quires 2 to 4 and there is a catchword on folio 25v, Quire 5 cannot be an independent unit. This item is the Mechthild "Information"; it provides for devotions in the morning on rising and before each of the day hours. Item 11 follows immediately, marked off only by a centered and indented heading that could well be mistaken for a subheading. It is a brief form of self-examination to be conducted in the morning and covers some of the same ground, essentially, as the opening of Item 6 (the *Diurnal* adaptation) and the beginning of Item 10. Although it recommends contemplation of Christ in his Godhead, the prayers it suggests in honor of the Five Wounds (a typically Bridgettine devotion) are very simple: five Paters, a Creed, the versicle

Adoramus te, and the collect *Domine Jesu Christe fili dei, pone Passionem*. Both Items 10 and 11 are essentially morning devotions, similar to those often found at the beginning of books of hours and *preces privatae*.

Item 12 is quite distinct from the previous item in that it has a different source, but this is by no means obvious as it begins mid-line with nothing more noticeable than a slightly larger capital B for "Because." The connection with the end of Item 11 seems to be that this text, too, is about prayer. It is rather heavily adapted from Richard Whitford's version of *The Golden Epistle*. Item 13, still part of the same quire, is set off by an indented title and presents a set of four intercessory prayers, of which three come from William Bonde's *Pilgrimage of Perfection* (Bk III, 6th Day, cap. 54). The fourth is very similar in style but unidentified and could well have been composed by the compiler.

Item 13 ends at the top of signature E8r; the rest of the page is blank, and Item 14 (still in Hand E) begins on the verso. This text, entitled "For your receiving of þe sacrament," occupies the rest of Quire 5, all of Quire 6, and the first few leaves of Quire 7. It is the longest text in the manuscript and up to the bottom of folio 57r is adapted with varying degrees of freedom from parts of Richard Whitford's *Due Preparation unto Houseling*. The ten prayers that follow, however, are not by Whitford. The Whitford text gives instructions on preparation for communion that are somewhat similar to those of Item 9 in stressing the need for recollection and solitude. However, it also proffers a very structured meditation, first on the goodness of God, then on Christ's Passion and death. This preparatory meditation is followed by a series of vocal prayers to be recited at different stages of the Mass, culminating in an office for Corpus Christi. After this we find a brief explanation of spiritual communion, which twice expressly addresses the reader as "madam" (the only occurrences of the word in the whole manuscript).[42] This section has no parallel in Whitford's text and is followed by a series of non-Whitfordian prayers. The centered heading "To the blissed Seyntes" on folio 57 is perhaps slightly largely than earlier headings, and the prayers that follow have nothing to do with the Mass or reception of communion except that they are penitential in tone. The first three prayers appear to be a set, addressed respectively to the saints, the apostles, and the angels; each invokes the "love" or "charite" that the saints and so forth have toward one of the Persons of the Trinity (the first invoking the Holy Spirit, the second Jesus, the third the Father), and prays for grace, pity, and mercy respectively for the supplicant, whose sinfulness is stressed. The next prayer is also part of this series: addressed to the Virgin, it invokes the love she has for the Trinity and again prays for "mercy and grace" for the suppliant's "innumerable wrechednes & synnes."

There then follow four more prayers that focus on the Trinity itself: the first, "to the glorious and mercyfull Trynite," is a long prayer for mercy, invoking the merits of the Virgin, the angels, and the saints, and the prayers of the Church. Three short prayers follow to the separate Persons of the Trinity, specifically requesting from each in turn "the water of contricion." There is then a series of very short prayers under the heading "To the Trinite," praying for mercy on "all rightouse peple," on sinners, on those in purgatory, and on "the infidels." This ends with the Latin invocation *Sancta Trinitas vnus deus miserere nobis*, taken from the opening common to various litanies. Generally there is a similarity between the preceding prayers and the tropes and final collects that follow the Litany in books of hours such as the Burnet Psalter (Aberdeen University Library MS 25), which follows the Litany with prayers to the Persons of the Trinity, the Virgin, the saints, the angels, and the apostles, among others.

The rest of signature G3r (with room for four lines) is left blank. On the verso of the leaf there is an exhortation to hear Mass, which has come from the *Liber Specialis gratiae*, promising as many saints at one's deathbed as one has heard Masses. Next is a long prayer to be said at the *beginning* of Mass. This last ends with the prayer "Jesu Jesu Jesu esto mihi Jesu." (These are probably distinct items, but for convenience I regard them as continuations of Item 14.)

Items 15 and 16 follow, in Hands H and I respectively, but they are apparently *not* "fillers" as they do not occur at the end of a quire. Item 15 occupies the verso of signature G4 and half the recto of signature G5 (Quire 7 consists of twenty leaves in all). This is the English adaptation of Marie d'Oisterwijk's Five Wounds exercise, discussed earlier, and fits in very well with this manuscript's preoccupation with the Wounds.

Item 16 follows in a new hand (Hand I), filling the remainder of signature G5r-v (this leaf is torn and approximately the bottom third is missing). This is a set of prayers to God the Father, in the name of the Son, for the Seven Gifts of the Holy Spirit. It will be recalled that Item 3 was a set of Latin prayers for the Gifts, addressed to the Holy Spirit, but it seems otherwise unconnected with the English text. There is an underlying Trinitarian emphasis in a number of the texts that is worth noting (compare the prayers added to the version of Whitford's *Due Preparation* [Item 14], and several of the items derived from Mechthild's *Liber specialis gratiae*).

The main hand resumes with the next Item, 17, which starts in the middle of Quire 7 (sig. G). Even if Quire 7 is not a single quire of twenty but two quires of ten (and given the tightness of the binding it is impossible to be sure), this item would still begin in the middle of a quire, which reinforces the argument that the two items that precede it are not merely fillers but integral elements in the collection as a whole. Certainly their preoccupations are consonant with it. Item 17, "Meditacions for tyme of the masse," resumes the dominant theme of the eucharist and the Blessed Sacrament (compare Items

1, 9, and 14). This text is one of the longer items in the manuscript, second only to the Whitford *Due Preparation*, and is again adapted from an early printed text, William Bonde's *Pilgrimage of Perfection*. It interprets the unfolding of the liturgical action of the mass exclusively as an allegory of the Passion and the priest as a figure of Christ; this approach makes it transitional between the various eucharistic texts that have so far appeared in Harley 494 (Items 1, 9, 14) and the texts to come that focus on Christ's Passion (although this is a theme already announced by part of Item 10 centering on the Hours of the Cross, and by Item 15, Marie d'Oisterwijk's devotion to the Wounds).

After the Bonde material ends, Item 17 continues without a break (fol. 72v) with a consideration of four reasons why Christ gives himself in the form of bread. This is similar to a section of Gherit van der Goude's 1532 *Interpretacyon and sygnyfycacyon of the Masse* (STC 11549), which gives not four but no fewer than twenty-five ingenious reasons for the use of bread as a symbol. This addition ends with "Amen." Then follows another non-Bonde extract, a highly rhetorical passage urging the reader to concentrate on devotion to the Passion. (The reader is here addressed as "thou": in the Bonde material the address is to "you.") Again, this stresses the more mystical side of religious devotion, referring to a desire to be "enflawmed in holy meditacion . . . replenysshed with spirituall joye and gostly gladnesse and to be raptt & taken vp in excesse of mynde." J. T. Rhodes has identified this as a version of a text found in the Swiss Cistercian Nicholas Salicetus's devotional anthology *Anthidotarius animae* (first printed in 1490, frequently reprinted).[43]

Item 17 ends with both "Amen" and "Finis" and is followed at the bottom of the same page by Item 18, "a devout meditation and a thankful orison to Our Lord," again written by Hand E, which completes Quire 7 and carries over into Quire 8 and continues the theme of Christ's Passion. This lengthy prayer thanks Christ for his earthly life, with a pronounced emphasis on the events of his suffering and death. It is followed by a series of shorter prayers, the first two of which contain numerous invocations beginning with "O," reminiscent of the pseudo-Bridgettine Seven Oes (which is otherwise noticeable by its absence from Harley 494) or the prayer O *bone Jesu*, attributed to Saint Bernardine of Siena. The next prayer is addressed to the three Persons of the Trinity, and the sixth and last, invoking the three Persons, prays for the gifts of might, wisdom, and good will – the attributes of the Trinity.

Hand E continues, writing Item 19, a translation of the O *intemerata*, one of the most popular of medieval prayers addressed to the Virgin and a regular feature in books of hours. This is not the first Marian devotion to appear in Harley 494: we have already had Items 5, 7, and the non-Whitfordian section of 14, but this one introduces a whole string of Marian devotions. In fact, devotion to the Blessed Virgin, along with devotion to the

sacrament of the Mass, is one of the leading themes that gives the manuscript its coherence. Item 20, a salutation to the Virgin based on her Ten
Virtues, is also written by Hand E. Each short prayer, invoking the Virgin by
naming each of her virtues in turn, introduces a recitation of the Ave Maria
(cf. Item 15 and also the structure of the early printed *Rosary of Our Lady*, STC
1754). Starting on a fresh page, but still written by Hand E and continuing the
Marian theme, is Item 21, "Contemplation for the Feast of the Assumption."
This is a rather unusual text on the Joys of the Virgin, not the usual set but
focusing specifically on the Seven Joys of the Assumption, followed by
another seven joys now possessed by the Virgin in heaven. These are followed by a lengthy prayer marked off by a blank line and also marked in the
margin as separate by an open *a* (but referring back to her Joys). This contains
references to the Trinity at the beginning and end. Item 22, again written by
Hand E, follows without any introduction or title. It is a translation of a single
chapter from the revelations of Saint Bridget, in which the Virgin instructs the
visionary how she may suitably praise her by praising God for his various
interactions with the Virgin.

Item 23 ends on signature H12v and is followed by Item 24. As Item
24 ends on signature H13r and the verso of that leaf and the last leaf in the
quire are blank, we may justifiably conclude that this item is indeed a "filler."
Nonetheless, thematically it follows on seamlessly from Items 19 to 23: it
records a somewhat eccentric and quasi-magical devotion that involves
saying a hundred Aves a day for ten days, followed by the prayer *Adonai domine
deus* (often found in books of hours) and the gift of alms to a poor person.
This will ensure ("ye may not fayle with owte dout") the granting of one's wish
or prayer.

Item 24, which begins a new quire and is once again in Hand E, is the
first of two penitential pieces, "a short confessional for religious persons."
Penance up to this point has not been the prominent theme that it so often
is in medieval collections of devotions, although Item 11 encourages self-
examination first thing in the morning. Rather, the stress is on the positive,
on the cultivation of the virtues (cf. Items 15 and 20) and the acquisition of
the Gifts of the Holy Ghost (Items 3, 16). Confessional formulae are common
enough, but the interest of this one lies in its being specifically tailored for a
religious. (The very first sin confessed relates to inadequate saying or singing
of the office.) Although the formula is said by the manuscript to derive from
the Franciscan saint Bonaventure, the confession specifically addresses
"beatam Birgittam," the only mention of Saint Bridget in the manuscript apart
from the translation of the chapter from her revelations. (This is a little surprising if the manuscript was indeed compiled at Syon Abbey.) After enumer-
ating eight types of sin, a short note follows, citing Saint Bernard "& oþer
deuout doctours" on the dangers of boring one's confessor by being too

prolix if one makes frequent confession. This part of Item 24 does not seem to be particularly applicable to religious and offers a kind of general round-up of sins in conclusion.

This item ends in the middle of a leaf, and Item 25, written again by Hand E, begins at the top of the next leaf (sig. J6v). This is another penitential text, "an exclamation of a penitent sinner." Reverting to the manuscript's Marian preoccupations, Item 25, a Latin text of the O *intemerata* (though a different version from that earlier translated into English), follows immediately, written by Hand E. This version includes a reference to the reception of communion, which the suppliant laments to have received too often unworthily, hence linking the penitential and eucharistic themes.

This is the last item to be written by Hand E. There remain six more leaves in Quire 9 at this point, and the four-leaf Quire 10, which seems to be a slightly later addition. Items 27, 28, and 29 complete Quire 9. Item 27, written by Hand K, continues the Marian theme of Taylor's final contribution. It is a set of prayers invoking the Seven Sorrows of the Virgin, each followed by a Pater and an Ave. Item 15 enumerates the Five Sorrows of the Virgin, but all are confined to the events of Christ's Passion. In contrast, this set of seven is more wide-ranging, including three drawn from the infancy and childhood of Christ: the prophecy of Simeon; the Flight into Egypt; the Loss of the Child Jesus; Christ's arrest, scourging, and condemnation; the Crucifixion and Death of Christ; the Deposition; and the Entombment. The final sorrow concludes with a Pater, Ave and Credo, so the devotion is in form a type of rosary.

Signature J13v is blank, and a new hand, Hand L, writes the next item, Item 28. This calls itself "the beads of pardon of Saint Gregory's pity" and is a variant on a well-known devotion, often called "the Pardon Beads of Syon Abbey,"that makes use of a set of prayer beads. It consists of a set of seven separate prayers, each addressed to "swete blessyde Jhesu," focused on the Name of Jesus, each with a common repeated prayer, a Pater, an Ave, and a Credo, a similar pattern to that of the previous item. The Name of Jesus devotion is characteristic of Syon. It is immediately followed without a break by a set of prayers to the Virgin (briefly invoking Saint Anne) written in the same hand. These prayers, in English and Latin, derive from the Mechthildian *Liber specialis gratiae* and show both Marian and Trinitarian preoccupations; thus in various respects they fit in with the preoccupations of Harley 494 as a whole. At the bottom of the last page of this quire (sig. J16v) a new hand, Hand M, has written Item 29, a brief Latin prayer in a rather untidy textura. This prayer refers to the protection of one's guardian angel: again, devotion to the angels seems to have been a Syon cult in the early sixteenth century.

Quire 10, the final quire, which consists of four leaves, seems to be written on different paper stock and so may be a later addition. On the first leaf is Item 30, two prayers: the first, a brief act of contrition, and the second, the familiar Compline prayer, "Visit, we beseech thee, O Lord," so these might constitute suitable evening devotions, making an appropriate end to the collection. A different hand, Hand O, has scribbled, possibly much later, another prayer or note at the bottom of the first leaf, listing four virtues.

In the top margin of the next six leaves, another hand has written the sacred monogram J*hc*. Hand P (probably not the same as the hand that writes the running head) has written Item 31, three pairs of prayers in Latin and English, each pair to be followed by a Pater and an Ave. The English prayers are each somewhat free translations of the preceding Latin. The first set is a lament for lost time and a request for spiritual insight. The second set addresses Christ as the Good Shepherd, while the third prays for temperance and the avoidance of gluttony. The third Latin prayer is followed by a hexameter couplet addressed to one's guardian angel which is found independently elsewhere, for instance in books of hours, and then by an expansion or exegesis of the second half of the last line. The Latin prayers are written in italic or in a hand with humanistic or italic influences, while the English versions are in anglicana, but I think the same scribe P wrote both.

The final item, 32, is written by Hand Q. It is a salutation addressed to Christ, the opening words of which seem derived from a salutation found in the very popular pseudo-Bridgettine Fifteen Oes. The prayer goes on to invoke Christ's Passion, wounds, body, and blood, hence gathering up so many of the themes of the collection as a whole.

Taken as a whole, the manuscript has the general shape one would expect of a *preces privatae* volume. It has morning prayers at the beginning and evening prayers at the end (as do, of course, books of hours); it has prayers and devotions associated with the Mass in the first half of the book – attendance at Mass always took place in the morning — and prayers centered on the Virgin and on penance, appropriate to any time of the day, later in the book. J. T. Rhodes discusses the overall shape of this collection, and her identification of many of the texts has proved invaluable.[44] She concludes that "Dame Anna's collection provided her with plenty of devotional material, although it was not particularly well organized."[45] It is my hope that further investigation of the context and sources of the texts will clarify the principles of organization. Certainly there can be no question here of a random accretion of devotional material; someone has gone to considerable lengths to seek out texts from a variety of sources, some quite rare. Indeed, many of the items are, as far as we know at present, unique. There is a very distinctive discrimination at work in Harley 494, possibly that of the eponymous if elusive Dame Anne Bulkeley but it may also be that of the compiler. The really intriguing question is: were any of the texts composed by Anne Bulkeley herself, or by her friends?

University of Waikato

NOTES

1. Mary C. Erler, "Devotional Literature," in *The Cambridge History of the Book in Britain III: 1400-1557* (Cambridge: Cambridge University Press, 1999), 495-525, 509-10.
2. Mary C. Erler, "The Books and Lives of Three Tudor Women," in *Privileging Gender in Early Modern England*, vol. XXIII, *Sixteenth Century Essays and Studies* (Sixteenth Century Journals Publishers: Kirksville, MI), 4-17, 5.
3. See, for instance, Virginia R. Bainbridge, "Women and the Transmission of Religious Culture: Benefactresses of Three Bridgettine Convents *c.* 1400-1600," *Birgittiana* 3 (1997): 55-76, and Veronica Lawrence, 'The role of the monasteries of Syon and Sheen in the production, ownership and circulation of mystical literature in the late Middle Ages," in *The Mystical Tradition and the Carthusians* 10, Analecta Cartusiana 130 (1996): 101-115.
4. Brian Stock, *The Implications of Literacy: written language and models of interpretation in the eleventh and twelfth centuries* (Princeton, NJ: Princeton University Press, 1983), 89, 90.
5. Felicity Riddy, "'Women talking about the things of God': a late medieval sub-culture," in Carol M. Meale, ed., *Women and Literature in Britain 1150-1500*, 2nd ed. (Cambridge: Cambridge University Press, 1996), 104-127.
6. Riddy, "'Women talking about the things of God,'" 107-111.
7. Carol Wyvill, "Five Sixteenth-Century Devotional Texts from Anne Bulkeley's Book: British Library MS Harley 494," MA thesis, University of Otago, 2005, viii.
8. Greg Waite, University of Otago, in a private communication. I am most grateful to Dr Waite for this information about the physical makeup of the manuscript.
9. Rebecca Krug, *Reading Families: women's literate practice in late medieval England* (Ithaca and London: Cornell University Press, 2002), 157.
10. Kathleen Scott, "*Caveat Lector*: Ownership and Standardization in the Illustration of Fifteenth-Century English Manuscripts," in Peter Beal and Jeremy Griffiths, eds., *English Manuscript Studies 1100-1700* (Oxford: Basil Blackwell, 1989), 19-63, 20.
11. A.I. Doyle in a 1999 letter to Charity Scott Stokes. See also David N. Bell, *What Nuns Read* (Kalamazoo, MI: Cistercian Publications, 1995), 176, citing R. W. Dunning, "The Building of Syon Abbey," *Transactions of the Ancient Monuments Society* 20 (1975): 16-26, 21. Christopher de Hamel, however, remarks that

Taylor was apparently an outside scribe, as "there is no record of him at Syon" (de Hamel, *Syon Abbey: The Library of the Bridgettine Nuns and their Peregrinations after the Reformation* [London: Roxburghe Club, 1991], 98), but Ian Doyle assures me that he was indeed at Syon.

12. Dunning, "The Building of Syon Abbey," 21.

13. See Bell, *What Nuns Read*, 175-6. On the Aberdeen manuscript, see also Henry Hargreaves, "'The Mirror of Our Lady': Aberdeen University Library MS. 134," *Aberdeen University Review* 62 (1968): 267-80.

14. Lorna Stevenson, in her 1992 University of Liverpool Ph.D. thesis, "Fifteenth-Century Chastity and Virginity: Texts, Contexts, Audiences," argues that Hand G and Hand I are the same, and further that they are identical to the "correcting hand" found in MS Harley 554 and may be that of Anne Bulkeley herself. In my opinion, however, Hands G and I are quite distinct.

15. Mary Erler, "Syon Abbey's Care for Books: Its Sacristan's Account Rolls 1506/7-1535/6," *Scriptorium* 39 (1986): 293-307, 294.

16. Erler, "Syon Abbey's Care for Books," 301.

17. Kirsten M. Christensen, "Maria van Hout and Her Carthusian Editor," *Ons geestelijk erf: driemaandewlijks* 72 (1998): 105-121, 118.

18. Christensen, "Maria van Hout and Her Carthusian Editor," 11, 116.

19. See Charity Scott-Stokes's review of *Dom Gérard Kalckbrenner: Mélanges de Spiritualité*. Texte établi, traduit et présenté par Dom Augustin Devaux, Analecta Cartusiana 158, ed. by James Hogg, Alain Girard, Daniel Le Blèves (Salzburg: Institut für Anglistik und Amerikanistik, Universität Salzburg, 1999), *Mystics Quarterly* 26 (2000): 131.

20. Christensen, "Maria van Hout and Her Carthusian Editor,"109.

21. See further Kirsten M. Christensen, "The Gender of Epistemology in Confessional Europe: The Reception of Maria van Hout's Ways of Knowing," in Anneke B. Mulder-Bakker, ed., *Seeing and Knowing in Medieval Europe 1200-1550* (Turnhout: Brepols, 2004), 97-120. I should like to thank Professor Christensen for generously providing me with photocopies of the various texts of the exercises in Latin and Ripuarian.

22. Christensen, "Maria van Hout and Her Carthusian Editor,"117.

23. Christensen, "Maria van Hout and Her Carthusian Editor,"111.

24. G. R. Elton, *Policy and Police: The Enforcement of the Reformation in the Age of Thomas Cromwell* (Cambridge: Cambridge University Press, 1972), 231-32.

25. Humfrey Wanley, *A Catalogue of the Harleian Collection of Manuscripts in Two Volumes* (London, 1759): I.

26. C. E. Wright and Ruth C. Wright, eds., *The Diary of Humfrey Wanley 1715-1726* (London: The Bibliographical Society, 1966), 2 vols., I, xviii.

27. See Andrew G. Watson, *The Library of Sir Simonds D'Ewes* (London: Trustees of the British Museum, 1966), 329. Watson suggests that D'Ewes's hand may

appear on fol. 98v writing the phrase "in æternum" (in the margin of the "O intemerata").

28. See E. Wilson, "Sir Robert Shottesbrook (1400-1471): Translator," *Notes & Queries*, n.s. 28 (1981): 303-5.

29. See also J. T. Rhodes, "The body of Christ in English eucharistic devotion, *c.*1500-*c.*1620," in Richard Beadle and A.J. Piper, eds., *New Science Out of Old Books: studies in manuscripts and early printed books in honour of* A. I. Doyle (Aldershot, UK: Scholar, 1995), 388-417, 414, n. 71.

30. De Hamel, *Syon Abbey*, 81.

31. Ian Doyle, in a private communication.

32. W. Dugdale, *Monasticon Anglicanum*, 6 vols in 8 (London: Bohn, 1946), II: 340.

33. G. A. J. Hodgett, ed., *The State of the Ex-Religious and Former Chantry Priests in the Diocese of Lincoln* 1547-1574 (Hereford, UK: Lincoln Record Society, 1959), xvii.

34. F. A. Gasquet, *Henry VIII and the English Monasteries: an attempt to illustrate the history of their suppression*, 6th ed. (London: G. Bell, 1902), 305 ff.

35. E. G. Jones, transcribed and ed., W. Williams, "A history of the Bulkeley family," 1673/4, *Transactions of the Anglesey Antiquarian Society* (1948): 7-99; D. C. Jones, "The Bulkeleys of Baron Hill, 1440-1621," MA diss., University of Wales, Bangor, 1958.

36. D.A. Crowley, ed., *A History of the County of Wiltshire, The Victoria History of the Counties of England*, vol. 3 of 16 vols (Oxford: Oxford University Press, 1999), 242.

37. Yvonne Parrey, "'Devoted disciples of Christ': Early Sixteenth-Century Religious Life in the Nunnery at Amesbury," *Bulletin of the Institute of Historical Research* 67, 164 (1994): 240-248.

38. Carol M. Meale and Julia Boffey, "Gentlewomen's reading,"in Lotte Hellinga and J.B. Trapp, eds., *The Cambridge History of the Book in Britain* III: 1400-1557 (Cambridge: Cambridge University Press, 1999), 526-540, 528.

39. Caroline Barron and Mary Erler, "The Making of Syon Abbey's Altar Table of Our Lady *c.*1490-96," in John Mitchell, ed., *England and the Continent in the Middle Ages: Studies in Memory of Andrew Martindale*, Harlaxton Medieval Studies VIII (Stamford, UK: Shaun Tyas, 2000), 318-335, 322, n. 20.

40. Mary Erler, "The Books and Lives of Three Tudor Women," 4-17.

41. First identified by J. T. Rhodes, "The body of Christ in English eucharistic devotion," 413, n. 62.

42. Unfortunately this term throws no light on the question of Anne Bulkeley's status, as both nuns and laywomen could be addressed in this way. Sir Thomas More, for instance, addressed Elizabeth Barton, the Nun of Kent, as "madam" or "good madam" several times in the letter he wrote her.

43. "The body of Christ in English eucharistic devotion," 414-5, n. 88.

44. "The body of Christ in English eucharistic devotion," 398-400.
45. "The body of Christ in English eucharistic devotion," 400.

WORKS CITED

Bainbridge, Virginia R. "Women and the Transmission of Religious Culture: Benefactresses of Three Bridgettine Convents c. 1400-1600." *Birgittiana* 3 (1997): 55-76.
Bell, David N. *What Nuns Read*. Kalamazoo, MI: Cistercian Publications, 1995.
Christensen, K. "Maria van Hout and Her Carthusian Editor." *Ons geestelijk erf: driemaandewlijks* 72 (1998): 105-121.
———. "The Gender of Epistemology in Confessional Europe: The Reception of Maria van Hout's Ways of Knowing." In *Seeing and Knowing in Medieval Europe* 1200-1550. Ed. Anneke B. Mulder-Bakker. Turnhout: Brepols, 2004, 97-120.
Crowley, D.A., ed. *A History of the County of Wiltshire, The Victoria History of the Counties of England*. Vol. 3. 16 vols. Oxford: Oxford University Press, 1999.
De Hamel, Christopher. *Syon Abbey: The Library of the Bridgettine Nuns and their Peregrinations after the Reformation*. London: Roxburghe Club, 1991.
Dugdale, William. *Monasticon Anglicanum*. Vol. II. 6 vols. in 8. London: Bohn, 1846.
Dunning, R. W. "The Building of Syon Abbey." *Transactions of the Ancient Monuments Society*. 25 (1981): 16-26.
Elton, G. R. *Policy and Police: The Enforcement of the Reformation in the Age of Thomas Cromwell*. Cambridge: Cambridge University Press, 1972.
Erler, Mary. "Syon Abbey's Care for Books: Its Sacristan's Account Rolls 1506/7-1535/6." *Scriptorium* 39 (1986): 293-307.
———. "The Books and Lives of Three Tudor Women." In *Privileging Gender in Early Modern England*. Ed. Jean R. Brink. Sixteenth Century Essays and Studies 23. Kirksville, MI: Sixteenth Century Journals Publishers, 1993, 4-17.
———. "Devotional Literature." In *The Cambridge History of the Book in Britain*. Vol. III: 1400-1557. Ed. Lotte Hellinga and J. B. Trapp. Cambridge: Cambridge University Press, 1999, 495-525.
———. "The Making of Syon Abbey's Altar Table of Our Lady c.1490-96." In *England and the Continent in the Middle Ages: Studies in Memory of Andrew Martindale*. Ed. John Mitchell. Harlaxton Medieval Studies VIII. Stamford, UK: Shaun Tyas, 2000, 318-335.
Gasquet, F. A. *Henry VIII and the English Monasteries: an attempt to illustrate the history of their suppression*. 6th. ed. London: G. Bell, 1902.
Hargreaves, Henry. "'The Mirror of Our Lady': Aberdeen University Library MS. 134." *Aberdeen University Review* 62 (1968): 267-280.
Hodgett, G. A. J., ed. *The State of the Ex-Religious and Former Chantry Priests in the*

Diocese of Lincoln 1547-1574. Hereford, UK: Lincoln Record Society, 1959.

Jones, D. C. "The Bulkeleys of Baron Hill, 1440-1621." MA diss., University of Wales, Bangor, 1958.

Jones, E. G., and W. Williams. "A history of the Bulkeley family, 1673/4." *Transactions of the Anglesey Antiquarian Society* (1948): 7-99.

Krug, Rebecca. *Reading Families: women's literate practice in late medieval England.* Ithaca and London: Cornell University Press, 2002.

Lawrence, Veronica. "The role of the monasteries of Syon and Sheen in the production, ownership and circulation of mystical literature in the late Middle Ages." In *The Mystical Tradition and the Carthusians* 10. Analecta Cartusiana 130. Salzburg: Institut für Anglistik und Amerikanistik, Universität Salzburg, 1996, 101-115.

Meale, Carol M., and Julia Boffey. "Gentlewomen's Reading." In *The Cambridge History of the Book in Britain III: 1400-1557.* Ed. Lotte Hellinga and J. B. Trapp. Cambridge: Cambridge University Press, 1999, 526-540.

Parrey, Yvonne. "'Devoted disciples of Christ': Early Sixteenth-Century Religious Life in the Nunnery at Amesbury." *Bulletin of the Institute of Historical Research* 67.164 (1994): 240-248.

Rhodes, J. T. "The body of Christ in English eucharistic devotion, c.1500- c.1620." In *New Science Out of Old Books: studies in manuscripts and early printed books in honour of* A. I. *Doyle.* Ed. Richard Beadle and A.J. Piper. Aldershot, UK: Scholar, 1995, 388-417.

Riddy, Felicity. "'Women talking about the things of God': a late medieval subculture." In *Women and Literature in Britain* 1150-1500. Ed. Carol M. Meale. 2nd ed. Cambridge: Cambridge University Press, 1996, 104-127.

Salter, Elizabeth. "Ludolphus of Saxony and his English Translator." *Medium Aevum* 33 (1964): 26-35.

Scott, Kathleen L. "*Caveat Lector*: Ownership and Standardization in the Illustration of Fifteenth-Century English Manuscripts." In *English Manuscript Studies* 1100-1700. Ed. Peter Beal and Jeremy Griffiths. Oxford: Basil Blackwell, 1989, 19-63.

Scott-Stokes, Charity. Review of *Dom Gérard Kalckbrenner: Mélanges de Spiritualité.* Texte établi, traduit et présenté par Dom Augustin Devaux. Analecta Cartusiana 158. Salzburg: Institut für Anglistik und Amerikanistik, Universität Salzburg, 1999. *Mystics Quarterly* 26 (2000): 131.

Stevenson, Lorna. "Fifteenth-Century Chastity and Virginity: Texts, Contexts, Audiences." Ph.D. diss., University of Liverpool, 1992.

Stock, Brian. *The Implications of Literacy: written language and models of interpretation in the eleventh and twelfth centuries.* Princeton, NJ: Princeton University Press, 1983.

Wanley, Humfrey. *Catalogue of the Harleian Collection of Manuscripts in Two Volumes.* London, 1759.

Watson, Andrew G. *The Library of Sir Simonds* D'Ewes. London: Trustees of the British Museum, 1966.

Wilson, E. "Sir Robert Shottesbrook (1400-1471): Translator." *Notes &Queries* 28 (1981): 303-305.

Wright, C. E., and Ruth C. Wright, eds. *The Diary of Humfrey Wanley* 1715-1726. 2 vols. London: Bibliographical Society, 1966.

Wyvill, Carol. "Five Sixteenth-Century Devotional Texts from Anne Bulkeley's Book: British Library MS Harley 494". MA thesis, University of Otago, 2005.

Dating the Manuscripts of the "Hammond Scribe": What the Paper Evidence Tells Us

DANIEL W. MOSSER

The "Hammond scribe" is named for Eleanor Prescott Hammond, who first identified his work and diagnostic features in six manuscripts.[1] To date, the Hammond scribe's hand and distinctive spellings[2] have been identified in fifteen manuscripts, all copied on paper. Two of these are single-leaf fragments that lack a watermark: a fragment of the English prose *Merlin* on folio 43 of Bodleian Library MS Rawlinson D.913;[3] and British Library MS Harley 78, "one of the historical and poetical collections made by John Stow," of which folio 3r, containing *Piers the Ploughman's Creed*,[4] can be attributed to the Hammond scribe. C. Paul Christianson tentatively identified this scribe as John Multon (d. 1475) on the basis of "Quod Multon 1458" on folio 215r and "Quod Multon" on folios 217r, 219r, and 222r in Trinity College, Cambridge MS R.14.52.[5] Linne R. Mooney, however, argues that the identification is incorrect since the name occurs only in one text, "a tract on making and using a quadrant," and suggests that Multon may instead identify the source of the quadrant text. Simon Horobin rejects the Multon identification on linguistic grounds: "The dialect features found in this scribe's usage suggest a localisation in Kent, and it seems likely that this scribe was an immigrant to London from this region."[6]

Because the Hammond scribe and his collaborators wrote exclusively on paper instead of parchment, and because at least some of the papers are datable, it is possible to propose a sequence for these manuscripts' production. In several instances, two MSS share some paper stocks; it is reasonable to infer that those portions of MSS that share paper stocks were copied either in parallel or in close succession. While being able to match a given paper stock with dated examples gives us an approximate date for the paper's production, it does not necessarily pinpoint a time of use. However, it does seem reasonable to think that a datable paper stock that has a date earlier than another datable paper stock would be used before the later paper stock (or at least would be available for use earlier). In fact, the dates of the Hammond scribe's paper stocks do fall into the period proposed for his active career (the reign of Edward IV), so it is likely that the dates of those papers correspond fairly closely to the dates for their use, especially where they occur in significant "runs."

The Paper Stocks Used by the Hammond Scribe

In this section, the paper stocks found in MSS identified with the Hammond scribe are described and, when possible, identified and dated.[7] Examples of many of the watermarks are reproduced in figures 1–13.

1. British Library MS Royal 17.D.xv: *Canterbury Tales*, folios 1r–301r; "Somnium vigilantis" (by John Fortescue? Latin-English-French, after 1459): folios 302r–310r (IPMEP 5391); "Declaration upon Certayn Wrytinges Sent Oute of Scotteland," by John Fortescue (after October, 1471): folios 311r–326r (IPMEP 10); "The Balet of the Kynge" (poem on Edward IV's return to London, 1471): folios 327r–332r (NIMEV 2808); "Boke of Kervyng & Nortur" (by John Russell?): folios 333r–348r (NIMEV 1514). The Hammond scribe copies only folios 167r–301r, but note that the work of Scribe 1 and part of that of the Hammond scribe use the same paper stock.[8]

   See figure 1:
   a. Bull's head/"Tête de Boeuf," similar to Briquet 15054 (1441–1445), centered between chain lines 3.8 cm apart. The mark is 6 cm high by ca. 4 cm at its widest point: folios 1–272 [Scribe 1 copies fols. 1–166].
   b. "Armoires Deux Pals," similar to Briquet 2064 (1464), but each tip of the crown has a series of three circles: folios 273–284.
   c. Scissors with post horn/"Ciseaux," similar to Briquet 3694 (1433–1434), but with different chain-line widths and the detached element more upright); cf. Ms Briquet xxx, no. 6622 (Catane 1463) [fig. 1d]. Cf. also *Wasserzeichenkartei*

Piccard "Shere—Scheidershere mit Beizeichen," number 122557 (Genova 1476). Chain lines are 3.5 and 3 cm apart, with the middle chain line bisecting the mark. The scissors element is 5 cm high: folios 285–301 (i.e., to the end of Hammond scribe's stint, except for 241r, where Scribe 3 supplies VII.891–917 [B^2 2081–2107]).

The remainder of the MS contains material by or associated with John Fortescue. As the paper stocks have no apparent connection with the Hammond scribe, they are not illustrated but are described below:

Unicorn/"Licorne Simple," closest to Briquet 10015 (Dijon 1448; variants from 1440 to 1450), but the tail is more like that of Briquet 10014 (Paris 1446) and 10024 (Cuy 1477).[9] See also UNI.001 and UNI.002 (*The Thomas L. Gravell Watermark Archive*) from Caxton's first edition of the *Canterbury Tales* (STC 5083 [1476–1477]). Chain lines are 3.8 and 3.6 cm apart, and the relationship of the mark to the chains is as in #10015: folios 302–310.

Unicorn/"Licorne Simple": the twin of the preceding mark. Very close to Ms Briquet xxx, no. 13247 (Saint-Omer 1469).

Unicorn/"Licorne Simple," near Briquet 9997 (1477–1478), but the mark is 9.4 cm long, while the Briquet mark is only 8.3 cm. Both have chain lines 3.6 cm apart, and the orientation is identical: folios 311–316; 333–348.

Unicorn/"Licorne Simple": the twin of the preceding mark.

Anchor/"Ancre," very near Piccard "Anker," II.704–707 (1474–1478): folios 327–332.

Anchor/"Ancre": the twin of the preceding mark.

2. British Library MS Harley 2251: a collection of 133 items, many of which are by or attributed to Lydgate, as well as Chaucer's *Prioress's Tale*, "Fortune," "Gentilesse," "The ABC," "Complaint to His Purse."[10]

See figure 2:

a/b. A pair of "Armoire Deux Pals," similar to Briquet 2064 (1464): one of the twins is centered between chain lines 3.8 cm apart, the other between chain lines 3.5 cm apart: folios 1–238; 260? (an unmarked leaf with chain lines 3.8 cm apart).

c. Scissors with post horn/"Ciseaux," near Briquet 3700 (1469); cf. Ms Briquet xxx, no. 6622 (Catane 1463: see above under MS Royal 17.D.xv and fig. 1d); bisected by a

chain line with attendant chain lines 2.8 cm apart: folios
240–256; 261–273.
d. Bull's head with cross/"Tête de Boeuf," bisected by a chain
line, with attendant chains 2.7 cm apart: folios 239,
274–293.

3. British Library MS Additional 34360 (formerly Phillipps 9053): contains a
number of shorter works by Chaucer and Lydgate, and Lydgate and
Burgh's *Secrees of old Philisoffres* (NIMEV 935). Cf. the contents of MS Harley
2251.[11]
See figure 3:
a. The first section (Q [1]: fols. 4–23) and the final section
(Qq [5–6]: folios 78–116) both have the same pair of
Hand/"Main" watermarks and the same blacker ink. The
mark is 4 cm tall and the attendant chain lines are 2.8
cm apart. Undated.
b. Cart/"Char"—not pictured—very similar if not identical to
that in Oxford, MS Bodley 414 (*Canterbury Tales*; see fig.
1b); very near Briquet 3546 (Catane 1466). In MS
Additional 34360, the paper stock occurs in a run in Q
[2]: folios 24–43. The mark is 7 cm tall, bisected by a
chain line, with attendant chain lines 3.3 and 3.5 cm
apart. Undated.
c. Wheel/"Roue," undated, Q [3] (folios 44–57); p. "109" (the
blank between fols. 57 and 58). Attendant chain lines are
4 cm apart. None of the examples in Briquet or the Ms
Briquet xxx feature the two projecting elements.
d. Bull's head with cross/"Tête de Boeuf" with a very symmetrical structure. Q [4] (folios 58–73). Undated.

4. British Library MS Additional 29901: "Tracts on State Ceremonials," in Latin
and French (identified by the late Jeremy J. Griffiths).[12]
See figure 4:
a. The paper stock is all of the same Ring/"Anneau" type,
identical with that in MS Bodley 414 (see fig. 4b). The
mark is 3.8 x 2.5 cm; the attendant chain lines 3.3 cm
apart. Examples in Ms Briquet xxx are from the late
1450s to early 1460s, for example, number 6622 (Catane
1462; see fig. 4c). The *Wasserzeichenkartei Piccard* has thirteen examples—none exact matches—ranging from
1458 to 1577, the closest being number 032339 ("Ringe";
Düsseldorf 1460).

5. Royal College of Physicians MS 388 (formerly MS 13): *Canterbury Tales*.[13]
     See figure 5:
     a. Two Arrows crossed (saltire) over a circle/"Deux flèches en
        sautoir" (4°), with a structure similar to Briquet 6303
        (1462–1474), but the attendant chain lines are 3.2 cm
        apart, and one of the chain lines bisects the circle. Cf.
        Ms Briquet xxx, no. |9012?| (Augsberg 1465; see fig. 5b):
        folios 1–120.
     c. Scissors with post horn/"Ciseaux" (4°): a pair of twins,
        somewhat similar to Briquet 3694–3696 (1433–1456):
        folios 121–290.
     d. Scissors/"Ciseaux" (4°) similar to the previous, but with no
        post horn element. The attendant chain lines are 3 and
        2.5 cm from the line that bisects the mark: folios
        291–354.
     e. Scissors/"Ciseaux" (4°) with a separate cinquefoil/five-
        pointed star instead of a post horn element at the blade-
        end of the scissors. The attendant chain lines are 2.5 and
        3.2 cm from the line that bisects the mark. Cf. Ms
        Briquet xxx, no. 3666 (1475; see fig. 5f). Some later
        examples with this morphology are recorded in
        Wasserzeichenkartei Piccard, "Shere—Shneiderschere mit
        Beizeichen," number 122541 (Genova 1481) and number
        122543 (Parma 1483): folios 355–362.

6. Trinity College, Cambridge MS R.14.52: Treatises of Roger Bacon ("a collec-
     tion of treatises, recipes, lists, and problems, principally related to the
     practice of medicine, but also strong in the related sciences of mathe-
     matics and astronomy/astrology").[14]
     Hand with five-pointed star: folio 3 (one of the fly leaves at
        the front); Qq |10–14; 16–17|; mixed in Q |15| (not repro-
        duced, the same as in Trinity College, Cambridge, MS
        O.3.11; see below and Fig. 7a).
     Gothic P (not reproduced, the same as in MS O.3.11; see
        below and Fig. 7c): folio 5 (last of the fly leaves at the
        front); Qq |7–9; 22–23|.
     Gothic P with cross (not reproduced, the same as in MS
        O.3.11): Qq |1–6|.
     See figure 6:
     a. Crown with trefoil. The attendant chain lines are 3.7 cm
        apart; the mark measures 4.4 x 2.4 cm. Very similar to

WM I 61491 (Haarlem, Netherlands [October 25, 1484–May 5, 1485]: *Watermarks in Incunabula Printed in the Low Countries*): Qq [18–21].

Church (not reproduced, the same as in British Library MS Harley 4999; see below and Fig. 8a): the four folios inserted between 173 and 174 in Q [15]).

Monts in a circle surmounted by a cross (not reproduced; bisected by a chain line with attendant chain lines 3 cm apart; the mark is 8 cm tall): in the three inserted folios between 256 and 257.

7. Trinity College, Cambridge MS O.3.11.[15]

See figure 7

a. Hand with five-pointed star (same as MS R.14.52: bisected by a chain line with attendant chain lines 2.5 cm apart; the mark is 7.7 cm tall; the twin—for example, folio 55— is 8 cm tall and the attendant chain lines are 2.5 and 2.3 cm apart): Qq [1–7]; mixed in Q [10]; folio 157 (i.e., the first folio of Q [14]).

b. Scissors (bisected by a chain line with attendant chain lines 2.5 cm apart; the mark is 5.7 cm tall); close to Briquet 3687 (same chain line spacings; Gênes 1467–1470): folio 125r.

Gothic P with a cross (not reproduced, same as in MS R.14.52): Qq [8–10]

c. Gothic P (the same as in MS R.14.52): folio 126 in Q [11]; Qq [12–15] except folio 157.

d. Merchant's mark/monogram/cipher? Somewhat similar structure to Ms Briquet xxx, "Lettre A" no. 4522 (Lyon 1406). Also found in MS Harley 4999, folio 228 (the last folio).

8. British Library MS Harley 4999: *Statutes of the Realm*, 1 Edward III to 18 Henry VI.[16]

See figure 8:

a. Church (as in MS R.14.52); Heawood alludes to a "*Church. Letter of Richard III, 1484 (Sotheby tracing)*":[17] folios 1–197; 201–216; 218–227.

b. Hand with six-rayed star (7.5 cm high, bisected by chain lines 4 cm apart).

Merchant's mark? Same mark as in MS O.3.11, folio 6a (see fig. 7d), occurring here on the last folio, 228.

9. British Library MS Cotton Claudius A.viii (fols. 175r–197v are in the hand of
   the Hammond scribe): "a post-mediaeval assemblage of independent
   items and fragments of earlier books," including Sir John Fortescue's
   Governance of England.[18]
   See figure 9:
   a. Sun with *yhs* (one of the *nomina sacra* for Jesus)/"Lettres
      assemblés." The chain lines are 3.7 cm apart. This state
      of the mark differs from the one in British Library MS
      Arundel 59 (see below) primarily in the ray on the right-
      hand side that extends over the chain line. Very close to
      the Ms Briquet xxx mark shown in figure 9b, dated 1468
      (Savoie 1468; chain lines not traced but measured "37
      mm").

10. British Library MS Arundel 59: Hoccleve's *Regiment of Princes*, Lydgate and
    Burgh's translation of the *Secrees of old Philisoffres*, and "three miscellaneous
    literary collections."[19]
    See figure 10:
    a. The sun with *yhs* (one of the *nomina sacra* for Jesus)/"Lettres
       assemblés" mark occurs throughout Arundel 59; it is
       probably the same paper stock as that in MS Cotton
       Claudius A.viii, though a different state, and is very sim-
       ilar to that in British Library MS Egerton 2864
       (*Canterbury Tales*).

11. British Library MS Harley 372: two unrelated MSS bound together, the rel-
    evant MS being folios 71r–112r, containing Hoccleve's *Regiment of Princes*,
    beginning at 3312: "[M]ercy aftir the word of Seynt Austyn | Of hert is a
    verray compassioun."[20]
    See figure 11:
    a. Bull/"Boeuf," similar to Briquet 2786 (Angoulême 1470);
       bisected by a chain line with attendant chain lines 3.6
       and 3.8 centimeters apart. Very close to Ms Briquet xxx,
       no. 9340 (Carpentras 1471; see fig. 11b). This paper stock
       is similar to or the same as stocks found in Princeton MS
       100 (the Helmingham *Canterbury Tales*) and Cambridge
       University Library MS Hh.4.11 (Hoccleve, *Regiment of
       Princes*): folios 71–85.
    b. Bull's head/"Tête de Boeuf"; very close to WM I 003329
       (Utrecht, [1474]), WM I 03357 (Utrecht, 1474), WM I
       60210 (Netherlands, [1474–1475]), WM I 51687 (Bruges,
       March 31, 1474), WM I 51688 (Bruges, March 31, 1474),

and WM 1 55864 (Bruges, [1473]) in the *Watermarks in Incunabula Printed in the Low Countries*). Folios 89–112.

12. Trinity College, Cambridge, MS R.3.21: folios 34r–49v, the section containing *Parce mihi domine* (NIMEV 561) and *Pety Job* (NIMEV 1854).[21]
See figure 12:
  a. Scissors, 4°, bisected by a chain line, attendant chain lines are 2.6 and 2.8 cm apart (cf. MS R.3.19, but this mark does not match any of those paper stocks): Qq [1–9]; mixed in [19, 29].
  b. Gothic P with quatrefoil: Qq [10–13, 33]; mixed in Qq [18, 21, 31] (the same stock as MS R.3.19, paper stock 5; cf. Ms Briquet xxx, no. 23501 [Namur 1476; see fig. 12c])
  d. "Splayed" Gothic P with quatrefoil: Qq [14–17]; mixed in Q [18].
  e. Shield with "A" (the same stock as in MS R.3.19, paper stock 7): Q [21], folios 175–178.
  f. Crown and scepter (4°; the same stock as in MS R.3.19, paper stock 8): mixed in Qq [19, 24]; Qq [22–23; 25].
  g. Gothic P: mixed in Qq [24, 28, 31]; throughout Q [27]. Crowned fleur-de-lis (not reproduced, the same stock as in MS R.3.19, paper stock 9; see fig. 12h): mixed in Q [28]; Qq [35–40].

Although the Hammond Scribe does not contribute to Trinity College, Cambridge MS R.3.19, the fact that he collaborates with the scribe of that MS elsewhere motivates the following discussion of the paper stocks in that MS, some of which, as noted above, are shared by MS R.3.21. The paper stocks detailed below are cross-referenced to betaradiographic reproductions in Fletcher's introduction to the facsimile volume, which in some cases are clearer than the ones reproduced here:
  Paper stock 1: Scissors, 4° (unidentified): folios 1–16; 67–81; 82–97 (Fletcher's figs. 5 & 6).
  Paper stock 2: Scissors with post horn (of the type similar to Briquet 3702, but not that mark), 4°: folios 17–25 (Fletcher's fig. 7).[22]
  Paper stock 3: Gothic P with quatrefoil: folios 26–41; 42+48; 55–66; 114–145; 146+153; 148–151; 179–191; 197–204; 217–232; 247–254 (Fletcher's fig. 1).
  Paper stock 4: Gothic P with quatrefoil: folios 49–54 (Fletcher's fig. 3).

Paper stock 5: Gothic P with quatrefoil: cf. Ms Briquet xxx, no. 23501 (Namur 1476: the mark is virtually identical to this tracing, but shifted to the left in relation to the chains, which are also of the same spacing; see fig. 12c); the same stock as MS R.3.21, e.g., folio 99; folios 154–161 (Fletcher's fig. 2).

Paper stock 6: Gothic P with quatrefoil, close to Piccard XI.154 (Bensberg [Köln] 1482): folios 170+179; 180–188; 189–191; 194–196 (Fletcher's fig. 4).

Paper stock 7: Shield with an "A" 2°, perhaps identical to Briquet 7690 (1476); the same stock occurs in MS R.3.21 (see fig. 12e): folios 43–47; 240–246 (Fletcher's fig. 9).

Paper stock 8: Crown with scepter(?) 4°; the same stock occurs in MS R.3.21 (see fig. 12f): folios 98–113; 162–178 205–216 (Fletcher's fig. 8).[23]

Paper stock 9: Crowned fleur-de-lis, 2°: cf. Briquet 7252 (Sens 1474, Paris 1475); closer to the unpublished Ms Briquet xxx, no. 11703 (Le Puy 1476), and perhaps identical with Ms Briquet xxx, no. 11648 (Montferrano 1477; see fig. 12h) folios 192+193 (Fletcher's fig. 11).

Paper stock 10: "Flag," 2°: (like Briquet "Etendard" 5989 [Palerme 1477]; somewhat closer to Ms Briquet xxx, no. 6622 [Catane 1489]): folios 233–246 (Fletcher's fig. 10).

Paper stock 11: Seated pope 2° (Briquet 7546–7550, 1451–1484: the same paper stock as Caxton's *History of Jason* [STC 15383 (1477)]; reproduced in Blades, vol. 2, pl. IX.9[24]): folios 147+152 (Fletcher's fig. 12).

13. Worcester Cathedral Library MS F.172: "English prose translations of Latin apocrypha and authentic books of scripture, exemplary tales, devotional and didactic treatises, and ecclesiastical decrees, with some vernacular contemplative compositions."[25]

See figure 13:

a. Gothic P with quatrefoil: a pair of twins; e.g., folio 32; the watermark is 7.5 cm tall with attendant chain lines 3.5 | 3.3| 3.3 | 3.3 | 3.3 | 1.8 cm apart. One of the pair (e.g., on fol. 32; fig. 13b)[26] is an identical match, including sewing dots, with Piccard IX.781 (Mechelen 1475): Qq [1–3].

c. Gothic P: e.g., folio 37, chain lines spaced 3.8 | 3.0 | 3.6 | 2 cm apart: no quatrefoil, diagonal cross on stem; mark is 5.5 cm; see MS O.3.11, fig. 7c, above, which is probably the same paper stock. Close to Ms Briquet xxx, no. 23161 (Colmar 1481; see fig. 13d): Qq [4–5].

e. Gothic P with quatrefoil and diagonal cross on stem: a pair of twins, e.g., folio 72. The mark is 5.9 cm tall with chain lines spaced 3.1 | 3 | 3.2 | 30 | 33 | 1.2 cm apart. One of the stocks (e.g., fol. 60) has a bent chain line (the chain-line spacing for this twin is 3 | 3.3 | 3 | 3 | 3.2 cm). Very close to Piccard XII.458 (Wesel, 1486): Qq [6–13].

f. Gothic P with small quatrefoil: a pair of twins, e.g., folios 165, 172, and 204; measuring 6 cm and 6.5 tall with very narrow chain-line spacing: 2.2 | 2 | 2 | 2 | 2.2 | 2.2 cm. Very close to Ms Briquet xxx, no. 23493 (Namur 1482; see fig. 13g): same chain-line spacing, same dimensions, probably a slightly different state: Qq [14–18], except for folios 206+209.

h.   Ring   with   a   crown   and   Maltese   cross/cross potent/"Anneau" (Briquet 694 [1479]):[27] folios 206+209.

What Does the Paper Evidence Tell Us?

MS Additional 34360 poses something of a problem. Even with the availability of the unpublished Briquet tracings and online databases, none of the paper stocks in this MS can be matched precisely with dated examples. The cart watermark that occurs in Q [2] is very similar to Briquet 3546, which is dated 1466. In a roundabout fashion, however, we can conjoin its dating with that of MS Additional 29901: both MSS appear to share paper stocks with *Canterbury Tales* MS Bodley 414, which has both the cart watermark and the ring watermark that occurs in MS Additional 29901. All the dated examples of watermarks with this morphology in Ms Briquet xxx are from the late 1450s and early 1460s, the closest being the example 6622 (Catane 1462). These pieces of information allow us tentatively to assign both MSS to the mid-1460s.

MS Royal 17.D.xv is a composite manuscript. The symmetrical bull's-head stock has a long run, covering all of the first scribe's stint (whose hand is as yet unidentified in other MSS) and over a hundred folios of the Hammond scribe's work. The Hammond scribe employs two more paper stocks: the "Armoires Deux Pals" mark and the scissors-and-post-horn stock. While I have not found a dated analogue of the bull's-head mark, the other two stocks are from the mid-1460s. The rest of the MS—unrelated to the first part—is datable on internal evidence to later than 1471, and the unicorn and anchor paper stocks are of the mid-to-late 1470s. MS Harley 2251 has paper stocks very similar to those of MS Royal 17.D.xv, though none appear to be exact matches. They may come from the same reams of papers but from different states of manufacture. All of the analogues for these papers (except for the elusive bull's-head marks) are the same as for MS Royal 17.D.xv and so also place MS Harley 2251 in the mid-1460s.

When the Hammond scribe copied his second *Canterbury Tales* MS, Royal College of Physicians MS 388, he accessioned a much more authoritative exemplar for the bulk of the text than what was available for the copying of MS Royal 17.D.xv.[28] For the *General Prologue* and *Parson's Tale*, however, Manly and Rickert believed that Physicians 388 "unmistakably" shares the ancestor of MS Bodley 414 and Bibliotheca Bodmeriana, Cod. Bodmer 48 (formerly Phillipps 8136), and that it uses the exemplar of MS Royal 17.D.xv for other pieces of text missing from Hengwrt.[29] Peter Robinson's analysis of the MSS relationships for the *General Prologue*, in contrast, groups the Physicians MS with a subgroup including MS Royal 17.D.xv, while classifying Bodley 414-Bodmer 48 as the only two witnesses of his e̲ ancestor in the *General Prologue*.[30] However, Robinson kindly carried out a VBase (database of variants) search of the subgroup for me with the following results (since the *Canterbury Tales* Project's lineation varies from Manly and Rickert's, I include theirs in brackets where they differ):[31]

        CollateDB="GP.db"

        Multiple Query, 17 hits:

        in Bo1 Ph2 Py: FROM \start TO \end

                AND in <7 of \all: FROM \start TO \end

                L346 [344] fressh | Bo1 Hg Ph2 Py

                L365 [363] And | Alle Bo1 Ph2 Py

                L365 [363] alle | Omitted Bo1 Ds1 Fi Ph2 Py Sl2

                L367 [365] apyked | ypyked Bo1 Mg Ph2 Py Se

                L505 [503] And | Omitted Bo1 Ph2 Py

                L536 [534] gamed | gramed Bo1 Ph2 Py

                L542 [540] of | in Bo1 Ph2 Py

                L559 [557] blake weere | weere blake Bo1 Dl Ph2 Py

                L590 [588] he | it Bo1 Ph2 Py

                L605 [603] nas | ne was Bo1 Dl Gl Ph2 Py

                L615 [613] he lerned | lerned he Bo1 Ph2 Py

                L625 [623] was ther | ther was Bo1 Cn Ph2 Py

                L629 [627] blake | Omitted Bo1 Ph2 Py

                L673 [673] This | The Bo1 Ha4 Ph2 Py

                L765 [is | be Bo1 Ph2 Py

                L789 I pray yow in desdeyn | in desdeyn I yow pray
                  Bo1 Ph2 Py

                L794 he | ye Bo1 Ph2 Py

Robinson comments:

> I must say that I can see why [Manly and Rickert] thought this is too many for simple coincidence. The variants *only* in Bo1 Ph2 Py are striking. I would not rule out contamination—occasional import of occasional readings, especially likely to occur in particular areas. If there is a known connection between Bo1 Ph2 Py then that would move contamination higher up the probability scale as an explanation.[32]

Since it appears that two of the Hammond scribe's earlier MSS shared paper stocks with Bodley 414, it would be very interesting if the Hammond scribe also had access to that MS's exemplar. The paper stocks in the Physicians MS are difficult to date, in no small part because they are in 4° format. My best guess is that this MS belongs to the period of the late 1460s: later than MS Royal 17.D.xv, but not much later.

The next three MSS must be considered together: Trinity College, Cambridge MSS R.14.52 and O.3.11, and British Library MS Harley 4999. Mooney describes close correspondence of physical features (size, format, scribal letter forms) in the two Trinity MSS and states: "both volumes were clearly conceived and produced as a whole, with works organized in a logical order, with scribal foliation throughout the volume, and with a detailed table of contents produced by the scribe at the front of each volume."[33] To this we can add the sharing of three paper stocks in long runs: the hand with five-pointed star, the Gothic P, and the Gothic P with a cross. The distribution of these stocks suggests that the two MSS were copied simultaneously. There is not much to help us with the dating. The scribe writes "Quod Multon 1458" on folio 215r in MS R.14.52, so the MS is certainly after that date. The scribe also attributes a recipe "(as if he were still living) to Roger Necton, M.D., of Oxford, a royal physician who is known to have died by 1484."[34] The attribution comes on folio 264v, on the stock for which an example is given from MS O.3.11, folio 126 (see fig. 7c). The crown-with-trefoil stock, which runs from folio 203 to folio 250 (i.e., preceding the attribution), likely derives from about 1484 or 1485. It is probable that these MSS were copied over a period of some time, perhaps from the late 1460s to the mid-1480s. The church paper stock in MS Harley 4999 also occurs in MS R.14.52 on four inserted folios containing drawings; they come between folio 173 and folio 174, foliated by the scribe as "clxxiiia–d." The stock with a mont in a circle surmounted by a cross in MS R.14.52 also constitutes an insertion of tables and music between folio 256 and folio 257, foliated "cclvia–c." The merchant's-mark stock occurs on the last folio of MS Harley 4999 and on folio 6a (a blank leaf ruled in violet) of MS O.3.11. Since the church stock is the primary stock in MS Harley 4999, I would speculate that this MS is for the most part of a later date than the Trinity pair, produced during the time that the inserted drawings were added to MS R.14.52, though the reverse order is certainly possible. The merchant's-mark singletons were apparently remnants.

MSS Arundel 59 and Cotton Claudius A.viii share very similar paper stocks, a sun with *yhs*, possibly dating from the late 1460s (the nearest analogue, which is very close, is from 1468), but they could date from as late as the mid-to-late 1470s. The Cotton MS, Doyle notes, "must be dated after 1471," when Fortescue first gave allegiance to King Edward IV. In the same place, Doyle suggests that this MS might be "anterior to that of Harley 78 and Worcester F.172, where the script is perhaps less firmly formed, if that by itself were a trustworthy sign, which it is not."[35] Arundel 59 might, then, be the earlier of the Hammond scribe's two *Regiment of Princes* MSS. The other, MS Harley 372, might have been produced before the three MSS discussed in the previous paragraph, but probably during a hiatus in that larger production. The first paper stock in that MS, a bull facing left, is from the early 1470s, and the bull's-head stock that completes the MS is likely from the early-to-mid 1470s. Although Seymour did not know Harley 372 was by the Hammond scribe, he does observe that "The Hoccleve text of MS. Arundel 59 is very close to that of MS. Harley 372."[36] A collation of the two MSS might reveal which was copied first.

The other two Trinity College, Cambridge MSS—R.3.19 and R.3.21— were, like R.14.52 and O.3.11, copied in tandem (or in parallel): "These two manuscripts have the common characteristic of having been created from booklets apparently produced separately, certainly foliated separately, and perhaps used separately before having been bound together. The booklets from which both were compiled were written in London in the 1460s, 1470s, and/or 1480s."[37] Based on the internal evidence of references to "Henry VI's death and burial at Chertsey (but not Windsor, whence his body was moved at the behest of Richard III in 1484)" and of "an address to Henry VI (the envoy to NIMEV 2218) changed to apply instead to Edward IV (fol. 245v)," at least a portion of MS R.3.21 "can be dated certainly after 1471 and probably—though not certainly—before 1484."[38] Though the Hammond scribe appears in only a portion of MS R.3.21, his main collaborator in that MS, Scribe A, copied MS R.3.19, and the production methods and shared paper stocks arguably link the MSS to the Hammond scribe's oeuvre. The dates for the paper stocks span a period from the mid-1470s to perhaps the early 1480s, overlapping at least in part with the production of the other two Trinity MSS. And perhaps that accounts for the appearance of Scribe A: the amount of work the Hammond scribe had contracted for came to exceed his ability to meet the demand and/or time constraints on the use of exemplars. Probably also during this same time frame, the Hammond scribe was engaged in copying Worcester

Cathedral Library MS F.172, with watermarks from 1475 to perhaps as late as the mid-1480s, one of which is shared by MS O.3.11.

In the following table, I present tentative suggestions for a sequence and dating of the Hammond scribe manuscripts, excluding British Library MS Harley 78 (fol. 3r) and Bodleian Library MS Rawlinson D.913 (fol. 43r–v), which lack watermarks.

Tentative Dating Sequence for the Hammond Scribe's Manuscripts

Royal 17.D.xv Harley 2251	1465–1469
Additional 34360 Additional 29901	1466–early 1470s
Royal College of Physicians MS 388	late 1460s
Trinity College, Cambridge R.14.52 Trinity College, Cambridge MS O.3.11 Harley 4999	late 1460s–mid-1480s
Cotton Claudius A.viii Arundel 59 Harley 372	early 1470s
Trinity College, Cambridge MS R.3.19 Trinity College, Cambridge MS R.3.21	mid-1470s–early 1480s
Worcester Cathedral MS F.172	1475–mid-1480s

Though many of these conclusions must remain provisional, my work has come to a point where further refinements will come only through the discovery of more and/or better-dated analogues. It is hoped that the publication of these watermark images and their accompanying data might allow others to make such identifications. Indeed, the present effort has already been greatly aided by access to three large archives of watermarks: the "Briquet Archive" (Ms Briquet xxx) in Geneva; the *Watermarks in Incunabula Printed in the*

Low Countries database mounted online by the *Koninklijke Bibliotheek*/National Library of the Netherlands; and the Piccard collection of watermarks (*Wasserzeichenkartei Piccard*, an online database at the Hauptstaatsarchiv Stuttgart). I had become frustrated earlier in my attempts to make identifications with the available albums and catalogues of watermarks, leaving the unfinished work in my files for some years before returning to it in the summer of 2005, with much happier results.

Figures 1–13: Images of Watermarks Found in the MSS of the Hammond Scribe

The images in the following "catalogue" of watermarks were reproduced by three different technologies. The images of watermarks in Oxford, MS Bodley 414 (not by the Hammond scribe, but used for purposes of comparison and illustration) are reproduced through betaradiography, a technology no longer in use in many institutions where it was once common. At the British Library and at Cambridge University Library, for example, watermarks are now reproduced using transmitted light: a cold-light source is used to illuminate the watermark, and the image is photographed, often using a digital camera. The image is then imported into a software program such as Adobe Photoshop, and adjustments are made to the levels, brightness, and/or contrast. The majority of watermarks used to illustrate this article were reproduced in this fashion. The results are not always as satisfactory as those provided by betaradiography, since parts of the watermark are obscured by the text on both sides of the leaf. The watermark images from the Royal College of Physicians MS 388 and Worcester Cathedral Library MS F.172 were made by me using transmitted light and digital image capture.[39] I have also used some examples of tracings from the Charles-Moïse Briquet Archive (Ms Briquet xxx) held by the Bibliothèque de Genève.[40] In 2000, I obtained digital copies of the more than 27,000 unpublished tracings that make up part of this large archive. The images made through the transmitted light method, unfortunately, were not reproduced at actual size or with a rule provided as part of the image. For this reason, and because reproducing all of these images as full- or near-full-sized images would be impracticable, I have not attempted to present these as full-scale images.

Virginia Tech

NOTES

1. Eleanor P. Hammond, "Two British Museum Manuscripts (Harley 2251 and Add. 34360): A Contribution to the Biography of John Lydgate," *Anglia: Zeitschrift für Englische Philologie* 28 (1905): 1–28; Eleanor P. Hammond, "A Scribe of Chaucer," *Modern Philology* 27 (1929): 27–33.

2. The most recent analyses of the Hammond Scribe's spellings are Simon Horobin, "Linguistic Features of the Hammond Scribe," *Poetica* 51 (1999): 1–10; Lister M. Matheson, "The Dialect of the Hammond Scribe," in *Sex, Aging, & Death in a Medieval Medical Compendium: Trinity College Cambridge MS R.14.52, Its Text, Language, and Scribe*, 2 vols., ed. M. Teresa Tavormina (Tempe: Arizona Center for Medieval and Renaissance Studies, 2006), I:65–93.

3. The rest of the MS consists of a collection of binding fragments and "larger excerpts"; A. I. Doyle, "An Unrecognized Piece of *Piers the Ploughman's Creed* and Other Work by Its Scribe," *Speculum* 34 (1959): 428–436, 433.

4. Julia Boffey and A. S. G. Edwards (London: British Library, 2005), no. 663 (hereafter NIMEV); Doyle, "An Unrecognized Piece of *Piers the Ploughman's Creed*" (facsimile of folio 3r) Humphrey Wanley, David Casley, et al., *Catalogue of the Harleian Manuscripts in the British Museum* (London: Record Commission, 1808–1812), I:20–21. For John Stow's ownership of and commentary in this and other Middle English MSS, see A. S. G. Edwards, "John Stow and Middle English Literature," in Ian Gadd and Alexandra Gillespie, eds., *John Stow (1525–1605) and the Making of the English Past* (London: British Library, 2004), 109–118.

5. C. Paul Christianson, "Evidence for the Study of London's Late Medieval Manuscript-Book Trade," in *Book Production and Publishing in Britain, 1375–1475*, ed. Jeremy Griffiths and Derek Pearsall (Cambridge: Cambridge University Press, 1989), 107, n. 43; Linne R. Mooney, "A Middle English Text on the Seven Liberal Arts," *Speculum* 68 (1993): 1027–1052, 1028 and n. 8. A. I. Doyle cites the Hammond scribe's connection with the John Multon, stationer of London, whose will is dated 1475 ("Commissary Court of London, reg. 6, f. 178v": "English Books in and out of Court from Edward III to Henry VII," in *English Court Culture in the Later Middle Ages*, ed. V. J. Scattergood and J. W. Sherborne [London: Duckworth, 1983], 163–181177 n. 42). Anthony Gross discusses the Multon connection extensively in *The Dissolution of the Lancastrian Kingship*: (Stamford, UK: Paul Watkins, 1996), 106–126.

6. Horobin, "Linguistic Features of the Hammond Scribe," 8. Lister Matheson, employing a larger corpus of the scribe's work, agrees with Horobin that "the scribe was an immigrant working in London" (Matheson, "The Dialect of the Hammond Scribe," I:83, n. 17), but localizes his language instead to "north-west Essex or even extreme southwest Suffolk" (I:82). Matheson's localization jibes with the association of some of the scribe's MSS with Sir Thomas Cook and John Vale (I:87; see also Linne R. Mooney, "The Scribe," in *Sex, Aging, &*

Death in a Medieval Medical Compendium: Trinity College Cambridge MS R.14.52, *Its Text, Language, and Scribe*, 2 vols., ed. M. Teresa Tavormina [Tempe: Arizona Center for Medieval and Renaissance Studies, 2006], I:55–63.)

7. In this section I make frequent use of the following references: Charles-Moïse Briquet, *Les filigranes: Dictionnaire historique des marques du papier dès leur apparition vers 1282 jusqu'en 1600* (Geneva: A. Jullien, 1907), hereafter "Briquet"; Charles-Moïse Briquet, Ms Briquet xxx (Bibliothèque de Genève; the unpublished tracings of Charles-Moïse Briquet); Daniel W. Mosser and Ernest W. Sullivan II with Len Hatfield, *The Thomas L. Gravell Watermark Archive* (1996–), available at http://www.gravell.org; the published catalogues of Gerhard Piccard listed in the Works Cited section; (Gerhard Piccard), *Wasserzeichenkartei Piccard*, available at http://www.landesarchiv-bw.de/piccard/sitemap.php (Hauptstaatsarchiv Stuttgart), an online database of watermarks collected by Piccard; and *Watermarks in Incunabula Printed in the Low Countries* (Koninklijke Bibliotheek /National Library of the Netherlands, 2000–), available at http://watermark.kb.nl/.

8. See Hammond, "A Scribe of Chaucer," for a reduced facsimile of the opening of folios 166v–167r; see Gross, *The Dissolution of the Lancastrian Kingship*, for reduced facsimiles of folios 312r, 304v, 307v, and 320v; for descriptions, see John Manly and Edith Rickert, *The Text of the Canterbury Tales* (Chicago: University of Chicago Press, 1940), I:476–484; Michael Seymour, *The Canterbury Tales*, vol. 2 of *A Catalogue of Chaucer Manuscripts* (Aldershot, UK, and Brookfield, VT: Scolar, 1997), 135–138; Daniel W. Mosser, "Witness Descriptions," in *The Nun's Priest's Tale on CD-ROM*, ed. Paul Thomas (Birmingham, UK: Scholarly Digital Editions, 2006). Note that Gross's "mid-century date for the paper" used in folios 302–310 ("Somnium vigilantis") should be revised to ca. 1469–1477 (Gross, *The Dissolution of the Lancastrian Kingship*, 98 and n. 35).

9. In "The Use of Caxton Texts and Paper Stocks in Manuscripts of the *Canterbury Tales*," in *Chaucer in Perspective: Middle English Essays in Honour of Norman Blake*, ed. Geoffrey Lester (Sheffield, UK: Sheffield Academic Press, 1999), 161–177, I erred in stating that the unicorn paper stock occurs in "a section of [MS Royal 17.D.xv] copied by the 'Hammond Scribe'" (169). Clearly, this section of the MS is in a different, slightly later hand.

10. See the listings of contents in Hammond, "Two British Museum Manuscripts"; Manly and Rickert, *The Text of the Canterbury Tales*, I:241–244 (reduced facsimile of folio 7r); Michael Seymour, *Works before the Canterbury Tales*, vol. 1 of *A Catalogue of Chaucer Manuscripts* (Aldershot, UK, and Brookfield, VT: Scolar, 1995), 140–143; Lori J. Dixon, "The *Canterbury Tales* Miscellanies: A Contextual Study of the Manuscripts Anthologizing Individual *Canterbury Tales*" (unpublished dissertation, University of Delaware, 1995), 227–233 and Appendix D; see also Linne R. Mooney, "John Shirley's Heirs," *Yearbook of English Studies* 33 (2003): 182–198.

11. For a listing of contents, see Hammond, "Two British Museum Manuscripts"; see Mooney, "John Shirley's Heirs." See Edwards, "John Stow and Middle English Literature," 113, for a facsimile of folio 19r.

12. See Linne R. Mooney, "A New Manuscript by the Hammond Scribe Discovered by Jeremy Griffiths," in *The English Medieval Book: Studies in Memory of Jeremy Griffiths*, ed. A. S. G. Edwards, Vincent Gillespie, and Ralph Hanna (London: British Library, 2000), 113–123.

13. For descriptions, see Manly and Rickert, *The Text of the Canterbury Tales*, 1:439–446; Seymour, *The Canterbury Tales*, 150–154; Mosser, "Witness Descriptions"; a reduced facsimile of folio 188r appears in Hammond, "A Scribe of Chaucer."

14. Identified by Doyle, "English Books in and out of Court," 177 n. 42; see Linne R. Mooney, "A Middle English Text on the Seven Liberal Arts," 1028 (Mooney presents an edition of the text on pp. 1037–1052, reprinted in M. Teresa Tavormina, ed., *Sex, Aging, & Death in a Medieval Medical Compendium: Trinity College Cambridge MS R.14.52, Its Text, Language, and Scribe*, 2 vols. [Tempe: Arizona Center for Medieval and Renaissance Studies, 2006], II:701–736); see Linne R. Mooney, *The Index of Middle English Prose: Handlist XI, Manuscripts in the Library of Trinity College, Cambridge* (Cambridge: D. S. Brewer, 1995), 53–64, for a full listing of contents; see also Linne R. Mooney, "More Manuscripts Written by a Chaucer Scribe," *Chaucer Review* 30 (1996): 401–407; see Gross, for reduced facsimiles of folios 1r, 215r, 218v–219r, 53r, and 57r; for a comprehensive study of the MS, see M. Teresa Tavormina, ed., *Sex, Aging, & Death in a Medieval Medical Compendium: Trinity College Cambridge MS R.14.52, Its Text, Language, and Scribe*, 2 vols. (Tempe: Arizona Center for Medieval and Renaissance Studies, 2006), with a reduced, color facsimile of folio 1r as a frontispiece (see especially the essays by Pahta, Kurtz and Voigts, Mooney, and Matheson listed separately in the Works Cited section).

15. Identified by Mooney, "More Manuscripts Written by a Chaucer Scribe" (facsimile of folio 1r); see also Mooney, *The Index of Middle English Prose*, 109–114, for a comprehensive listing of contents, consisting of "City and legal documents." See also Gross,*The Dissolution of the Lancastrian Kingship*, 110–112 n. 68; 116–117 n. 73; 121. After this article had passed the copy-editing stages, I engaged in a series of e-mail exchanges with Laura Wright, of the University of Cambridge, who reminded me that MS Trinity O.3.11 has the Church water-mark on one of the unfoliated fly leaves at the front of the MS. Wright has located a cognate in Oriol Valls i Subirà, *Paper and Watermarks in Catalonia*, 2 vols. (Amsterdam: Paper Publications Society, 1970), number 1604: "Iglesia/Church." Valls i Subirà dates the mark as 1470, based on "[a] number of leaves in a Santa Pau register [150]," in Olot, Spain. The Valls i Subirà tracing differs from the paper stock of MSS Harley 4999 (see figure 8a), Trinity R.14.52, and Trinity O.311 in several ways: the Hammond mark has a chain

line running through the spire of the church, while the Valls i Subirà tracing is centered between chain lines; the Hammond mark has two windows in its design, while the Valls i Subirà tracing has only a single window. But the two marks are very similar, and the dating does help to corroborate my dating of those MSS.

16. Identified by Doyle, "English Books in and out of Court"; see Mooney, "A New Manuscript by the Hammond Scribe," 121 n. 6.

17. Edward Heawood, "Sources of Early English Paper Supply," The Library 10 (1929–1930): 282–307, 290.

18. Doyle, "An Unrecognized Piece of Piers the Ploughman's Creed," 432 (includes a facsimile of folio 175r). See Gross,The Dissolution of the Lancastrian Kingship, 72 n. 9 (dating); 84 n. 60; 115–116 n. 72; 116–117 n. 73.

19. See Hammond, "A Scribe of Chaucer," 27; Michael C. Seymour, "The Manuscripts of Hoccleve's Regiment of Princes," Edinburgh Bibliographical Society Transactions 6 (1974): 255–297, 264–265; Richard Firth Green, "Notes on Some Manuscripts of Hoccleve's Regiment of Princes," British Library Journal 4 (1978): 39–41; a reduced facsimile of folio 80v is reproduced in Hammond, "A Scribe of Chaucer."

20. See Seymour, "The Manuscripts of Hoccleve's Regiment of Princes," 266–267; identified in Green, "Notes on Some Manuscripts of Hoccleve's Regiment of Princes," which includes a facsimile of folio 103r. See Edwards, "John Stow and Middle English Literature," 112, for a facsimile of folio 103r.

21. See Hammond, "A Scribe of Chaucer," 33; Linne R. Mooney "Scribes and Booklets of Trinity College, Cambridge, Manuscripts R.3.19 and R.3.21," in Middle English Poetry: Texts and Traditions, Essays in Honour of Derek Pearsall, ed. A. J. Minnis (Suffolk, UK, and Rochester, NY: York Medieval Press in association with the Boydell Press, 2001), 241–266, with facsimiles of folios 2v, 49v, 74r, 245v; see also Mooney, "John Shirley's Heirs"; Pamela R. Robinson, A Catalogue of Dated and Datable Manuscripts c. 737–1600 in Cambridge Libraries, 2 vols. (Cambridge: D. S. Brewer, 1988), I:96 (no. 344) and II:pl. 304. The majority of MS R.3.21 was written by a scribe labeled by Mooney as "Scribe A" ("Scribes and Booklets," 241). This same scribe copied Trinity College, Cambridge MS R.3.19 (reproduced in facsimile and described in Bradford Y. Fletcher, intro., "MS Trinity R.3.19," The Facsimile Series of the Works of Geoffrey Chaucer.

22. Fletcher's arrangement of the top and bottom elements in his fig. 7 is somewhat misleading: both elements should be rotated 180 degrees to illustrate their proper alignments to each other.

23. Here, too, Fletcher's arrangement of the top and bottom elements in his fig. 8 should be rotated 180 degrees to illustrate their proper alignments to each other.

24. William Blades, The Life and Typography of William Caxton, 2 vols. (London: J. Lilly, 1861–1863).

25. Doyle, "An Unrecognized Piece of *Piers the Ploughman's Creed*," 430–431; contents described in R. M. Thomson, *A Descriptive Catalogue of the Medieval Manuscripts in Worcester Cathedral Library* (Cambridge: D. S. Brewer, 2001), 114–116. An extensive study of MS F.172 is underway by Muriel Kasper: "Ms Worcester F.172, A Religious Miscellany by the Hammond Scribe, Containing the Only Known Middle English Version of Petrus Alphonsi's Disciplina Clericalis" (http://www.anglistik.uni-bonn.de/research/memo/KASPER.HTM; and e-mail to Mosser January 29, 2003).
26. The reproduction is somewhat distorted, as the camera angle was less than 90 degrees; a transparency reproduction of the Piccard mark fits exactly over the mark in MS F.172.
27. This watermark also appears in Trinity College, Cambridge MS R.3.15, folio 9r; another watermark in that MS, a dog/"Chien," is an identical match with Ms Briquet xxx, no. 23431 (Ecloo 1480).
28. Manly and Rickert believed that Physicians 388 was "derived, through many intermediaries, from a MS akin to Hg" (i.e., National Library of Wales MS 392D, the Hengwrt MS; *The Text of the Canterbury Tales*, 1:441). Peter Robinson's collations and stemmatic commentaries on the *Canterbury Tales* Project's CD-ROM editions see the text of the Royal College of Physicians MS in an even better light, if anything, than Manly and Rickert. On *The Nun's Priest's Tale* on CD-ROM, for example, Robinson identifies Physicians 388 as one of eleven MSS (including Hg) classified as ǫ (i.e., independent copies of the archetype) witnesses; Robinson, "The Witness Relations in The Nun's Priest's Tale and Related Links, § 5. Conclusions about the Textual Tradition," *The Nun's Priest's Tale on* CD-ROM, ed. Paul Thomas (Birmingham, UK: Scholarly Digital Editions, 2006).
29. Manly and Rickert, *The Text of the Canterbury Tales*, 1:441; 1:478–479.
30. Peter Robinson, "Analysis Workshop," *The General Prologue on* CD-ROM, ed. Elizabeth Solopova (Cambridge: Cambridge University Press, 2000), Analysis Workshop, Section 3.4.3, "Hg, El; ę; Manly and Rickert."
31. The sigla used below are standard in Chaucer studies. Expansions of the MSS cited by Robinson are: Bo[1] = MS Bodley 414; Ds[1] = Takamiya MS 24 (formerly "Devonshire"); Dl = Takamiya MS 32 (formerly "Delamere"); Fi = Cambridge, Fitzwilliam Museum MS McClean 181; Gl = Glasgow, Hunterian Museum MS 197 (formerly U.1.1); Hg = National Library of Wales MS 392D; Ph[2]= Bibliotheca Bodmeriana, Cod. Bodmer 48; Py = Royal College of Physicians MS 388; Sl[2]= British Library MS Sloane 1686.
32. Peter Robinson, e-mail to author, August 8, 2005.
33. Mooney, "More Manuscripts Written by a Chaucer Scribe," 403–404.
34. Mooney, "A Middle English Text on the Seven Liberal Arts," 1029.
35. Doyle, "An Unrecognized Piece of *Piers the Ploughman's Creed*," 432–433.

36. Michael C. Seymour, "The Manuscripts of Hoccleve's *Regiment of Princes*," 265.
37. Mooney, "A Middle English Text on the Seven Liberal Arts," 241. Pamela R. Robinson dates MS R.3.21 to "betw. 1471 & 1483": "Lydgate's verses on the kings of England ends with the death of Henry VI, d. 1471. The wording of his prayer for Henry (folio 245) has been emended in favour of Edward IV, d. 1483"; P. R. Robinson, A *Catalogue of Dated and Datable Manuscripts*, I:96.
38. Mooney, "Scribes and Booklets," 245.
39. I am very grateful to the Chapter of Worcester Cathedral for granting me permission to do this, in particular Alvyn Pettersen, Canon Librarian, and David Morrison, who assisted me in making the reproductions. I would also like to thank the Royal College of Physicians for allowing me to make images from MS 388, especially Pamela Forde, Archivist, for her kind assistance. The cold-light source I used is a Viewlight, a portable light sheet developed by Howard Eating Lighting, Ltd., in conjunction with Ian Christie-Miller. The British Library's light source is evidently brighter than that used to produce the Trinity College, Cambridge, images.
40. I describe the Briquet Archive and illustrate its usefulness in Mosser, "The Charles-Moïse Briquet Watermark Archive in Geneva," in *Looking at Paper: Evidence & Interpretation*, Symposium Proceedings, Toronto, 1999, ed. John Slavin, Linda Sutherland, John O'Neill, Margaret Haupt, and Janet Cowan. (Ottawa: Canadian Conservation Institute, 2001), 122–127. My annotated translation of the inventory of the *Papiers Briquet* (now "Ms Briquet xxx") at the Bibliothèque de Genève (1998), is available at http://ada.cath.vt.edu:591/dbs/gravell/briquet/briqeng.html.

WORKS CITED

Blades, William. *The Life and Typography of William Caxton*. 2 vols. London: J. Lilly, 1861–1863.
Briquet, Charles-Moïse. *Les filigranes: Dictionnaire historique des marques du papier dès leur apparition vers 1282 jusqu'en 1600*. Geneva: A. Jullien, 1907.
———. Ms Briquet xxx (formerly "Papiers Briquet"). Bibliothèque de Genève. (The unpublished tracings of Charles-Moïse Briquet).
Boffey, Julia, and A. S. G. Edwards. A *New Index of Middle English Verse*. London: British Library, 2005.
Christianson, C. Paul. "Evidence for the Study of London's Late Medieval Manuscript-Book Trade." In *Book Production and Publishing in Britain, 1375–1475*. Ed. Jeremy Griffiths and Derek Pearsall. Cambridge: Cambridge University Press, 1989. 87–108.

Dixon. Lori J. "The Canterbury Tales Miscellanies: A Contextual Study of the Manuscripts Anthologizing Individual Canterbury Tales." Unpublished dissertation. Univ. of Delaware, 1995.

Doyle, A. I. "An Unrecognized Piece of Piers the Ploughman's Creed and Other Work by Its Scribe." Speculum 34 (1959): 428–436.

———. "English Books in and out of Court from Edward III to Henry VII." In English Court Culture in the Later Middle Ages. Ed. V. J. Scattergood and J. W. Sherborne. London: Duckworth, 1983. 163–181.

Edwards, A. S. G. "John Stow and Middle English Literature." In John Stow (1525–1605) and the Making of the English Past. Ed. Ian Gadd and Alexandra Gillespie. London: British Library, 2004. 109–118.

Fletcher, Bradford Y., intro. "MS Trinity R.3.19." The Facsimile Series of the Works of Geoffrey Chaucer. Vol. 5. Norman, OK: Pilgrim Books, 1987.

Green, Richard Firth. "Notes on Some Manuscripts of Hoccleve's Regiment of Princes." British Library Journal 4 (1978): 39–41.

Hammond, Eleanor P. "Two British Museum Manuscripts (Harley 2251 and Add. 34360): A Contribution to the Biography of John Lydgate." Anglia: Zeitschrift für Englische Philologie 28 (1905): 1–28.

———. "A Scribe of Chaucer." Modern Philology 27 (1929): 27–33.

Heawood, Edward. "Sources of Early English Paper Supply." The Library 10 (1929–1930): 282–307.

Horobin, Simon. "Linguistic Features of the Hammond Scribe." Poetica 51 (1999): 1–10.

Kurtz, Patricia Deery, and Linda Ehrsam Voigts. "Contents, Unique Treatises, and Related Manuscripts." In Sex, Aging, & Death in a Medieval Medical Compendium: Trinity College Cambridge MS R.14.52, Its Text, Language, and Scribe. 2 vols. Ed. M. Teresa Tavormina. Tempe: Arizona Center for Medieval and Renaissance Studies, 2006. I:19–54.

Lewis, Robert E., N.F. Blake and A. S. G. Edwards. Index of Printed Middle English Prose. New York: Garland 1985. [IPMEP]

Manly, John M., and Edith Rickert, eds. The Text of the Canterbury Tales: Studied on the Basis of All Known Manuscripts. 8 vols. Chicago: University of Chicago Press, 1940.

Matheson, Lister M. "The Dialect of the Hammond Scribe." In Sex, Aging, & Death in a Medieval Medical Compendium: Trinity College Cambridge MS R.14.52, Its Text, Language, and Scribe. 2 vols. Ed. M. Teresa Tavormina. Tempe: Arizona Center for Medieval and Renaissance Studies, 2006. I:65–93.

Mooney, Linne R. "Lydgate's 'Kings of England' and Another Verse Chronicle of the Kings." Viator 20 (1989): 255–289.

———. "A Middle English Text on the Seven Liberal Arts." Speculum 68 (1993): 1027–1052.

————. *The Index of Middle English Prose: Handlist XI, Manuscripts in the Library of Trinity College, Cambridge.* Gen. ed. A. S. G. Edwards. Cambridge, UK: D. S. Brewer, 1995.

————. "More Manuscripts Written by a Chaucer Scribe." *Chaucer Review* 30 (1996): 401–407.

————. "A New Manuscript by the Hammond Scribe Discovered by Jeremy Griffiths." In *The English Medieval Book: Studies in Memory of Jeremy Griffiths.* Ed. A. S. G. Edwards, Vincent Gillespie, and Ralph Hanna. London: British Library, 2000. 113–123.

————. "Scribes and Booklets of Trinity College, Cambridge, Manuscripts R.3.19 and R.3.21." In *Middle English Poetry: Texts and Traditions, Essays in Honour of Derek Pearsall.* Ed. A. J. Minnis. Suffolk, UK, and Rochester, NY: York Medieval Press in association with the Boydell Press, 2001. 241–266.

————. "John Shirley's Heirs." *Yearbook of English Studies* 33 (2003): 182–198.

————. "The Scribe." In *Sex, Aging, & Death in a Medieval Medical Compendium: Trinity College Cambridge MS R.14.52, Its Text, Language, and Scribe.* 2 vols. Ed. M. Teresa Tavormina. Tempe: Arizona Center for Medieval and Renaissance Studies, 2006. I:55–63.

Mosser, Daniel W. Annotated translation of the inventory of the *Papiers Briquet* (now "Ms Briquet xxx") at the Bibliothèque de Genève. 1998. Available at http://ada.cath.vt.edu:591/dbs/gravell/briquet/briqeng.html.

————. "The Use of Caxton Texts and Paper Stocks in Manuscripts of the *Canterbury Tales.*" In *Chaucer in Perspective: Middle English Essays in Honour of Norman Blake.* Ed. Geoffrey Lester. Sheffield, UK: Sheffield Academic Press, 1999. 161–177.

————. "The Charles-Moïse Briquet Watermark Archive in Geneva." *Looking at Paper: Evidence & Interpretation.* Symposium Proceedings. Toronto, 1999. Ed. John Slavin, Linda Sutherland, John O'Neill, Margaret Haupt, and Janet Cowan. Ottawa: Canadian Conservation Institute, 2001. 122–127.

————. "Witness Descriptions." *The Nun's Priest's Tale on CD-ROM.* Ed. Paul Thomas. Birmingham, UK: Scholarly Digital Editions, 2006.

Mosser, Daniel W., and Ernest W. Sullivan II, with Len Hatfield. *The Thomas L. Gravell Watermark Archive.* 1996–. Available at http://www.gravell.org.

Pahta, Päivi. "Description of the Manuscript." In *Sex, Aging, & Death in a Medieval Medical Compendium: Trinity College Cambridge MS R.14.52, Its Text, Language, and Scribe.* 2 vols. Ed. M. Teresa Tavormina. Tempe: Arizona Center for Medieval and Renaissance Studies, 2006. I:1–17.

Piccard, Gerhard. *Ochsenkopf Wasserzeichen.* Findbuch II.3 of *Die Wasserzeichen Piccard im Hauptstaatsarchiv Stuttgart.* Stuttgart, Germany: Verlag W. Kohlhammer, 1966.

————. *Wasserzeichen Anker*. Findbuch VI of *Die Wasserzeichen Piccard im Hauptstaatsarchiv Stuttgart*. Stuttgart, Germany: Verlag W. Kohlhammer, 1978.

(Piccard, Gerhard.) *Wasserzeichenkartei Piccard*. Hauptstaatsarchiv Stuttgart [an online database of watermarks collected by Piccard]. Available at http://www.landesarchiv-bw.de/piccard/sitemap.php.

Robinson, Pamela R. A *Catalogue of Dated and Datable Manuscripts c. 737–1600 in Cambridge Libraries*. 2 vols. Cambridge, UK: D. S. Brewer, 1988.

Robinson, Peter. "Analysis Workshop." *The General Prologue on* CD-ROM. Ed. Elizabeth Solopova. Cambridge, UK: Cambridge University Press, 2000.

————. "The Witness Relations in The Nun's Priest's Tale and Related Links, § 5. Conclusions about the Textual Tradition." *The Nun's Priest's Tale on* CD-ROM. Ed. Paul Thomas. Birmingham, UK: Scholarly Digital Editions, 2006.

Seymour, Michael C. "The Manuscripts of Hoccleve's *Regiment of Princes*." *Edinburgh Bibliographical Society Transactions* 6 (1974): 255–297.

————. *Works before the Canterbury Tales*. Vol. 1 of A *Catalogue of Chaucer Manuscripts*. Aldershot, UK, and Brookfield, VT: Scolar, 1995.

————. *The Canterbury Tales*. Vol. 2 of A *Catalogue of Chaucer Manuscripts*. Aldershot, UK, and Brookfield, VT: Scolar, 1997.

Tavormina, M. Teresa (Ed.) *Sex, Aging, & Death in a Medieval Medical Compendium: Trinity College Cambridge MS R.14.52, Its Text, Language, and Scribe*. 2 vols. Tempe: Arizona Center for Medieval and Renaissance Studies, 2006.

Thomson, R. M. A *Descriptive Catalogue of the Medieval Manuscripts in Worcester Cathedral Library*. Cambridge, UK: D. S. Brewer, 2001.

Wanley, Humphrey, David Casley, et al. *Catalogue of the Harleian Manuscripts in the British Museum*. London: Record Commission, 1808–1812. 1:20–21.

Watermarks in Incunabula Printed in the Low Countries. Koninklijke Bibliotheek/National Library of the Netherlands. 2000–. Available at http://watermark.kb.nl/.

Fig. 1: British Library MS Royal 17.D.xv
(Hammond Scribe copies only fols. 167r-301r)

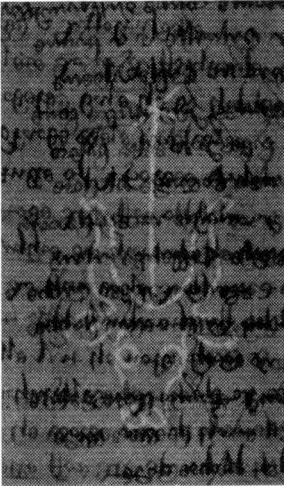

a. fol. 8v

b. fol. 277

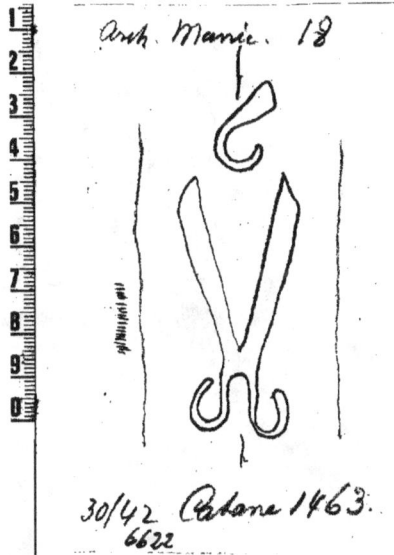

c. fol. 286

d. Ms Briquet xxx, no. 6622 (Catane 1463)

Figs. 1a-c reproduced by permission of the British Library; **Fig. 1d** by permission of the Bibliothèque de Genève.

Fig. 2: British Library MS Harley 2251

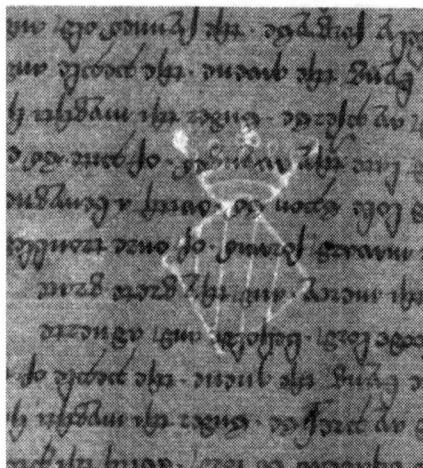

a. fol. 10v

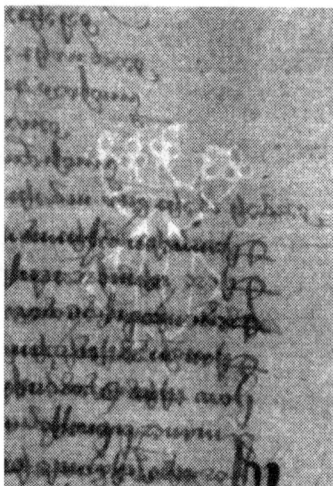

b. fol. 145

c. fol. 273

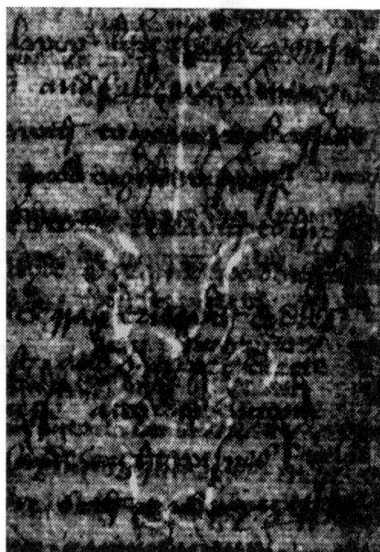

d. fol.292

Figs. 2a-d reproduced by permission of the British Library.

Fig. 3: British Library MS Additional 34360

a. fol. 87

b. Oxford, Bodleian Library MS 414,
fol. 163

c. fol. "109"

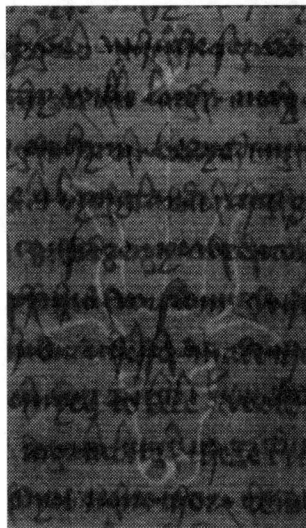

d. fol.66r

Figs. 3a, c-d reproduced by permission of the British Library; **Fig. 3b** by permission of the Bodleian Library, University of Oxford.

Fig. 4: British Library MS Additional 29901

 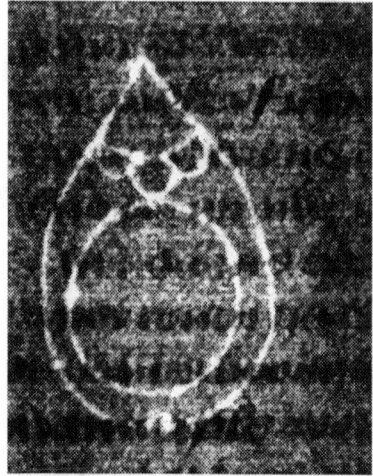

a. fol. 87   b. Oxford, MS Bodley 414, fol. 13v

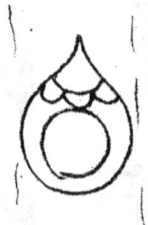

c. Ms Briquet xxx, no. 6622 (Catane
1462)

Fig. 4a reproduced by permission of the British Library; **Fig. 4b** by permission of the Bodleian Library, University of Oxford; **Fig. 4c** by permission of the Bibliothèque de Genève.

Fig. 5: Royal College of Physicians MS 388

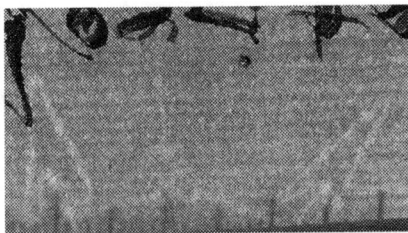

a. fol. 2 (upper) + fol. 4 (lower)

b. Ms Briquet xxx, no. [9012?],
Augsburg 1465

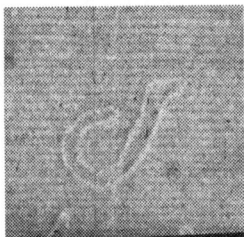

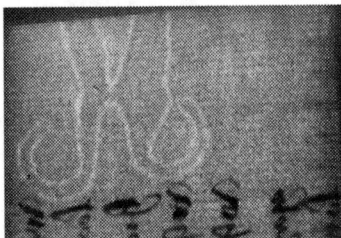

c. fol. 140v (upper) + fol. 121r (lower)   d. fol. 292r (upper) + fol. 307v (lower)

Fig. 5, cont.

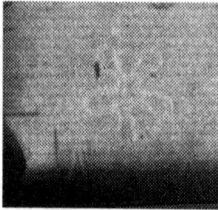
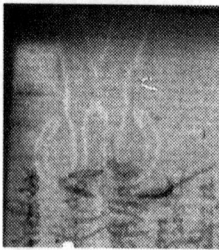
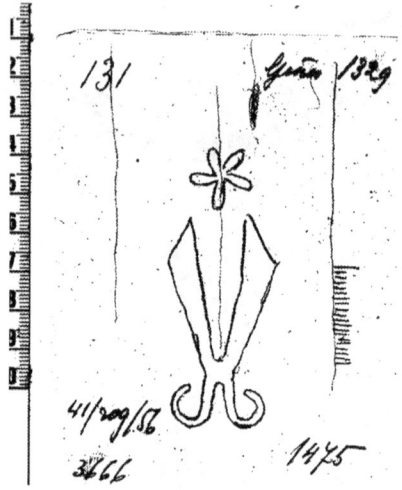

e. fol. 358r (upper) + fol. 361r (lower,   f. Ms Briquet xxx, no. 3666 (1475)
rotated horizontally)

Figs. 5a, c-e reproduced by permission of The Royal College of Physicians of London; **Figs. 5b & f** by permission of the Bibliothèque de Genève.

Fig. 6: Trinity College, Cambridge MS R.14.52

Fig. 6a reproduced by permission of the Master and Fellows of Trinity College, Cambridge.

Fig. 7: Trinity College, Cambridge MS O.3.11

a. fol. 52r

b. fol. 125r

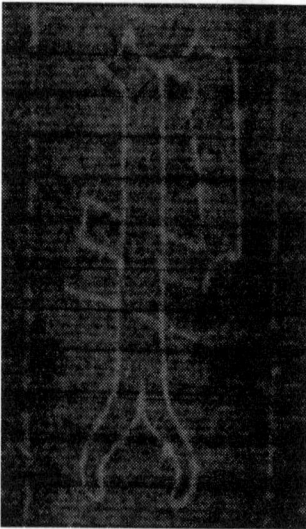

c. fol. 126r

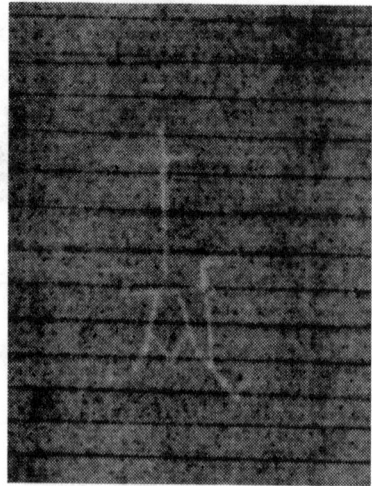

d. fol.6a (verso)

Figs. 7a-d reproduced by permission of the Master and Fellows of Trinity College, Cambridge.

Fig. 8: British Library MS Harley 4999

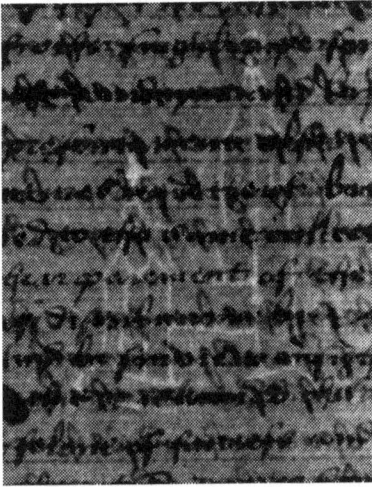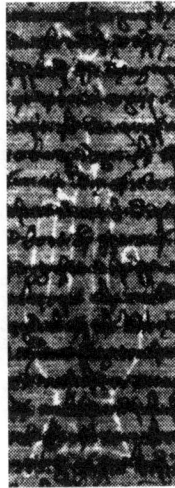

a. fol. 55r   b. fol. 198v

Figs. 8a-b reproduced by permission of the British Library.

Fig. 9: British Library MS Cotton Claudius A.viii

a. fol. 182v

b. Ms Briquet xxx no. 98 [?] (Savoie 1468)

Fig. 9a reproduced by permission of the British Library; Fig. 9b by permission of the Bibliothèque de Genève.

Fig. 10: British Library MS Arundel 59

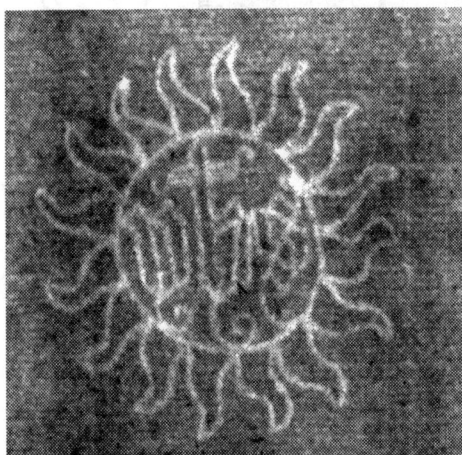

a. Blank fol. after fol. 89

Fig. 10a reproduced by permission of the British Library.

Fig. 11: British Library MS Harley 372

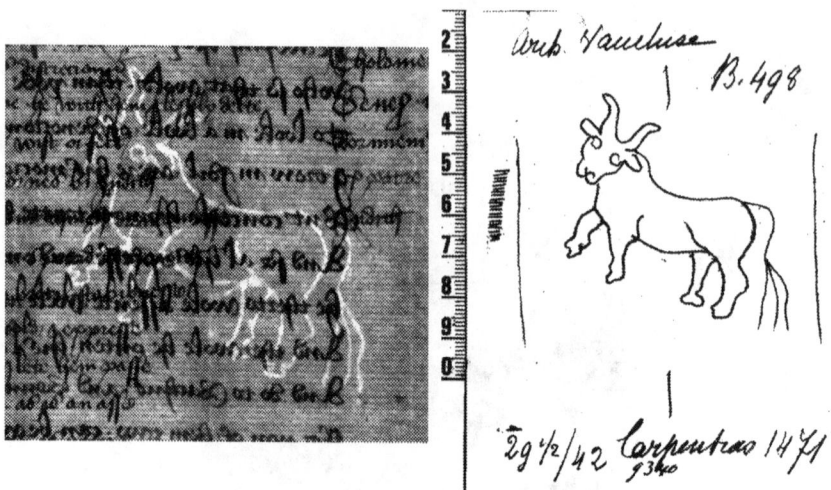

a. fol. 81

b. Ms Briquet xxx, no. 9340
(Carpentras 1741)

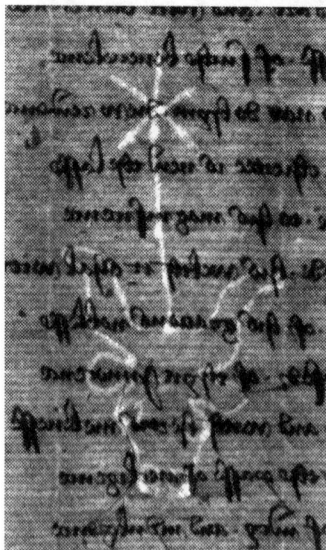

c. fol 112

Figs. 11a & c reproduced by permission of the British Library; **Fig. 11b** by permission of the Bibliothèque de Genève.

Fig. 12: Trinity College, Cambridge MS R.3.21

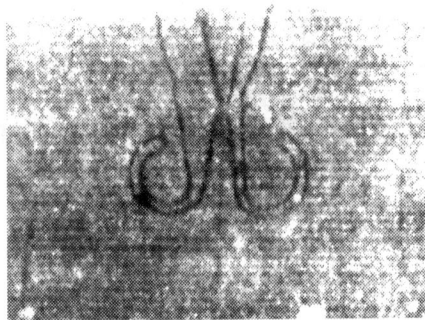

a. fol. 33v, lower half of mark

b. fol. 99v (mold side, mark inverted)

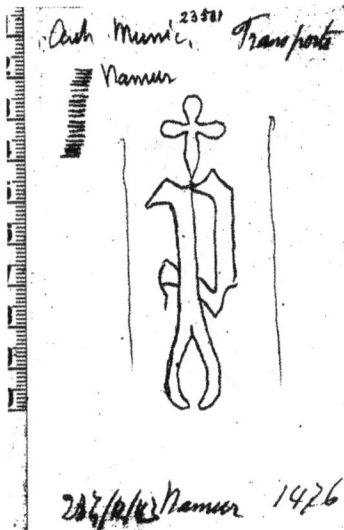

c. Ms Briquet xxx, no. 23501 (Namur 1476)

d. fol. 134r

Fig. 12, cont.

e. fol. 175v   f. fols 161v (lower)+160r(upper)

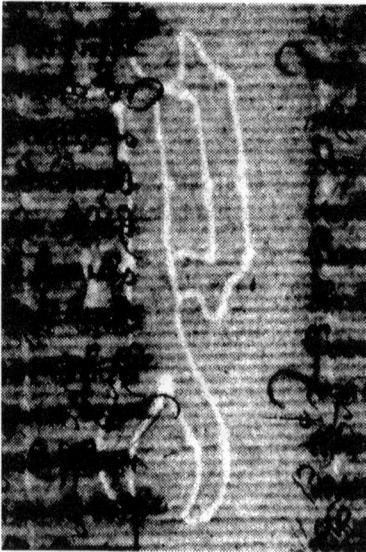

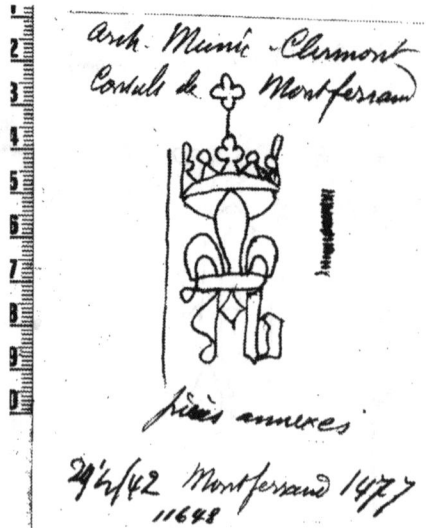

g. fol. 267r   h. Ms Briquet xxx, no. 11648
                           (Montferrano 1477)

Figs. 12a-b, d-g reproduced by permission of the Master and Fellows of Trinity College Cambridge; **Figs. 12c & h** by permission of the Bibliothèque de Genève.

Fig. 13: Worcester Cathedral Library MS F.172
(most of these reflect some distortion as the camera angle was not 90°)

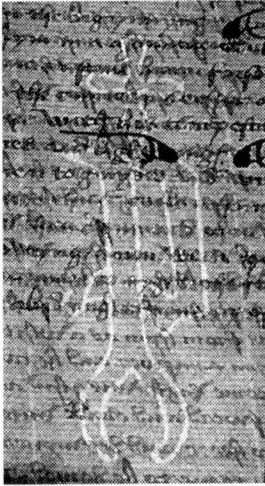

a. fol. 12v

b. fol. 32v

c. c. fol. 37v (rotated horizontally)

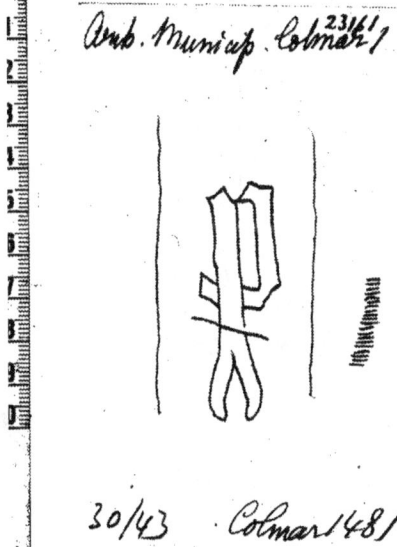

d. Ms Briquet xxx, no. 23161 (Colmar 1481)

Fig. 13, cont.

e. fol. 72v

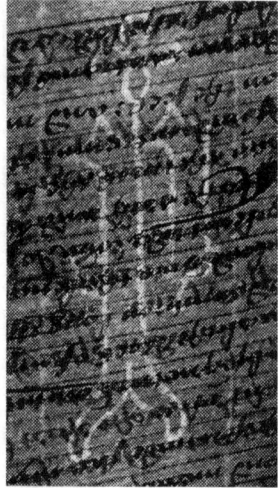

f. fol. 181r

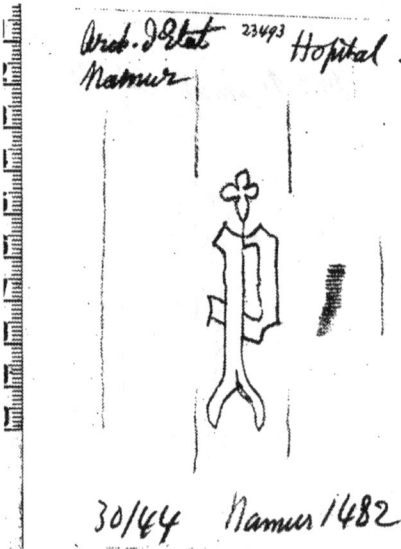

g. Ms Briquet xxx, no. 23493 (Namur 1482)

h. fol. 206

Figs. 13a-c, e-f, h reproduced by permission of the Chapter of Worcester Cathedral (U.K.); **Figs. 13d & g** by permission of the Bibliothèque de Genève.

The Clerk's "Unscholarly Bow": Seeing and Reading Chaucer's Clerk from the Ellesmere MS to Caxton

MAIDIE HILMO

In the Prologue to his second edition of the *Canterbury Tales*, printed in 1483, William Caxton praised Chaucer for his "short, quyck and hye sentences" and commended the book in which may be found "many a noble hystorye of every astate and degree."[1] Caxton hoped that all who "shal *see* and rede therin may so take and understonde" the tales as to profit their own souls (emphasis added).[2] This echoes his stated reason for including woodcuts in the first English printed book with illustrations, his 1481 edition of the *Mirror of the World*: without them the text "may not lightly be understande."[3]

In view of Caxton's emphasis on seeing and understanding, it would be quixotic if he went to the expense and trouble of having twenty-three woodcuts made for Chaucer's text if they were not intended to help his audience understand the text. Given their plain, unadorned style, it is most likely that they were meant as visual aids that enhanced the prestige and marketability of the book for late-fifteenth-century readers. Whether the manuscript provided for the second edition by the "gentylman" mentioned in the Prologue contained illustrations remains speculative – very few manuscripts of the *Canterbury Tales* are illustrated, though a good number are decorated. The woodcuts made specifically for the *Canterbury Tales* reveal the political climate and the literary contexts in which they were produced. Until recently, critical opinion of the woodcuts has been rather low, still ringing with Edward Hodnett's estimation of them as so "miserably executed" that they are "some of the poorest cuts ever inserted between covers," despite the fact that this "inexperienced" block-cutter illustrated "some of the most important works from our first press."[4] This same block-cutter made the woodcuts not only for the *Canterbury Tales* and the *Mirror of the World* but also for the *Game and Playe of the Chesse*, as well as some of those for the *Golden Legend*, the last two also published in 1483.

Elsewhere I examine a number of the woodcuts designed for the *Canterbury Tales*—including those of the Pardoner, the Nun's Priest, the Manciple, and Chaucer—to demonstrate how specific details in the portrayal of the pilgrims are emblematic, deal with speech issues, and affect how the tales can be understood in light of the characterizations ascribed to the tellers. The woodcut of the Clerk is singled out on the British Library web site of *Caxton's Chaucer* to support the generally held opinion that not all the woodcuts represent the pilgrims whose tales they precede: "It seems especially strange that a woodcut more suitable for a well-armed gamekeeper is used to illustrate the virtuous and studious Clerk from Oxford."[5] Because the meaning of the Clerk's apparently incongruous visual portrayal is perhaps the most difficult to recover, I will deal with it as a special case here. Viewed in the context of other selected illustrations, for example, from the Ellesmere Manuscript, the manuscripts of *Vox Clamantis* and *Confessio Amantis*, and Caxton's printed version of the *Game and Playe of the Chesse*, the woodcut reflects Caxton's concerns with issues of authority raised by the historical events of 1483. Dynastic changes resulting from those events were not entirely dissimilar from those that occurred at the beginning of the fifteenth century, when the Ellesmere manuscript was made. Though the intended audience and the technologies of manuscript and print differ, there is a decided connection in the visual language of these works.

More familiar to Chaucerian scholars than the Caxton woodcut is the illustration of the Clerk in San Marino, Huntington Library, MS Ellesmere 26 C9, 1400–1410, folio 88r (fig. 1). Obvious differences between the printed page and the manuscript folio are in the ordinatio: a lavish demivinet border frames the hand-lettered vernacular text; a running title above indicates who the narrator is; a large decorated letter introduces the tale itself; and two levels of Latin annotations in the margins give authoritative quotations in Latin from Petrarch's original text or, in the Clerk's Prologue, indicate stanza pauses. The unframed marginal illustration of the mounted pilgrim narrator interacts directly with the text of his tale.

The use of color and gold leaf "illuminate" the text just as Petrarch's "rethorike sweete / Enlumyned al Ytaille of poetrie."[6] This ornamentation visually translates the verbal "colours" of rhetoric employed by the Italian poet laureate[7] and rendered into English by Chaucer's Clerk—even though he had been asked by the Host to refrain from speaking in "heigh style, as whan that men to kynges write" (16, 18). Corresponding to Chaucer's verbal style, the lavish visual style of the Ellesmere Manuscript, of which the Clerk's portrait page is only a sample, suggests that it was likely intended for an aristocratic or even kingly audience.[8]

     The painted portrait of the Clerk draws attention by the line of his vision to the "delitable sighte" (ClT 62) of the setting of his tale, which, by his pleased facial expression, he is envisioning as he remembers the tale taught to him by Petrarch (ClP 40). As if in confirmation of his Petrarchan source, he reverently holds up a book toward the same line at which his gaze is directed. This book would seem to contain not "Aristotle and his philosophye" (GP 295), which the other two books under his arm might suggest, but the authoritative text of Petrarch himself. In a further intertextual enrichment, the beginning of the "prohemye" of Petrarch's original Latin text is conveniently laid out for the viewer's gaze in the gloss at the top right of the page beside the stanza referring to Petrarch (ClP 39–46). Every visual and verbal feature of the page's apparatus enriches the perceived value of the vernacular text: the Latin annotation at the top transfers the authority of its source to the translation, which the illustration of the narrating Clerk holding up his book reiterates pictorially.

     But not only the source text and the English translation are featured. That the Ellesmere illustrates the English storyteller, not the setting or subject of each tale, calls attention to the filtering effect the individual pilgrim "author" has on the form and tone of the story itself. In the General Prologue, the pilgrim Chaucer has announced that he will describe the pilgrims' "condicioun," who and of what "degree" they are, and how they are dressed (GP 38–41). The Ellesmere illustrations likewise seem to take account of these, albeit with some changes of emphasis in recasting the text for its aristocratic audience. In the case of the miniature of the Clerk, can his pleased expression suggest not only his envisioning of the delightful setting but also his moral approbation of the content of the tale he has chosen, against the Host's request for a merry tale?

     Yet this rosy-cheeked Clerk (fig. 2) does not look "Holwe and thereto sobrely," contradicting Chaucer's description that he is "nat right fat" (GP 288–289). His facial features recall the description of the Oxford clerk in the Miller's Tale who is "lyk a mayden" (MilT 3202); in fact, when the Host asks the Clerk to tell a merry tale, he says to him that he rides "as coye and stille as dooth a mayde" (ClP 2). In the illustration even his lips are painted red and, as Richard K. Emmerson points out, he wears red hose.[9] He also has a fringe of reddish hair in front of what appears to be a tonsure. Nor is his attire "thredbare" (GP 290). His gown and cape are edged with white fur. In her study of estates satire, Jill Mann traces the Latin descriptions of clerks who display maidenly qualities and who exhibit pride by showing off their fringed garments.[10] While the General Prologue description of the Clerk appears to indicate humility, the Ellesmere illustration of him does not preclude a touch of intellectual pride, perhaps his pride in knowing and translating the high style of Petrarch.

His mount with ribs showing, however, graphically illustrates the General Prologue description: "As leene was his hors as is a rake" (GP 287). This Clerk, who would rather spend his money on books (GP 293–294, 300), is not inclined to feed his horse overmuch. How would an audience accustomed to fine horses view a round-cheeked owner and a starving horse? The Clerk's horse seems to glare at the first line of the second stanza that introduces Walter, the lord of the delightful land. The horse seems to anticipate Walter's shortcomings: its forehoof points at the third stanza, which ends with the authorial admission that "in somme thinges . . . he was to blame" (ClT 76).

While the Ellesmere portrait of the Clerk is sometimes considered to reflect the notion of an ideal Clerk as implied in the General Prologue,[11] it may be that some of the details of the Ellesmere portrait are intended to modify this impression and to convey contradictory impulses. The placement of the Ellesmere storytellers at the beginnings of their tales rather than beside the General Prologue descriptions allows for the choice and tone of the tale to be indicative of the pilgrim who chooses to tell a particular story in a particular manner. In this case, the visual portrait tilts the reader toward the alternate, competing interpretations offered at the end of the tale. The portrait can be seen as undercutting with subtle irony the tale of extreme wifely obedience and anticipating the change of tone when the Clerk says "lat us stynte of ernestful matere" and inverts his own moral in his concluding song (Lenvoy de Chaucer) to "noble wyves" (ClT 1175, 1183). The object of the tale's exemplarity is now open to interpretation, depending on which of the series of constructions is preferred. Serious pilgrims can stay with the spiritual reading about the necessity of virtuous sufferance, while ironically-inclined clerkly misogynists can see the unrealistic Griselde as an inversion of the comedy of wicked wives, and men the likes of the Host or Merchant, laughingly or somewhat bitterly (albeit amusingly for the readers of the text), can see it as a tale they wish their own wives had heard.

Even serious readings are moderated considerably by the alternate interpretations. With the Envoy, the suffering of any flesh-and-blood Griselde is denied validation and practically disappears from consideration. A sense of amused superiority over innkeepers and merchants is confirmed for aristocratic readers. The Ellesmere illustration of this ingratiating, maidenly Clerk, whose portrayal would recall estates satire to educated late-medieval readers, hints that the story does not have to be taken with excessive seriousness, as might have been the case if a sober-faced Clerk had introduced it and therefore accorded its marital and spiritual exemplarity more authority.

In the Ellesmere illustrations the countenances of the Clerk and of the pilgrim Chaucer, both tellers of serious moral tales, are very different: the one is sweet and dreamy, the other serious and grave, as befits the narrator of the weighty Tale of Melibee (fig. 3). Unlike that of the Clerk, the Ellesmere illustration of Chaucer does not suggest any ambiguity about this allegory, which J. Allan Mitchell describes as "one of Chaucer's least equivocal exemplary pieces."[12] The seriousness of the Tale of Melibee is indicated on the Ellesmere page by the block of dense prose as opposed to the separated rime royal stanzas of the Clerk's Tale. This feature of the ordinatio links the Melibee author with the Parson, whose prose is similarly laid out and and who declares that he is interested in truth rather than fiction. The illustrated and ornamented vellum pages marking the beginnings of the tales in the Ellesmere manuscript offer multifaceted aesthetic, sensuous, and authoritative accompaniments that present Chaucer's vernacular text for the leisurely, holistic perusal of its aristocratic readers at the beginning of the fifteenth century.

All of this apparatus is absent from Caxton's first printed edition of the *Canterbury Tales* in 1476. In addition to a corrected text and Caxton's own prologue mentioning the fact, the second edition gives evidence of Caxton's reevaluation of the needed enhancements of this new printing. By using a smaller version of the same typeface as the first for the main text, he reduced the number and size of the pages and therefore the size of the book. The dense texture of rows of heavy black type is also lightened by this reduction in size. Practical reading aids improve the visual appeal of the page, as in the case of the running titles such as "The clerkis tale of oxenford," at the tops of the relevant pages (fig. 4). Additional spaces between items, and in the case of the Clerk's Tale, spaces between the rime royal stanzas, as in the Ellesmere, allow the reader a greater appreciation of their poetic value and an opportunity to pause and linger. The monotony and tedium of endless type is decreased somewhat, at least for a modern eye, from that presented in the first edition. This may not, however, have been how all early readers would have experienced the new look and density of texture, as indicated by a near contemporary who exhibits an aesthetics of standardization as he waxes enthusiastic about printed books and the "uniform letters and lines . . . that adorn these books."[13]

Most significant, however, is the addition of woodcuts to the second edition. The primary advantage of woodcuts is that they can be reused. During the early period of printed books, as Martha Driver so aptly points out, "movable pictures illustrate books printed with movable type, and word and image have equal power to convey meaning."[14] In the case of the *Canterbury Tales*, Caxton for the first time was able to insert "movable pictures" portraying the pilgrims at the relevant places both in the General Prologue and before their tales. The woodcuts would have already begun to shape how readers interpreted character descriptions in the General Prologue because the woodcuts precede the texts. This method of linking the General Prologue and the tales closely together engenders a different reading experience and prioritizing of parts than, for example, in the Ellesmere Manuscript. In that work, greater weight is accorded to the tales by the addition of the pilgrim portraits that are specifically placed at the start of each tale.

Since the woodcut of the Clerk has proven the most problematic, it is of some importance to determine if it typifies a lack of relevance between woodcut and text in Caxton's second edition. N. F. Blake states that the woodcut "for the Clerk is inappropriate since he carries a bow and arrows, and it may have been meant in the first instance for the Yeoman."[15] David R. Carlson puts it most memorably, saying that the Clerk is shown "equipped with an unscholarly bow and arrows."[16] Carlson also expresses the commonly held opinion that "this unsuitable illustration" was "perhaps designed for a yeoman and misplaced in the text."[17] In his appendix, he further points out that it was used for the Clerk by Caxton's successors and was copied in the Pynson series.[18] Such repeated use suggests that the woodcut was, in fact, properly placed and that modern evaluations are missing some aspect of visual literacy that Caxton and subsequent printers took for granted. Yet the key to understanding this woodcut is a question of literacy, *visual* literacy.

There was already a woodcut for the Yeoman (fig. 5) preceding that of the Clerk in the General Prologue, indicating that the Clerk illustration could never have been intended for that of the Yeoman pilgrim. It is instructive to compare the two figures, each with a longbow. The posture of the Knight's Yeoman and horse indicate pride of bearing, suitably reflecting the Knight's status. The woodcut of the Yeoman faces that of the Squire and repeats, in a minor key, the posture and look of the Squire. This Yeoman echoes the General Prologue description of his having the best-cared-for and most complete equipment, from the "myghty bowe" and the "bright" arrows with their peacock feathers, to his sword and horn (Cx2: a5rv–a5v, GP 104–116). In this instance, the Yeoman's bow can be understood literally.

The woodcut of the Clerk, on the other hand, is quite different in aspect (fig. 4). While he has the troublesome bow, he does not have any other military equipment. Like all the other pilgrims portrayed in the woodcuts in Caxton's book, except for the Yeoman, who scarcely has room for it, the Clerk carries a rosary, in this case over one shoulder and under the opposite arm. The two items the Clerk carries are both contemporary, the longbow representing late-medieval English warfare and the rosary reflecting the growth of the cult of the rosary.[19] One is tempted to think of the Clerk as having metaphorically put on the armor of God to wrestle "not against flesh and blood" but against "spiritual wickedness" by always praying and watching (Eph. 6:11–18). If read in this light, the bow and accompanying arrows present the physical image and the rosary the spiritual intent. Given the Clerk's practice of praying for the souls of his donors (GP 301–102), there may well be some religious resonance of this sort to the image. Perhaps further evidence about the significance of the bow and arrows might be uncovered by examining the larger contexts of its publication.

Unlike the fine hat with upturned brim worn by the Yeoman, linking him to the Squire, who has a similar one with the addition of a feather, the peasant's straw hat worn by the Clerk helps to establish his poverty, referred to in the General Prologue. Despite his humble hat and plain clothes in the Caxton illustration, the Clerk's head is not bent in deference as are the heads of the Yeoman and the Squire. He does not have long points on his shoes as they do. His horse is not starved, as is the one in the Ellesmere, but it is by no means the sort of curly-maned specimen featured in the woodcuts of the Yeoman and the Squire. They appear ready for tournament entry in a way the Clerk's splay-footed horse does not. The Clerk's horse would hardly be found in the retinue of any self-respecting knight, except maybe as a packhorse. The Clerk himself does look somewhat "holow and therto sobyrly" (Cx2: b1r, GP 291), perhaps because he is thinking about speaking of some "moral vertu" (Cx2: b1v, GP 309) or, suggestively, because he is studying "some sophyme" (Cx2: aa1r, ClP 5).

In comparison with the Ellesmere Clerk, the Clerk in print is not distinguished by carrying any expensive books bound in "whyt and reed" (Cx2: b1r, GP 296).[20] The absence of books allows for the main feature in the woodcut to come into sharp focus: the bow and arrows that are instrumental in signaling how the Clerk and his tale should be read. It will be helpful to look first at Chaucer's text and then at late-medieval visual iconography to understand the multiple meanings offered by the woodcut of the Clerk.

In drawing the universal moral of his tale when he refers to the "sharpe scorgis" (Cx2: cc3r; ClT 1157) with which God allows us to be beaten, the Clerk introduces language featuring sharp instruments. The Clerk turns, as Kittredge points out, to the Wife of Bath and applies the substance of his tale "to the purpose of an ironical answer, of crushing force, to her whole heresy."[21] Kittredge sees "nothing inappropriate to his character" in this because clerks "were always satirizing women," as the Wife had said, and this particular clerk has "no scruples against using the powerful weapon of irony in the service of religion and 'moral vertu.'" In this case, "the satire is particularly poignant," as Kittredge continues, "because it comes with all the suddenness of a complete change of tone (from high seriousness to biting irony, and from the impersonal to the personal)."[22] In this marital "bateyll," wives should not dread, as the Clerk declares:

> For though thy husbond armyd be in mayl
> Thy *arowes* of thy crabbyd *eloquence*
> Shal perse his brest and eke his auentayl
> (emphasis added; Cx2: 33v; Lenvoy de Chaucer 22, 26–28)

This is an effective double use of satirical "arrows" as exemplified by the Clerk's verbal assault against wives whose own armory consists of such weapons of speech. The imagery of scourges or whips, used by the Wife when she recalls that she was the "whippe" against her old husbands (WBPro 175), is also employed in the Merchant's Tale (which precedes the tales of the Wife of Bath and the Clerk in Caxton's editions) when Justinius counsels old January against marriage to a young woman because:

> She may be goddys mene and goddis whippe
> Than shal your soule vp to heuyn skyppe
> Swyfter than *an arow doth out of a bowe.*
> (emphasis added; Cx2: m6r; MerT 427–429)

By this argument, a young wife is likely to be turned into God's instrument to speed the old fool's soul to heaven, arrow-like, in a reversal of his expectations of marital life as a "heuen in erthe" (Cx2: m5v; MerT 403).

In Chaucer's Manciple's Tale, Phoebus shoots his unfaithful wife with the bow he had formerly used to kill the Python (264-265; 108-110, 128-129). By introducing the Python into this story of the tell-tale crow Chaucer identifies the lecherous wife with this serpent.[23] The bow and arrow wielded by the god of poetry likely has metaphoric reference to speech acts as in Jeremiah 9.8 in which the deceitful tongue is equated with an arrow. This weapon with which the "archer-god" Phoebus slays his wife in the Manciple's Tale is described by David Wallace as a bow of the mind made into "a killing instrument."[24]

Chaucer's text supplies the figurative associations of the imagery of the bow and arrows, but it is the visual iconography that is most relevant. This derives from such works as the illustrated *Vox Clamantis,* a popular Latin work by the "moral Gower," as his contemporary Chaucer referred to him in *Troilus and Criseyde* and as he was still known in Caxton's day.[25] Of the nine independent manuscripts of the *Vox* (plus two that are copied),[26] four include illustrations of an archer with a longbow.[27] "The moral satirist aims his arrows at the world," according to Alan T. Gaylord's description of the one in San

Marino, Huntington Library, MS HM 150, folio 13v (fig. 6).[28] The Latin verse above the image of the archer identifies the intent of this portrait:

> Ad mundum mitto mea jacula, dumque sagitto | Att vbi justus erit, nulla sagitta ferit | Sed male viventes hos vulnero transgredientes | Conscius ergo sibi se speculetur ibi.
>
> (I throw my darts and shoot my arrows at the world, but where there is a righteous man, no arrow strikes. But I wound those who live wickedly. Therefore, let him who recognizes himself there look to himself.)[29]

This might echo the metaphor of the bow applied in the thirteenth century by Hugh of St-Cher to describe the skill required by Dominican preachers: "Arcus tenditur in studio, postea sagittatur in praedicatione" ("First the bow is bent in study, then the bow is released in preaching").[30] In the mid-fourteenth century the bow metaphor also appears in Boccaccio's *Decameron* in a reference to the current lack of virtuous rulers who "l'arco reso dello 'nteletto" ("can train the bowstrings of their minds").[31]

In Gower's case, the metaphor developed into one that was more polemic and satiric. As C. G. Macaulay describes it, "the main substance of the *Vox Clamantis* is an indictment of human society, the corruptions of which are said to be the cause of all the evils in the world. The picture which appears in several manuscripts of the author aiming his arrows at the world fairly represents its scope."[32] The tripartite globe depicts the sky with its moon and stars in the top left segment, the green earth in the top right, and the swirling water in the bottom. Since there would be no point in shooting at the elements, the tripartite globe is more likely to refer, as Hsy suggests, to the three estates at which the poet, represented by the archer, takes aim in the *Vox*.[33] The globe is surmounted by a cross with a resurrection banner, alluding to the world that was redeemed by Christ. Taken together with the text, these features imply that the satirist is performing a corrective function.

The same basic iconography of the archer is used in the other illustrated *Vox Clamantis* manuscripts.[34] The one in London, British Library, MS Cotton Tiberius A.IV, folio 9v (fig. 7) was the basis of an engraving that was added, probably in the late seventeenth or early eighteenth century, as suggested to me by John Goldfinch,[35] to the blank page preceding Caxton's edition of John Gower's *Confessio Amantis* (fig. 8). If the seventeenth- or eighteenth-century owner of Caxton's Gower knew of the author image in Tiberius A.IV and had an engraving made from a copy of it or knew where to obtain such an engraving, then it could have been added to the *Confessio* printed edition to emphasize its value and to highlight the authority of the original and by then antique author. The addition of the archer image presents the *Confessio* as something of a satire just as it did originally for the *Vox*, thereby placing the former as an early example of a genre that was fashion-able at the turn of the eighteenth century. It may be that the first Vox artist adapted iconography associated with representations of the planets, as seen, for example, in a Continental drawing of a similar but blindfolded archer in aristocratic dress who has just shot an arrow into the planet Venus, which contains within its circumference the nude goddess pierced in her rib cage.[36] Because the Confessio deals with the confessions of the poet-lover involving sins against love, the Continental iconography of the archer is not foreign to the concept of Gower's text, and so knowledge of such a work might in some fashion have been another influencing factor in the decision to add the engraving of the Vox archer to the Caxton's Confessio.[37]

Although the engraving of the archer added to Caxton's Gower was obviously the result of a later impulse, in view of Caxton's intimate knowledge of the English literary landscape, which was, after all, his business, he was likely familiar with the popular illustrated Latin Vox Clamantis manuscripts. Since he preferred to publish mainly English literary works, the Confessio was more suitable for Caxton's purposes. The archer figure with his longbow was relevant to the late fourteenth and early fifteenth centuries because it was a weapon that was used by the English to devastating effect against the French during the Battle of Crecy in 1346 and the Battle of Agincourt in 1415.[38] As such, it became a meaningful English symbol[39] at the time it was applied to verbal as well as martial weaponry in the Vox manuscript illuminations. When, later in the fifteenth century, Chaucer's Clerk was illustrated with a bow in the woodcut, it seems plausible that, since Chaucer and Gower were both pub-lished in 1483, there was a crossover effect in the minds of the Caxton print team in the preparation of the work of these two literary moralists.

Whether or not Caxton intended originally to include a woodcut, pos-sibly even one with the archer, at the beginning of his printed edition of the English Confessio Amantis—there are gaps possibly intended for woodcuts[40]—the circumstances surrounding its publication link it to his 1483 edition of the Canterbury Tales. This was the year in which there were three different kings, which might have been the reason that Caxton was circumspect in not naming the "gentylman" whose father's copy inspired the Caxton's second edition of the Canterbury Tales. The dedications in his Prologues of 1483, or sometimes the lack of specific dedications, reflect Caxton's various attempts to position himself according to the rapid political shifts of the times.[41] A change of tactics showing some expedient maneuvering is evident in his colophon to the Confessio, which, he says, was finished on September 2, 1483, "the first yere of the regne of Kyng Richard the Thyrd," echoing Caxton's ear-lier reference in the Prologue to King Richard II, as if the legitimacy of the latter were transferable.[42] Although the Confessio was originally written during the time of Richard II, Gower revised the Prologue in the later manuscript versions so that it was dedicated to Richard's usurper, Henry IV[43] (Caxton printed this revised dedication to Henry); similarly, Caxton adapted his Prologue to appeal to the third of the kings in 1483, the usurper Richard III. In this politically fraught climate Caxton probably found Gower's work especially appropriate concerning issues of authority and a good model for the new king. As Winthrop Wetherbee says, "The many tales which draw the line between authority and coercive brutality in the relations of parents and children, husbands and wives, are at once powerful metaphors for the use and abuse of royal authority and expressions of Gower's pervasive, Boethian concern with love as the foundation of the social order."[44]

Issues of authority are likewise evoked by the woodcut portrayal of Chaucer's Clerk with the symbolic bow and arrows. Just as Griselde is reclothed in new garments upon her marriage and as Petrarch's text is reclothed by Chaucer's translation,[45] so this woodcut re-equips the Clerk with the satirist's bow instead of the token books. This portrayal of the narrator therefore has the potential of reshaping the tale itself, not only the various and alternative moral applications at the end. It imparts to the story an edge and invites the sophisticated late-medieval viewer to puzzle over the object of his satiric attack. If a satirist tells a story, is that story ipso facto a satire? This tale, as J. Allan Mitchell suggests, "may feel more like a parody than parable, and indeed I would suggest the tale has about it the sort of rhetorical excess characteristic of both the ridiculous and the sublime."[46] In the woodcut, the neighing horse suitably projects derision. The figure of the archer can be seen as potentially striking at the tale's foundations, not only at the marital relationship portrayed but, by extension, the social order and political governance that it models.

The latter was a concern reflected in the second edition of the *Game and Playe of the Chesse*, which Caxton also published in 1483, without a specific dedication except that he mentions it pertains to "every astate and degree."[47] It is of interest here because he added twenty-four woodcuts carved by the same block-cutter who made those for the *Canterbury Tales*.[48] The allegory begins with a king who killed his predecessor and had him chopped into three hundred pieces. A philosopher, upon being asked by the people to teach the new tyrant good governance, invented the game of chess. As Jenny Adams points out, Caxton's prologue to this second edition places emphasis on every estate that can benefit from the examples in the "book of the chesse moralysed" and so differs from the first edition, which endorses royal authority.[49] The first woodcut in the second edition depicts the assassinated king's body being chopped up by man with a mighty axe and consumed by birds flying off with pieces of his corpse (fig. 9). As Adams argues, it serves "as a warning to any monarch who arrogates excessive power."[50]

What is especially provocative is that the badge on the hat of the supervising figure now holding the scepter appears to be the white rose of York, surely a less than subtle reference to Richard III! Many of Caxton's noble patrons suffered in consequence of the usurpation of Richard III, who had himself crowned on July 6, 1483—Earl Rivers was executed, and Elizabeth Woodville, Edward IV's queen, took sanctuary at Westminster near Caxton's shop, while her young sons, Edward V and his brother the Duke of York, were seized by Richard, imprisoned, and very probably murdered. In her discussion of these events, Louise Gill suggests that there may have been a connection between Caxton's suing for and being granted a pardon the following spring and the failed rebellion against the Crown in October 1483.[51] Caxton's petition, like those of his immediate circle, could have been just a cautionary measure to ensure the security of his business,[52] but it is indicative of the turmoil of these years.

Works such as Chaucer's *Canterbury Tales*, Gower's *Confessio Amantis*, and the *Game and Playe of the Chesse* are all concerned with issues of authority and the functions (or failures in function) of the three estates, issues that also clearly occupied Caxton, his educated contemporaries, and his patrons. Seen within a larger literary and historical context, the Caxton woodcut of Chaucer's Clerk likewise participates in the exploration of authority that the tale details in the person of Lord Walter. The figure of the satirist is now intelligible as promoting a reading that aims a challenge at the absolutist, irresponsible, and cruel behavior of this marital and political tyrant who extracts unreasonable promises not only from his wife but also from his people, who are not to "grutche ne stryue" (Cx2: aa3v; ClT 170) against his choice.

In view of the inflammatory woodcut of the regicide introducing the *Game and Playe of the Chesse* and of the woodcut of Chaucer's Clerk as a moral satirist, it is obvious that the block-cutter was also something of a satirist, stimulating the viewer to decipher the significance of the illustrations. And that is what many of the woodcuts do in emblematic fashion:[53] they pose a moral riddle to be unraveled by a visually sophisticated audience. The second woodcut in the *Game and Playe of the Chesse* is interesting because the philosopher who modeled the game on "a state based on reason and law" sits frontally behind the checkered board and looks directly at the viewer, inviting participation in the game (fig. 10).[54]

An exploration of the renderings of Chaucer's Clerk would be incomplete without considering those of the antagonist he takes on, the Wife of Bath, beaten for a book by her fifth husband, also an Oxford clerk. The Caxton block-cutter depicts her frontally, like the philosopher just mentioned, so that she too looks at the viewer (fig 11), the only pilgrim in this edition to do so. She presents a slim figure elegantly dressed, with her flowing skirt neatly draped over her horse as she sits sidesaddle. Her rosary, not overlarge in comparison to some others of the same period,[55] is draped in accessory fashion over her right arm. Her right hand rests eye-catchingly on her belly, while her left hand delicately holds the reins of her pleasant-looking horse. As worn by her manuscript predecessor in the Ellesmere,[56] her coverchiefs and her hat, a practical travel hat, are not as large as described in the General Prologue or as featured in the illustration in Cambridge University Library, MS Gg.4.27, folio 22r.[57] Nor does the woodcut include her characteristic metaphoric whip, which both manuscripts highlight. Her purpose in Caxton is not to demonstrate her hard-won sovereignty over her old husbands or her interest in extravagant headgear. Rather, it is revealed in the way she displays herself to the viewer for extended inspection. Her expression is somewhat difficult to describe. It is at once demure and bold, complacent and benign, as if to say, "Wel come the sixte when that euer he shal" (Cx2: q7v; WBPro 45). It is also somewhat thoughtful, as is fitting for an experienced woman who is of "fyue husbondis scolyng" (Cx2: q7v; WBPro 44), in that a "Womman of many a scole half a clerk is" (Cx2: m2v; MerT 184). Placed before her tale as well as before her General Prologue description, the woodcut of this clerkly Wife also functions as the narrator of a tale involving the abuse of his position by a rapist knight and his subsequent education by the old woman who details behavior proper to a gentleman: openness, generosity, compassion, and courtesy. Caxton was concerned, as Blake puts it, with reviving chivalric society.[58] Caxton's Wife of Bath is shown as a woman of some depth. There is a sense that she too, like the Clerk, is holding something back, if not a satiric arrow then at least a kind of knowingness. Like the philosopher, this Wife of Bath invites the viewer to the game.

The portrayal of the Wife of Bath provides, as she does in the program of the fictional pilgrimage, a suitably strong and complex presence more than balancing that of the Clerk. She draws in the audience, compelling attention. Having gained that, Caxton's Wife of Bath presents herself not only to someone who might be "fressh a bedde"(Cx2: s7v; WBT 1232) but also to any clerk or reader willing to enter the discourse on issues of sovereignty and authority, which is really her main, serious theme.

Visual analysis of a few of the woodcuts made by Caxton's blockcutter demonstrates that he does not simply echo the text but makes its authority discursive, even while subtly guiding the readings. The woodcuts solicit a participatory response from the reader. The more they are examined, the more nuanced and layered the readings become. As the Prologue to the *Game and Playe of the Chesse* reminds the reader, echoing Chaucer's "Retraction" and the medieval commonplace assumption, "Saynt Poule sayth in his epistle: alle that is wryten is wryten unto our doctryne and for our lernyng."[59] These woodcuts, like the illustrations in literary manuscripts such as the Ellesmere, not only invite interaction with the text but also encourage the reader to consider the impact of the character and intentions of the narrator about the ways the tale is to be understood. The Ellesmere Clerk's countenance and expression might indicate that he is ravished by the imagined beauty of his story's setting and by making the work of the Italian poet laureate available in English, an illuminating process that is bound to cast some of its glow on the translator. It also anticipates his change of tone near the end when he says that he will "with lusty herte, fressh and grene" sing a song to "glade" his audience (ClT 1173–1174), thereby shifting attention away from the unpalatable cruelty of Griselde's treatment. His pleasant expression distances him, and therefore his audience, from the exemplarity of the wife's spiritual fortitude. Caxton's Clerk, however, does more than just anticipate the alternative readings at the end of the tale. The portrait of the Clerk as satirist stimulates a more evaluative reading of the story itself, not just in terms of its exemplarity of spiritual fortitude but in terms of its presentation of the authority of earthly lords, at whatever level. Intervisually appropriating the iconography of the poet as moral satirist and so alluding to Gower's literary oeuvre, the woodcut of the Clerk as satirist opens up the story's meanings and places it within a broader social and political landscape.

Given the other works published by Caxton in a period of shifting power and alliances, the Clerk's Tale is one of many that raise questions about the power of earthly lords and the role of all the estates within the Christian community, questions that must have been on people's minds, no matter their allegiances. Given also the many roles played by Caxton in the preparatory stages of publishing, including soliciting patrons and selecting books, often translating them, not to mention purchasing supplies and then marketing the finished product, it is reasonable to suppose that the roles of some of the others involved in that vast and busy enterprise have often been overlooked. This includes the role of the compositors, as N. F. Blake rightly asserts with respect to the *Canterbury Tales*.[60] It should also include the role of the block-cutters. It is not inconceivable that a block-cutter might also have been a compositor, just as a scribe might also have been an illustrator,[61] or a designer of the layout, or a corrector, or any of the other employments required in the pioneering period of revolutionizing the book industry. Against the white paper surface, the printed black outlines of the woodcuts are as variously thick as those of the text, encouraging the perception that they too were to be "read." They may lack the fine delicacy of Continental woodcuts and engravings, but the sturdy woodcuts of the Caxton Chaucer give strong evidence that this artist had more than a superficial understanding of English cultural traditions and contemporary issues. Further, there was an assumption on the part of Caxton and his block-cutter that the readers who mattered were visually literate, sufficiently so that the scholarly bent of the Clerk's bow was unmistakable. That was likely why Wynken de Worde continued to use the woodcut of the mounted figure with the bow for Chaucer's Clerk, whose speech was "Short and quyk and ful of hygh sentence" (Cx2: b1v; GP 308). Caxton's woodcut of the Clerk may even have inspired one of de Worde's own devices: a centaur with a bow, sometimes shooting an arrow.[62]

University of Victoria

ACKNOWLEDGMENTS

An earlier version of this paper was presented at the Medieval Association of the Pacific Conference on March 12, 2005, at San Francisco State University. The research for this study was funded in part by the Social Sciences and Humanities Research Council of Canada and by the Department of Humanities at the University of Victoria. I am grateful to Mary Robertson at the Huntington Library for the special privilege of being allowed to examine the Ellesmere manuscript. Many of the detailed observations in this paper would not have been possible if the British Library had not made Caxton's two editions of Chaucer's *Canterbury Tales* available online. Corinna Gilliland kindly helped me in the preliminary research for this study. For her enthusiastic support and good ideas, I thank Margot Louis. For information concerning the archer engraving added to Caxton's printed version of John Gower's *Confessio Amantis*, I am grateful to Siân Echard and John Goldfinch. Many particularly helpful suggestions were made by those who read this paper with care, including Kathryn Kerby-Fulton, Linda Olson, Martha W. Driver, Charlotte C. Morse, and Wayne Hilmo.

NOTES

1. For the Prologue, see N. F. Blake, ed., *Caxton's Own Prose* (London: Andre Deutsch, 1973), 61–63; the other Prologues from which I quote are also available in this publication. The date 1483 is now generally considered to be correct and is the one stated online in "Caxton's Chaucer: British Library Treasures in Full," text by Kristian Jensen, ed. Colin Wight (London: British Library, 2003), available at http://www.bl.uk/treasures/caxton/homepage.html. See, however, N. F. Blake, "Caxton's Second Edition of the *Canterbury Tales*," in *The English Medieval Book: Studies in Memory of Jeremy Griffiths*, ed. Vincent Gillespie, A. S. G. Edwards, and Ralph Hanna (London: British Library, 2000), 135, who suggests 1482. This date is arrived at by Caxton's statement that the first edition was based on a manuscript "brought to me vi yere passyd"; Prologue to the second edition in *Caxton's Own Prose*, 62. Of course, this does not say when he actually printed it. The dating is further complicated by the

fact that the calendar year began on March 25 in Caxton's time. See also George Duncan Painter, *William Caxton: A Quincentenary Biography of England's First Printer* (London: Chatto & Windus, 1976), 135, in which he suggests it was printed in 1483 close to the time Caxton printed Gower's *Confessio Amantis*.

2. Blake, *Caxton's Own Prose*, 62–63.

3. The *Mirror* was first printed in 1481 with woodcuts and reprinted in 1490 also with woodcuts. In the Prologue to the *Mirror*, Caxton mentions that he translated it from a French manuscript. See N. F. Blake, "The 'Mirror of the World' and MS Royal A ix," *Notes and Queries* 212 (1967): 86–87. This manuscript contains the models for many but not all the woodcuts; even so, there are distinct differences in the woodcuts.

4. Edward Hodnett, *English Woodcuts 1480–1535* (Oxford: Oxford University Press, 1973), 2.

5. "Caxton's Chaucer," http://www.bl.uk/treasures/caxton.homepage.html. Accessed December 2006.

6. Line 33 of the Clerk's head-link, given in the Ellesmere Manuscript on the page preceding the portrait of the Clerk. The line numbers are from Geoffrey Chaucer, *The Canterbury Tales*, in *The Riverside Chaucer*, ed. Larry Benson, 3rd ed. (Oxford: Oxford University Press, 1990). Line numbers will henceforth be enclosed in brackets in my text using the conventional abbreviations for the tales. If there is a noteworthy difference in Caxton's text, I will indicate it accordingly.

7. On the use of ornamental borders to emphasize laureate status, see Jane Griffiths, "What's in a Name? The Transmission of 'John Skelton, Laureate,'" in *Manuscript and Print*," in *Manuscript, Print, and Early Tudor Literature*, ed. Alexandra Gillespie, *Huntington Library Quarterly* 67.2 (2004): 229. See also Robert J. Meyer-Lee, "Laureates and Beggars in Fifteenth-Century English Poetry: The Case of George Ashby," *Speculum* 79.3 (July 2004): 694–695. On the metaphoric function of the Ellesmere borders, especially as an analogue to Chaucer's rhetorical finesse, see Maidie Hilmo, *Medieval Images, Icons, and Illustrated English Literary Texts: From Ruthwell Cross to the Ellesmere Chaucer* (Aldershot, UK; Burlington, VT: Ashgate, 2004), 164–167; or the earlier version of the chapter on the Ellesmere, published as Hilmo, "Framing the Canterbury Pilgrims for the Aristocratic Readers of the Ellesmere Manuscript," in *The Medieval Professional Reader at Work: Evidence from the Manuscripts of Chaucer, Langland, Kempe, and Gower*, ed. Kathryn Kerby-Fulton and Maidie Hilmo, English Literary Studies Monograph Series (Victoria, BC: University of Victoria, 2001), 15–17.

8. See Hilmo, *Medieval Images, Icons, and Illustrated English Literary Texts*, 160—199; or Hilmo, "Framing the Canterbury Pilgrims for the Aristocratic Readers of the Ellesmere Manuscript," 14–71. See also Joseph Rosenblum and William K.

Finley, "Chaucer Gentrified: The Nexus of Art and Politics in the Ellesmere Miniatures," *The Chaucer Review* 38 (2003): 142 and154, n. 12.

9. Richard K. Emmerson, "Text and Image in the Ellesmere Portraits of the Tale-Tellers," in *The Ellesmere Chaucer: Essays in Interpretation*, ed. Martin Stevens and Daniel Woodward (San Marino, CA: Huntington Library; Tokyo: Yushodo Co., 1995), 160.

10. Jill Mann, *Chaucer and Medieval Estates Satire: The Literature of Social Classes and the General Prologue to the Canterbury Tales* (London: Cambridge University Press, 1973), 76–78.

11. See Rosenblum and Finley, "Chaucer Gentrified," 147, who state that "the Clerk and the Parson of Chaucer's text are ideal characters" and that "Such details as the artist changes or adds render these characters even more sympathetic."

12. J. Allan Mitchell, *Ethics and Exemplary Narrative in Chaucer and Gower* (Cambridge: D. S. Brewer, 2004), 84.

13. Translated by Nicolas Barker, "A Contemporary Panegyrist of the Invention of Printing: The Author of the *Grammatica Rhythmica*," in *Incunabula: Studies in Fifteenth-Century Printed Books Presented to Lotte Hellinga*, ed. Martin Davies (London: British Library, 1999), 198.

14. Martha W. Driver, *The Image in Print: Book Illustration in Late Medieval England and Its Sources* (London: British Library, 2004), 75.

15. Blake, "Caxton's Second Edition," 140.

16. David R. Carlson, "The Woodcut Illustrations in Early Printed Editions," in *Chaucer Illustrated: Five Hundred Years of the Canterbury Tales in Pictures*, ed. William K. Finley and Joseph Rosenblum (Newcastle, DE; London: Oak Knoll Press and British Library, 2003), 82

17. Carlson, "The Woodcut Illustrations," 82.

18. See Carlson, "Catalogue of Woodcuts Used to Illustrate the *Canterbury Tales* 1483–1602," an appendix in "The Woodcut Illustrations," 106–17. As evident from Carlson's valuable "Catalogue," it wasn't until 1532, when close to half the Caxton woodcuts were lost or worn out, that Thynne used this woodcut not only for the Clerk but also for the Canon's Yeoman. The Pynson copy was used until 1561 solely for the Clerk.

19. See Plates 22a and b and the discussion in Annette Wickham, "Two Rosaries," in *Gothic Art for England 1400–1547*, ed. Eleanor Townsend (London: V&A Publications, 2003), 343. Turned wooden beads, as seem to be indicated in the Caxton woodcuts, were available to all levels of society. Wickham points out that rosaries were "frowned upon by reformers."

20. The fifteenth-century author of the *Grammatica Rhythmica* mentions that texts were more easily available to clerks, giving them no excuse for ignorance; see Barker, "A Contemporary Panegyrist of the Invention of Printing,"

197–198. If books were more available, then there is less reason to portray the Clerk with books because such ownership could be assumed.

21. George Lyman Kittredge, "The Debate on Marriage in the *Canterbury Tales*," *Modern Philology* 9.4 (April, 1912): 14. The other quotations from Kittredge in my paragraph are from the same source.

22. Kittredge, "The Debate on Marriage," 14.

23. Britton J. Harwood, "Language and the Real: Chaucer's Manciple," *Chaucer Review* 6.4 (1972): 269. In his list of the ways in which Chaucer's version differs from the analogues, Harwood points out that the account of the slaying of the Python occurs in Book I of Ovid's *Metamorphoses*; the story of the tell-tale bird is from Book II (Books I.438-567 and II.654-776 respectively).

24. David Wallace, *Chaucerian Polity: Absolutist Lineages and Associated Forms in England and Italy* (Stanford: Stanford University Press, 1997), 279; references to Phoebus Apollo as the "archer-god," 251, 257, and 258.

25. On the continuing use of this epithet from Chaucer's *Troilus and Criseyde*, V.1856–1859, see Siân Echard, "Introduction: Gower's Reputation," in *A Companion to Gower*, ed. Siân Echard (Cambridge: D. S. Brewer, 2004), 2–6.

26. Derek Pearsall, "The Manuscripts and Illustrations of Gower's Works," in Echard, *A Companion to Gower*, 78 and 84.

27. Kathleen L. Scott, *Later Gothic Manuscripts 1390–1490*, vol. 2 (London: Harvey Miller, 1996), 65–66.

28. Alan T. Gaylord, "Portrait of a Poet," in Stevens and Woodward, *The Ellesmere Chaucer: Essays in Interpretation*, 135–136. This manuscript was made in the last decade of the fourteenth century.

29. Translation from Jonathan H. Hsy, "Images of John Gower and His Works: Medieval to Modern," available at http://www.english.upenn.edu/~jhsy/gower.html. Hsy refers to the similar image with the same inscription in London, British Library, MS Cotton Tiberius A.IV, fol. 9v.

30. This quotation provides the title for M. Michèle Mulchahey, *"First the Bow Is Bent in Study. . . ." Dominican Education before 1350* (Toronto: Pontifical Institute of Medieval Studies, 1998), ix. It is from Hugh of St-Cher's *Postillae in totam bibliam*, extant in dozens of manuscripts and then in numerous printed editions between the fifteenth and seventeenth century; see Mulchahey, 500. She uses Hugh's metaphor to describe preachers as "bowmen who let fly the arrows of the Lord to pierce the hearts of sinners" (Mulchahey, 553). I thank Kathryn Kerby-Fulton for drawing my attention to Michèle Mulchahey's book.

31. Giovanni Boccaccio, *The Decameron*, trans. G. H. McWilliam (Harmondsworth: Penguin, 1972), 10.7.49; p.775. This is quoted by Wallace, *Chaucerian Polity*, 279. The quotation is from the story of King Peter of Aragon, which is told on the tenth day when the story of Griselde is also told. Referring to Boccaccio's version of the Griselde story, Wallace discusses the

restraint of personal desire that should be exercised by lords when necessary for the common good.

32. C. G. Macaulay, "John Gower: The Latin Vox Clamantis," in The End of the Middle Ages, vol. 2 of The Cambridge History of English and American Literature (New York: G. P. Putnam's Sons, 1907–1921; New York: Bartleby.com, 2000), available at www.bartleby.com/cambridge.

33. Hsy, Images of Gower.

34. Scott, Later Gothic Manuscripts, 66.

35. John Goldfinch, Head, Incunabula and Early Western Printed Collections, British Library, January 31, 2006, in answer to my email inquiry.

36. Scott, Later Gothic Manuscripts, 66, refers to this as an example of Continental archer figures. See Grete Ring, A Century of French Painting, 1400–1500 (London: Phaidon, 1949), cat. no. 70, Plate 30. Ring suggests that this drawing, from a Series of Planets, Franco-Burgundian School, now in Dresden, Kupferstichkabinett, was made after 1416. It cannot, therefore, be the specific source of the HM 150 Vox artist's adaptation, but an earlier version might have been known. The placement and the relative proportions of archer and planet are very similar in both.

37. Adding a portrait of the author was not unknown, as evidenced by another eighteenth-century portrait, this time of Chaucer (similar in aspect to the Ellesmere portrait), hand-painted on vellum and inserted into the front of a first edition of Caxton's Canterbury Tales now in the British Library. It may be that collectors were motivated to own a complete or perfected copy of a book, as discussed by Toshiyuki Takamiya, "John Harris the Pen-and-Ink Facsimilist," in "Caxton's Chaucer: British Library Treasures in Full," ed. Colin Wight (London: British Library, 2003), available at http://www.bl.uk/treasures/caxton/homepage.html.

38. On the effectiveness of the longbow, see Andrea Hopkins, Knights (New York: Artabras, 1990), 127–128.

39. For a discussion of the significance of the symbolism of the bow in connection with Richard II, see Wallace, Chaucerian Polity, 257-258.

40. Echard, "Gower in Print," 116. See also Martha W. Driver, "Printing the Confessio Amantis: Caxton's Edition in Context," in Re-Visioning Gower, ed. R. F. Yeager (Asheville, NC: Pegasus Press, 1998), 269–303, esp. 269–273.

41. Painter, William Caxton, 130–131, refers to this among a number of other manuscripts that "can be assigned with confidence to the period from July to December 1483," the motive being Caxton's "continuing reluctance to give the regnal year of the usurping Richard III." See also Louise Gill, "William Caxton and the Rebellion of 1483," English Historical Review 112.445 (1997): 116; and Jenny Adams, Power Play: The Literature and Politics of Chess in the Late Middle Ages (Philadelphia: Univerity of Pennsylvania Press, 2006), 144-155.

42. Blake, *Caxton's Own Prose*, 69–70. For a discussion of Caxton and the political context in which he worked see Painter, *William Caxton*, 121–140.

43. For a discussion see Kathryn Kerby-Fulton and Steven Justice, "Scribe D and the Marketing of Ricardian Literature, in Kerby-Fulton and Hilmo, *The Medieval Professional Reader at Work*, 218-222.

44. Winthrop Wetherbee, "John Gower," in *The Cambridge History of Medieval English Literature*, ed. David Wallace (Cambridge: Cambridge University Press, 1999), 601.

45. See Emma Campbell, "Sexual Poetics and the Politics of Translation in the Tale of Griselda," *Literature* 55.3 (2003): 191–216. See also David Wallace's chapter on the Clerk's Tale, "'Whan She Translated Was': Humanism, Tyranny, and the Petrarchan Academy," in *Chaucerian Polity*, 261-298.

46. Mitchell, *Ethics and Exemplary Narrative in Chaucer and Gower*, 120.

47. Blake, *Caxton's Own Prose*, 88.

48. Hodnett, *English Woodcuts*, 1.

49. Jenny Adams, "'Longene to the Playe': Caxton, Chess and the Boundaries of Political Order," *Essays in Medieval Studies* 21 (2004): 156–160. See also Caxton's Prologues to the first and second editions in Blake, *Caxton's Own Prose*, 85–88.

50. Adams, "'Longene to the Playe,'" 159.

51. Gill, "William Caxton and the Rebellion of 1483," 111–112. As Gill mentions, there were 1,100 petitioners for a pardon, many of whom were linked with the rising.

52. Gill, "William Caxton and the Rebellion of 1483," 113. See, however, Adams, *Power Play*, 155, in which she suggests that the "threat to the new regime" of which Caxton sought "to indemnify himself" was "raised most tangibly by the woodcuts."

53. Driver, *The Image in Print*, 157, observes that English woodcut images "are emblematic, almost totemic, rather than naturalistic representations of reality."

54. In "'Longene to the Playe,'" 159, Adams calls attention to the way the patterned floor beneath the philosopher repeats the pattern of the chessboard so that "Life resembles a chessboard to such an extent that Philometer becomes quite literally a piece on one."

55. As seen in the late-fifteenth-century alabaster relief of St. Sitha, who holds a similar rosary, with a tassel instead of a cross at the end; see Plate 28 and the discussion in Paul Williamson, "St. Sitha," *Gothic Art for England*, 51.

56. For a more extensive discussion, see Hilmo, *Medieval Images*, 187—189; or Hilmo, "Framing the Canterbury Pilgrims," 28–30.

57. For a discussion of this illustration, see Phillipa Hardman, "Presenting the Text: Pictorial Tradition in Fifteenth-Century Manuscripts of the *Canterbury Tales*," in *Chaucer Illustrated: Five Hundred Years of the Canterbury Tales in Pictures*, ed.

William K. Finley and Joseph Rosenblum (Delaware, DE; London: Oak Knoll Press and British Library, 2003), 55–56 and Color Plate 25.

58. Blake, Introduction to *Caxton's Own Prose*, 24. In his Epilogue to *the Order of Chivalry*, published in 1484, Caxton presents the book to the "most dradde soverayne lord" King Richard III hoping that he will order young lords, nobles, and gentleman to read the book so that the order of chivalry will be followed better than in "late dayes passed."

59. Blake, *Caxton's Own Prose*, 87.

60. Blake, "Caxton's Second Edition," 152.

61. See Kathryn Kerby-Fulton and Denise L. Despres, *Iconography and the Professional Reader: The Politics of Book Production and the Douce Piers Plowman* (Minneapolis, MN: University of Minnesota Press, 1999).

62. There may have been an association of ideas and images that led to Wynken de Worde's choice for his devices with the archer figure. Wynken de Worde's shop, which he brought to Fleet Street around 1500, was under the sign of the Sun. At the top of his devices, the sun with accompanying stars likely identifies the place of his shop. This may, in turn, have brought to mind the centaur, or Sagittarius (Latin: "archer") figure shooting at the stars. There might also have been some suggestion of the archer Phoebus Apollo, not only a sun god but also the god of poetry. In de Worde's device, the archer figure is usually shown in the register below Caxton's initials where he is depicted shooting his arrow up toward Caxton's mark. In de Worde's device used for his edition of *Familiarium colloquiorum formulae* by Erasmus, he holds Caxton's mark. Perhaps there was some hint in all this that de Worde (Anglicized version of Wörth in Alsace) was aiming to reach the standards set by his predecessor. It is agreeable to think that there was also some resonance with the scholarly Clerk portrayed as archer whose arrows were words. See Ronald B. McKerrow, *Printers' and Publishers' Devices in England and Scotland, 1485–1640* (1913; repr. London: Bibliographical Society, 1949), xi–xlvii, and Nos. 19–21, 23a–c, 25, and 30.

WORKS CITED

Adams, Jenny. "'Longene to the Playe': Caxton, Chess and the Boundaries of Political Order." *Essays in Medieval Studies* 21 (2004): 151–166.

———. *Power Play: The Literature and Politics of Chess in the Late Middle Ages*.Philadelphia: University of Pennsylvania Press, 2006.

Barker, Nicolas. "A Contemporary Panegyrist of the Invention of Printing: The Author of the *Grammatica Rhythmica*." In *Incunabula: Studies in Fifteenth-Century Printed Books Presented to Lotte Hellinga*. Ed. Martin Davies. London: British Library, 1999. 187–214.

Blake, N. F. "Caxton's Second Edition of the *Canterbury Tales*." In *The English Medieval Book: Studies in Memory of Jeremy Griffiths*. Ed. Vincent Gillespie A. S. G. Edwards, and Ralph Hanna. London: The British Library, 2000. 135–153.

———. (Ed.) *Caxton's Own Prose*. London: Andre Deutsch, 1973.

———. "The 'Mirror of the World' and MS Royal A ix." *Notes and Queries* 212 (1967): 86–87.

Boccaccio, Giovanni. *The Decameron*. Trans. G.H. McWilliam. Harmondsworth: Penguin, 1972.

Campbell, Emma. "Sexual Poetics and the Politics of Translation in the Tale of Griselda." *Literature* 55.3 (2003): 191–216.

Carlson, David R. "The Woodcut Illustrations in Early Printed Editions." In *Chaucer Illustrated: Five Hundred Years of the Canterbury Tales in Pictures*. Ed. William K. Finley and Joseph Rosenblum. Newcastle, DE; London: Oak Knoll Press and the British Library, 2003. 73–120.

"Caxton's Chaucer: British Library Treasures in Full." Text by Kristian Jensen. Ed. Colin Wight. London: British Library, 2003. Available at http://www.bl.uk/treasures/caxton/homepage.html.

Chaucer, Geoffrey. *The Canterbury Tales*. In *The Riverside Chaucer*. Ed. Larry Benson. 3rd ed. Oxford: Oxford University Press, 1990.

Driver, Martha W. *The Image in Print: Book Illustration in Late Medieval England and Its Sources*. London: British Library, 2004.

———. "Printing the Confessio Amantis: Caxton's Edition in Context." In *Re-Visioning Gower*. Ed. R. F. Yeager. Asheville, NC: Pegasus Press, 1998. 269–303.

Echard, Siân (Ed.) *A Companion to Gower*. Cambridge: D. S. Brewer, 2004.

———. "Gower in Print." In *A Companion to Gower*. Ed. Siân Echard. Cambridge: D. S. Brewer, 2004. 115–135.

———. "Introduction: Gower's Reputation." In *A Companion to Gower*. Ed. Siân Echard. Cambridge: D. S. Brewer, 2004. 1–22.

Emmerson, Richard K. "Text and Image in the Ellesmere Portraits of the Tale-Tellers." In *The Ellesmere Chaucer: Essays in Interpretation*. Ed. Martin Stevens and Daniel Woodward. San Marino, CA; Tokyo: Huntington Library and Yushodo, 1995. 143–170.

Gaylord, Alan T. "Portrait of a Poet." In *The Ellesmere Chaucer: Essays in Interpretation*. Martin Stevens and Daniel Woodward. San Marino, CA; Tokyo: Huntington Library and Yushodo, 1995. 121–142.

Gill, Louise. "William Caxton and the Rebellion of 1483." *English Historical Review* 112.445 (1997): 106–118.

Griffiths, Jane. "What's in a Name? The Transmission of 'John Skelton, Laureate,' in Manuscript and Print." In *Manuscript, Print, and Early Tudor*

Literature. Ed. Alexandra Gillespie. Huntington Library Quarterly 67.2 (2004): 215–235.

Hardman, Phillipa. "Presenting the Text: Pictorial Tradition in Fifteenth-Century Manuscripts of the Canterbury Tales." In Chaucer Illustrated: Five Hundred Years of the Canterbury Tales in Pictures. Ed. William K. Finley and Joseph Rosenblum. Delaware, DE; London: Oak Knoll Press and The British Library, 2003. 37–72.

Harwood, Britton J. "Language and the Real: Chaucer's Manciple." Chaucer Review 6.4 (1972): 268-279.

Hilmo, Maidie. "Framing the Canterbury Pilgrims for the Aristocratic Readers of the Ellesmere Manuscript." In The Medieval Professional Reader at Work: Evidence from the Manuscripts of Chaucer, Langland, Kempe, and Gower. Ed. Kathryn Kerby-Fulton and Maidie Hilmo. Victoria, BC: University of Victoria, 2001. 14–71.

———. Medieval Images, Icons, and Illustrated English Literary Texts: From the Ruthwell Cross to the Ellesmere Chaucer. Aldershot, UK; Burlington, VT: Ashgate, 2004.

Hodnett, Edward. English Woodcuts 1480–1535. Oxford: Oxford University Press, 1973.

Hopkins, Andrea. Knights. New York: Artabras, 1990.

Hsy, Jonathan H. "Images of John Gower and His Works: Medieval to Modern." Available at http://www.english.upenn.edu/~jhsy/gower.html. (Accessed February 25, 2006).

Kerby-Fulton, Kathryn, and Denise L. Despres. Iconography and the Professional Reader: The Politics of Book Production and the Douce Piers Plowman. Minneapolis, MN: University of Minnesota Press, 1999.

Kerby-Fulton, Kathryn and Steven Justice, "Scribe D and the Marketing of Ricardian Literature. In The Medieval Professional Reader at Work: Evidence from the Manuscripts of Chaucer, Langland, Kempe, and Gower. Ed. Kathryn Kerby-Fulton and Maidie Hilmo. Victoria, BC: University of Victoria, 2001. 217-237.

Kittredge, George Lyman. "The Debate on Marriage in The Canterbury Tales." Modern Philology 9.4 (April, 1912): 435–467.

Mann, Jill. Chaucer and Medieval Estates Satire: The Literature of Social Classes and the General Prologue to the Canterbury Tales. London: Cambridge University Press, 1973.

Macaulay, C. G. "John Gower: The Latin Vox Clamantis." In The End of the Middle Ages. Vol. 2 of The Cambridge History of English and American Literature. New York: G. P. Putnam's Sons, 1907–1921; New York: Bartleby.com, 2000. Available at http://www.bartleby.com/212/0605.html.

McKerrow, Ronald B. Printers' and Publishers' Devices in England and Scotland, 1485–1640. 1913. Reprint, London: Bibliographical Society, 1949.

Meyer-Lee, Robert J. "Laureates and Beggars in Fifteenth-Century English Poetry: The Case of George Ashby." *Speculum* 79.3 (July 2004): 688–726.

Mitchell, J. Allan. *Ethics and Exemplary Narrative in Chaucer and Gower.* Cambridge: D. S. Brewer, 2004.

Mulchahey, M. Michèle. "*First the Bow Is Bent in Study. . . .*" *Dominican Education before* 1350. Toronto: Pontifical Institute of Medieval Studies, 1998.

Painter, George Duncan. *William Caxton: A Quincentenary Biography of England's First Printer.* London: Chatto & Windus, 1976.

Pearsall, Derek. "The Manuscripts and Illustrations of Gower's Works." In *A Companion to Gower.* Ed. Siân Echard. Cambridge: D. S. Brewer, 2004. 73–97.

Ring, Grete. *A Century of French Painting*, 1400–1500. London: Phaidon, 1949.

Rosenblum, Joseph, and William K. Finley. "Chaucer Gentrified: The Nexus of Art and Politics in the Ellesmere Miniatures." *Chaucer Review* 38 (2003): 140–157.

Scott, Kathleen L. *Later Gothic Manuscripts* 1390–1490. Vol. 2. London: Harvey Miller, 1996.

Stevens, Martin, and Daniel Woodward. (Eds.) *The Ellesmere Chaucer: Essays in Interpretation.* San Marino, CA; Tokyo: Huntington Library and Yushodo, 1995.

Takamiya Toshiyuki. "John Harris the Pen-and-Ink Facsimilist." In "Caxton's Chaucer: British Library Treasures in Full." Ed. Colin Wight. London: British Library, 2003. Available at http://www.bl.uk/treasures/caxton/homepage.html.

Townsend, Eleanor. (Ed.) *Gothic Art for England*, 1400–1547. London: V&A Publications, 2003.

Wallace, David. *Chaucerian Polity: Absolutist Lineages and Associated Forms in England and Italy.* Stanford: Stanford University Press, 1997.

Wetherbee, Winthrop. "John Gower." In *The Cambridge History of Medieval English Literature.* Ed. David Wallace. Cambridge: Cambridge University Press, 1999. 589–609.

Wickham, Annette. "Two Rosaries." In *Gothic Art for England*, 1400–1547. Ed. Eleanor Townsend. London: V&A Publications, 2003. 343.

Williamson, Paul. "St. Sitha." In *Gothic Art for England*, 1400–1547. Ed. Eleanor Townsend. London: V&A Publications, 2003. 395.

Figure 1. The Clerk. Geoffrey Chaucer, *Canterbury Tales*. San Marino, CA, Huntington Library, MS Ellesmere 26 C9, c.1500-1510, fol. 88r. (This item is reproduced by permission of the Huntington Library, San Marino, California.)

Figure 2. The Clerk (detail). Geoffrey Chaucer, *Canterbury Tales*. San Marino, CA, Huntington Library, MS Ellesmere 26 C9, c.1500-1510, fol. 88r. (This item is reproduced by permission of the Huntington Library, San Marino, California.)

Figure 3. Chaucer. Geoffrey Chaucer, *Canterbury Tales*. San Marino, CA, Huntington Library, MS Ellesmere 26 C9, c. 1500-1510, fol. 153v. (This item is reproduced by permission of the Huntington Library, San Marino, California.)

The clerkis tale of oxenford

And begynneth the clerkis
tale of Oxenford

Ther is in the west syde of Itayle
Doun at the rote of Vesulus the colde
A lusty playn habundaunt of vitayle
Wher many a toun and tour thou mayst beholde
That foundëd were in tyme of faders olde
And many another delectable sight
And Saluces this noble contre hight

A markis somtyme lord was of that londe
As were his worthy eldris hym before
And obeysaunt ay redy to his honde
Were al his lieges bothe lasse and more
Thus in delyt he lyued and doth so yore
Beloued & drad thorough fauour of fortune
Both of his lordes and eke of his comune

aa ij

Figure 4. The Clerk. Geoffrey Chaucer, *Canterbury Tales* (Westminster: William Caxton, 1483), STC (2nd ed.) 5083; BL G.11586, sig. aa2r. (By permission of the British Library.)

Figure 5. The Yeoman. Geoffrey Chaucer, *Canterbury Tales* (Westminster: William Caxton, 1483), STC (2nd ed.) 5083; BL G.11586, sig. a5r. (By permission of the British Library.)

Figure 6. The Poet as moral satirist aims his arrow at the world. John Gower, *Vox Clamantis*. San Marino, CA, Huntington Library, MS HM 150, c. 1392-1399, fol. 13v. (This item is reproduced by permission of the Huntington Library, San Marino, California.)

Figure 7. The poet as moral satirist aims his arrow at the world. John Gower, *Vox Clamantis*. London, British Library, MS Cotton Tiberius A.IV, c. 1408, flor. 9v. (By permission of the British Library.)

The Portrait of John Gower from a MS. preserved in the Cotton Library.

CNC

Figure 8. The poet as moral satirist aims his arrow at the world. Late seventeenth- or early eighteenth-century engraving added as frontispiece to the 1483 edition of *Confessio Amantis*. (Westminster: William Caxton), STC (2nd ed.) 12142; BLIB.55077. (By permission of the British Library.)

Figure 9. Regicide. William Caxton, *Game and Playe of the Chesse*, trans. of Jacobus de Cessolis, *Liber de moribus hominum et officiis nobilium super ludo scacchorum* (Westminster: William Caxton, 1483), book I, chap. 1. (Courtesy of Project Gutenberg.)

Figure 10. Philometer (the Philosopher). William Caxton, *Game and Playe of the Chesse*, trans. of Jacobus de Cessolis, *Liber de moribus hominum et officiis nobilium super ludo scacchorum* (Westminster: William Caxton, 1483), book 1, chap. 2. (Courtesy of Project Gutenberg.)

Good wyf ther was of beside Bathe
And she was somdel deef & that was scathe
Of cloth makynge had she suche an haunt
She passed them of ypre and of gaunt
In al the parisshe wyf was ther non
That to the offrynge before hyr sholde goon
And yf ther dyd certayn wroth r. as she
Than was she oute of al charyte
Her kercheups ful fyn were of grounde
I durste swere they weyed thre pounde
That on a sonday were on hyr hed
Hyr hosyn were of fyne scarlet red
Ful streyte I teyd and shoos ful moyst and newe
Bold was her face fayr and rede of hewe
She was a worthy woman al hyr lyue
Husbondes at the chyrche dore had she fyue
Wythoute other companye in youthe
But her of nedyth not to speke as nowthe

Figure 11. The Wife of Bath. Geoffrey Chaucer, *Canterbury Tales* (Westminster: William Caxton, 1483), STC (2nd ed.) 5083: BL G. 11586, sig. b5v. (By permission of the British Library)

"A Good Reder and a Deuout": Instruction, Reading, and Devotion in the *Wise Book of Philosophy and Astronomy*

CARRIE GRIFFIN

The quotation forming part of the title of this paper, "a good reder and a deuout," is found in an astrological/astronomical text known as *The Wise Book of Philosophy and Astronomy*,[1] occurring in an instruction advising that time be measured by specific acts of devotional reading. Written in Middle English and surviving (both in its fullest form and in abridged versions) in thirty-three late-medieval manuscripts, *The Wise Book of Philosophy and Astronomy* (hereafter *Wise Book*) was arguably one of the most accessible—and widely accessed—scientific texts written in the vernacular circulating throughout the fourteenth and fifteenth centuries.

The records of its circulation and reception demonstrate that this prose text reached a varied public and coexisted with texts of surprising variety and in books whose contents, significantly, were interpreted and used by "publics variously limited."[2] Moreover, because the *Wise Book*—habitually classified as a scientific or "utilitarian" text[3]—is not exclusively concerned with the dissemination of practically applicable knowledge and because (based both on the types of books that preserve it and the textual instructions embedded therein) it appears to have been compiled with certain reading practices and a number of different types of reader in mind, we must imagine that the text, or at least parts of it, was accessed by a readership that is not immediately discernible by just examining the text itself. Furthermore, since the Wise Book appears to have been constructed to cater for or facilitate access by different types of reader, it allows these readers to interpret and utilize the text in an appropriate manner; in other words, it is "writerly,"[4] and just as it constructs a multifaceted audience, so also does it allow for the lectoris arbitrium—the discernment—of the audience or readership.

This paper argues, then, for varying levels of interaction with the Wise Book; it uses the evidence provided both by the manuscript books and by the directions within the text to consider that the information may have had a wide and varied discourse community, as opposed to what has previously been imagined as a fairly narrow and limited readership or audience. Specifically, it considers that the structures, ordinatio, and instructions associated with the process of reading secular, scientific, and utilitarian texts such as the Wise Book were not dissimilar to the manner in which spiritual or devotional materials were approached; the directions to readers with varying levels of literacy, for example, either to read certain devotional texts or recall them from memory and the contexts in which the Wise Book may have been consulted are examined to suggest that the author-compiler was conscious of his audience, their requirements, and their different levels of intellectual sophistication.

The Wise Book has suffered from a lack of meaningful critical and editorial attention; despite its undoubted centrality in the canon of scientific and utilitarian texts circulating in English toward the end of the Middle Ages and regardless of recent and sustained scholarly focus on similar texts and genres, it has generally and until recently only been mentioned as deserving of a full critical examination. The text has been fully published only twice: one version, edited from Cambridge, University Library, MS Ll.4.14, contains, among other tracts, a version of the B-text of Piers Plowman.[5] Here, the Wise Book is included in an anthology of texts that circulated alongside or were associated with Piers—"popularized, abridged, sometimes confused and fragmentary versions of high learning that circulated widely and often constituted the sole access to collections of formal learning of writers whose works colored the thought of the later Middle Ages"—with a view to providing "a new understanding of the intellectual and social atmosphere of fourteenth-century England."[6] A second version of the Wise Book was transcribed by Richard Grothé in his unpublished doctoral thesis.[7] Both, however, print versions from just one manuscript apiece, without considering the Wise Book directly in terms of context or speculating on possible audiences for or readers of the Book.[8]

Essentially, the Wise Book has been the subject of assessment largely only in terms of similar texts, and commentary on it has almost exclusively involved efforts at classification or has focused on the accuracy and sophistication of the instructions and information it contains. Crucially, it is in their consideration of the latter that commentators have reached conclusions on the nature and sophistication of the intended audience and actual readership of the text. Despite their concern with the important and revealing contemporary concepts disseminated by the text, Krochalis and Peters stress that the popular appeal of the Wise Book as "a handy compendium of astronomical, astrological, and characterological information" indicates an audience that was "not too learned,"[9] while Taavitsainen, more recently, classifies the text as "an astrological encyclopaedia . . . [representing] the lower end of the scale of compilations in prose . . . [and which] imitates the more learned type."[10] Thus many scholars have tended to speculate on the sophistication of both the text and its imagined or implied audience while failing to take into account either the nature of the manuscript witnesses or the internal textual evidence regarding an intended contemporary readership. Both of these important factors not only complicate the textual history of the Wise Book but also allow for a less narrow consideration of its audience and readership.[11]

As I have argued in my recent thesis on this text, the manuscripts that preserve the text reveal what must have been a varied and diverse readership for the Wise Book. Contrary to what has been hitherto speculated—that the Wise Book was a text accessed by the curious but amateur reader—it has been demonstrated that the range of codices in which the text circulated reveals a variety of reading contexts and discourse communities in which the text was encountered.[12] It is found, for example, embedded into professional medical treatises, such as those in London, Wellcome Medical Historical Medical Library, MS 564, in a gentleman compiler's miscellany such as New Haven, Yale University, MS Beinecke 163 (The "Wagstaff Miscellany"), and in the collection of legal, religious, and grammatical material at one time owned by the house of Augustinian canons at Creake, near Walsingham (London, British Library, MS Add. 12195). These contexts, moreover, negate the received view that the author-compiler cannot have been a learned man nor can have expected his audience to be. Most important to this discussion, the notion that the text was encountered by a varied audience must imply that it was not always read or interpreted in the same way by all.

Generally, the scholar must look primarily to a text's prologue in order to imagine or ascertain the readers of that text. The prologue fulfills many functions; it is the first point of contact between reader and text and was therefore important to the contemporary circulation and reception of a text. However, it also positions a text and is thereby instrumental in its transmission and circulation, locating it in a tradition that would be familiar to its likely audience and indicating the "principles of interpretation that might be applied" to it.[13] The prologue to the Wise Book, initially at least, appears to fulfill some of these criteria:

> Here begynneth the wise boke of philosophie *and* astronamye, contryued and made of the wisest philosophre *and* astronomyer þat euer was sethe the worlde was begunne, that is forto saie of the londe of Greece. For in that londe was an Englische man, ful wise and wel vnderstondinge of philosophie and astronomie, studied and compiled this boke oute of Grewe graciously into Englisch (fol. 59r).

The claims made here invest the subsequent information with authority by locating it in a learned, translated tradition of philosophical writing and by ensuring that the translator figure, the "Englische man," is both reliable and scholarly (fol. 59r). The prologue is focused on the term "wise book," presenting the reader with a text that has been compiled and written by the "wisest philosophre and astronomyer þat euer was." It is suggested, thereby, that the scope of the book is encyclopedic and that the prologue attempts to project the text outside the boundaries of what is inferred by just astronomy and philosophy. In so doing, the prologue and the ensuing text both demonstrate a deliberate awareness of a multifaceted audience that is necessarily and variously debilitated—in terms of literacy, education, status, or gender—and that, because of one or a combination of these factors, approaches the text in a unique way and with a specific purpose or to specific ends.

Despite this, the remainder of the prologue introducing the Wise Book is apparently addressed to and focused on one very restricted audience:

> withoute whiche sciens and knowynge no man may come to perfit wurchinge of astronomye, ne philosophie, ne surgerie, ne of non othir science. For ther is no leche in þe worlde that may treuly wirche his crafte, but if he haue the science and kunnynge of this booke (fol. 59v).

Albeit this occurs as a secondary directive of sorts (since it appears after both the initial prologue and the brief list of contents), it complicates possible contemporary responses to the Wise Book. In its evocation of an exclusive audience of literate medical professionals—surgeons and leech doctors—it suggests merely *one* community of readers that may have had recourse to the Book, all the while locating that potential audience within a wider, more heterogeneous discourse community. The nature of the literary prologue was such that:

most prologues reflect self-consciously on a crucial medieval understanding of 'literature,' one that relates not to the status of the text but to that of the reader. This understanding is derived from a common distinction between *litterati* and *illiterati*—roughly 'educated' and 'uneducated.'[4]

The preface to the *Wise Book*, I contend, does not advocate a limited, specific function for the *Book*, nor does the *Book* itself limit its use to an audience composed exclusively of *literati*; on the contrary, the apparent encyclopedic and all-encompassing nature of the text suggests both selective consultation and professional usage. Rather than restricting readership to a specific audience, the prologue attempts to ensure that the *Wise Book* will have as wide and varied a public as possible.

Immediately we can imagine, as distinct from the narrow audience initially alluded to in the prologue, a diverse and multiple readership for the *Wise Book*; those who encountered the text would conceivably have consulted it or read it selectively, used all of it or parts of it, or simply just perused it. The text, however, will also achieve what is termed "perfit wurchinge" of astronomy, philosophy, and, indeed, of all other sciences for all readers, and not just for those of the medical community who might consult it. Effectively, then, the *Book* not only invites selective reading and consultation but also postures itself as a manual that not only provides instruction but supplements learning in many disciplines. This is supported by the internal structure of the *Book*—the more philosophical elements are self-contained and are found grouped together in certain parts (such as the debate at the beginning and the physiognomy at the end), while the technical, functional aspects of the text are often copied in a list format, follow a logical schema, and are frequently presented in brief, accessible, and distinct sections.

As noted above, received criticism on the *Wise Book* has emphasized that the workings and effects of heavenly bodies and the cosmic system and theories and structures of the universe are simplified and condensed. Notwithstanding, one of the most remarkable achievements of the *Book* is that in its purveyance of knowledge, it actively allows for an audience with various levels of education, with the effect that the simplicity of the text is "more apparent than real."[15] On the one hand, it is assumed that members of its audience will have no prior knowledge of the cosmos or the zodiacal system; thus the tract begins by outlining and naming basic structures and concepts: the seven planets and the days of the week for which they are named; the ten heavens and eleven orders of angels; the twelve signs of the zodiac and the months in which they reign. Simultaneously, however, it aims to be of interest to readers with some background knowledge in a variety of categories, including philosophical issues, such as the nature of providence and free will. Also, the text would have appealed to those with an interest in astronomical and astrological theory, the *computus*, and related Latin scholarship; significantly, too, readers with practical experience in the use of astronomical instruments would have benefited from the *Book*. Indeed, the nature of the text is such that it can reasonably be regarded either as a short introduction for the amateur or beginner or a summary for those with some experience and knowledge. This duality of function may account in no small part for sustained contemporary interest in the *Book* and for its impressive circulation history from the late fourteenth through the sixteenth century.

It is not just in the prologue that evocations of a multifaceted audience are apparent; the section of the *Book* dealing with the calculation of secular time has both explicit and tacit references to the various ways in which the information can be useful and applicable. In the part of the text specifically concerned with the measurement of the length of each planet's reign, it is apparent that levels of educational achievement and the technical proficiency of the audience are of some importance to the author, not least because the matter at hand has the potential to be technically complex. The formula for measurement is presented thus:

> it is to wete that the planet regneth bi estimacioun as longe tyme
> as a good reder and a deuout schulde rede twies the *seven* psalmis
> with the letanye . . . and for as muche as eche man may not haue
> the astrolabe, therfor it is chosen a mesure and poynte that men
> may lightly knowe þe houres of þe planetis (fols. 71v - 72r).

The inclusion of a methodology of this type is indicative of author-compiler awareness, or intention, that the *Wise Book* would have circulated within diverse discourse communities and a concern that the text be accessed not just by a narrow and limited professional "audience." This is especially relevant when we consider that since the latter portion of the instruction—that which mentions the astrolabe—is absent from some of the manuscript witnesses, both the author-compiler and subsequent copyists recognized the restrictions experienced or indeed the educational standards likely to have been reached by members of its intended audience. The *computus* section, in particular, makes many assumptions about its audience, but one is important: that it will most likely comprise people—both male and female—with dissimilar abilities.

On the one hand, these instructions are pitched at that element of the audience with some level of expertise in the calculation of time. They will either have access to or sufficient expertise in the use of an astrolabe, such as the intended audience of the *Wise Book* contained in Cambridge, Trinity College, MS R.14.51 and London, British Library, MS Egerton 2433, who are instructed to "be holde an astrolabe" in order to measure the hour of planetary reign.[16] Similarly, the tone of the instruction indicates that certain mem-

bers of the audience will have "access to manuscript material, literacy [and]
at least some basic knowledge of mathematics and astronomy," and may even
possess the "parchment and paper volvelles" that act as substitutes for the
astrolabe.[17] This implied learned audience is, on the other hand, engaged
alongside an audience lacking either skills or resources or in some cases,
both; as Braswell-Means puts it, "many texts addressed in the first instance
to a more learned audience reflect a self-conscious recognition" of the diffi-
culties that the absence of resources—either written material or linguistic
capability—might pose.[18] In most of its manuscript versions, hence, the *Wise
Book* advises that "a good reder and a deuout" can measure an hour by reading "twies the *seven* psalmis with the letanye (fol. 72r), thereby addressing an
audience that is literate, is able to read Latin well, and has recourse to the
appropriate written devotional materials to do so.[19] Here the intended audience is well-educated and widely read—and because of this, able to make use
of this alternative method for the calculation of time—but still probably had
neither the cause nor the means to purchase or use an astrolabe. The antici-
pated audience of London, Wellcome Historical Medical Library, MS 411, for
example, is likely to have neither: "for it is costelew ech man to haue an astir-
labre, or ellis lest eche man be not vndirstondynge and kunnynge þeron."[20]
This version of the *Wise Book*, therefore, advises that to measure a similar
length of time, the reader should:

> sette a space as longe as þou mayste goo in wynter tyme ij myle or
> lesse and in somertyme sett þe space of iij myle goynge, or elles
> sette as longe tyme as þou mayst say two nocturnes of the sautre.[21]

The above extract caters to a section of the audience that will have a
different relationship with the *Wise Book*. The instructions here—to measure
an hour by walking—are clearly intended to facilitate those who cannot read
or those with the ability to read in the vernacular only. This audience also has
the option to read or recite two nocturns from the Psalter.

Some recent studies of scientific and medical tracts and devotional
materials of the later Middle Ages have stressed that late-medieval concern
with human spiritual and physical well-being may have led to the co-location
of devotional and astrological or medical material in individual codices;
moreover, such texts are organized in ways that suggest they may have been
read and assimilated in similar ways. Middle English charms, for example,
frequently blend folkloric advice, Latin incantations or prayer fragments, and
astrological information, and the reader is sometimes advised to read, recite,
or write down holy names or words.[22] Similarly, Green identifies what she
calls "evidence . . . of the easy juxtaposition of physical and spiritual healing
in late medieval England" in a paper that, significantly, makes use of the term
"spiritual regimen," regimen, of course, being more usually associated with

medical or astrological information.[23] In an earlier study, Braswell-Means offers some examples of formulae similar to those contained in the Wise Book, including one that is found in a Wise Book companion text, the Dome of Urynes by Henry Daniel (in Cambridge, Trinity College Library, MS O.10.21), which advises the recitation of a Hail Mary and the Lord's Prayer (quickly) to measure a minute.[24]

It is apparent, then, that in some contexts, the processes of maintaining spiritual and physical well-being were not entirely divorced in Middle English writings; moreover, scientific, pseudo-scientific, and folkloric instruction frequently seems to be dependent for effect on texts with which their public would undoubtedly be familiar. However, what is far more interesting, in a consideration of the Wise Book at least, is whether the integration of these concerns, not just in individual volumes but within specific texts, had an influence on the reading process and, crucially, if this intertextualization encouraged readers to participate actively in the selection of suitable material for consumption; in other words, do the intertextual references—to the Bible, to other devotional materials, and to other traditions of writing—allow readers to experience the text in a variety of ways, to draw on more than one source of comfort or healing, even effectively to "read" more than one text at a time?

The self-conscious awareness of a varied public evidenced in the Wise Book is exemplified throughout by its overwhelming sense of a community of readers. Strikingly, the methodology employed in the text allows it, potentially, to be accessed and used by a substantial readership, and further means that it may be utilized by those who are illiterate. Physical action can be taken to measure time, and the methods given can be put into practice by almost anyone. Those unable to read can have the instructions read to them and can then measure time by carrying out an everyday activity—walking. The audience can also read certain texts—or recall them from memory, if they are members of a religious order, like the Augustinians at Creake—since they are instructed to "say," or recite, two nocturnes. The illiterate can also have the suggested texts read to them, so responses to or encounters with the text may not always have been private.[25]

Hence there are various ways in which different publics might make use of the text, whether or not they are "good" readers. Significantly, however, the reader must also be "deuout"—not only practiced at reading Latin (or, indeed, at reading) but perhaps able to memorize the relevant texts or able to come by them easily. That popular prayers and devotional materials are recommended to aid in the measurement of time is significant, primarily because they suggest a wide readership for "secular" instructional material. However, such practices also challenge modern academic ideas on the categorization of medieval texts, a process that is necessary but that often refuses intertextuality. Significantly, too, such references allow us to consider that traditional devotional reading, biblical allusions, and apocryphal material may have been referred to or included in secular texts not only to facilitate the reader in applying the instructions using familiar triggers or references to well-known texts but to allow the reader a devotional or spiritual experience while simultaneously being instructed in a science or technique. Moreover, the awareness of a multilayered audience suggests that the actual contemporary reading public may have had the shape of a discourse community, one that conceivably included members of the clergy as well as laypersons, people who had the text read to them as well as private readers, and those with a professional interests as well as those with amateur curiosities.

These formulae are also revealing when we come to think about the dissemination and context of devotional materials in Middle English vernacular traditions of writing, since they evidence accessible and practical alternative uses for well-known or readily available devotional materials. That a reading of devotional materials is advocated by an astrological/astronomical text like the Wise Book may have had more meaning for a fourteenth- or fifteenth-century readership than it has for modern scholarship, since both types of text are instructional, didactic, and advisory.

More important for a study of the Wise Book in particular, however, the common ground can perhaps be found in the philosophical aspects of the text. In a manner similar to Middle English lunary texts, the Wise Book refers to the Bible as a source in its association of biblical persons and events with particular signs; these characters or events, drawn from both the Old and New Testaments, are then connected to a prediction for each person or to specific character traits, according to birth sign. Aquarius, for example, is linked to John the Baptist, and Libra to Judas' betrayal of Jesus. The outcome of this association with Judas is, perhaps unsurprisingly, negative ("who so is borne in this signe schal be a wickid man *and* a traitour and of an euel dethe schal deie" (fol. 62v). Even predictions that feature more positive figures than Judas tend toward the negative; the prophet Daniel, appropriately, represents Leo, but the person born under Leo will be a "bolde theef and hardy" (fol. 62r). Taken at face value, the suggestion is that the events mentioned happened under similar positions of the skies.[26] However, the author-compiler has perhaps ensured that the reader is drawn to the structure of this section, which mimics a missal in its linking the signs of the zodiac with archetypes and saints. The readership would have been aware that Abraham, associated with March (and therefore Aries) had his feast day on March 25. The overall effect may have been that the reader is imaginatively engaged in the reading a missal, and devotional reading practice is both explicit in the references to Christian archetypes (Adam, Abraham, and Isaac) and saints (John the

Baptist) and implicit in the associations and connections made in the mind of the reader.[27]

Moreover, the reader is encouraged to imagine and understand the structure of the universe through reference to familiar biblical and apocryphal examples; for example, the fall of Lucifer is used to explain theories relating to the influence of various planets. Lucifer and his "felowes" owe their demise to sin, and they fell "summe heigher and summe lower" (fol. 65v), thus corrupting certain stars, elements, and planets. The fall of Lucifer was, as a motif, important in an understanding of the order of the cosmos; it provided a framework, or a pathway, through which man must progress in mortal life.[28] Here, however, biblical paraphrase is utilized in a specific manner and to a certain end: to emphasize that there are negative aspects to planetary influence and to expound on the resultant moral dilemma of good and evil influence. Everything made by God, stresses the text, is by nature good; it is only through the actions of individuals that this inherent goodness is compromised, despite the acknowledgment that God made man "after his owne schap" (fol. 65r).[29] Readers are given as much information as is necessary to imagine the workings—and the influence—of the planets, but they are sporadically reminded of the power and omnipotence of the Creator.

Similar impulses—those allowing readers not only to realize the authority of the Bible but effectively, through intertextual references, to remember the Christian calendar when thinking about the astrological and "read" the supporting devotional material—must have been behind the directions to consult specific texts that can be used to measure time. However, references to what would have been well-known—or easily accessible—texts, such as the seven penitential psalms, may have had another function along with drawing the reader's mind to spiritual responsibilities. Biblical motifs such as those in the Wise Book are commonly found in vernacular pseudo-scientific texts in both verse and prose. They are, as mentioned, also common to lunaries, such the prose text "The Thrytty Daies of the Mone," which precedes the Wise Book in London, British Library, MS Egerton 827. In this lunary, the secular prognostications are framed; the biblical person or event introduces and establishes the prediction, for example, "on þe fyrste day of þe mone was Adam made, þat day is good and profytabele all werkes to werke"(fol. 11r), and each ends with a fragment from each of the first thirty psalms.[30]

Ultimately, biblical motifs and psalmic line fragments infuse the text with authority, but they may also have enriched readings of texts such as the Wise Book and may have urged readers to turn to or to imagine a devotional text or texts. Fragments from psalms in a text are familiar; by their inclusion, they convince the reader that the text is safe and authoritative, and the prayer fragments ensure that readers are mindful of their devotional duties. They are also, however, comforting; Taavitsainen suggests that it was a common superstition that sentences or phrases from the Bible could act as amulets or charms of a sort, protecting the reader from evil.[31] However, it seems likely that motifs and references to psalms are also present to both inspire and instruct the reader; "The Thrytty Daies of the Mone" also exists in verse, the prologue to which claims that the text has been "wryttyn . . . for our profit / For our solas and oure delijt."[32] This threefold claim—to provide profit, "solas" or comfort, and delight—is a good indicator as to the reasoning behind the merging of religious and scientific material and the associated benefits of dual reading. We can imagine how this rationale may have applied to a "writerly" text like the Wise Book: the information can be profitable, in that the text is a manual that can be consulted by the reader, say, to plan actions for the best possible outcome. Comfort is perhaps provided by references to psalms and the reassurance that prayer will help the onset of a fated outcome; delight may come with the recognition of common biblical events and persons and with the assurances that everything is controlled, ultimately, by a benevolent Creator.

In this sense, parallels can be drawn with religious didactic literature, which, as Morey asserts, offers "wisdom and comfort: the wisdom to lead a Christian life, and the comfort of knowing that salvation accrues from so living."[33] It is likely that similar responses may have been evoked by the Wise Book, since the notion commonly found in literary texts—the intention to tell stories that instruct as well as provide consolation and amusement—apparently found its way into works of science and information too.[34]

It follows, therefore, that the intended audience suggested by the Wise Book's prologue must have been expanded and that this encourages modern scholars to imagine various ways of reading this text. To account for a wider readership and associated discourse communities is significant in recovering a reception history for the Wise Book. In other words, given the layers of possible interpretation, the levels of interaction on the part of the reader, and the various types of manuscript book—and cotexts—common to the Wise Book, that text was encountered, used, and read by more than just the medical practitioner. This is to some extent determined by the vernacularization and accessibility of texts of this type: since the monastic culture had given way to the culture of the schools, we find "new kinds of books—a more technical literature—and new kinds of readers"; thus the "scholastic lectio was a process of study which involved a more ratiocinative scrutiny of the text and consultation for reference purposes."[35]

Conceivably, then, since the Wise Book appears to invite them, its discourse communities were probably composed of different types of private readers and groups of listeners. The peculiar encounters with the text are thereby colored by the individual requirements of the private reader or by the diverse responses of communities of readers. The variety of these possible discourse communities must inform our discussion of the reading practices associated with the Wise Book. The structure of the text would support consultation; for example, the opening section, outlining the signs of the zodiac according to month and outcome, could easily be consulted both privately and for others, and the detail accorded to each sign is brief enough to be read aloud to a number of people (in effect, this information may be consulted in much the same way that modern horoscopes are). Although from the thirteenth century onwards:

> increasing reliance and importance was placed upon the written word . . . some of the formulas of oral delivery persisted in later medieval texts . . . because they would be appropriate to the situation of reading aloud, especially to the whole family.[36]

The concluding section to the Wise Book—the physiognomy—also lends itself to consultation and to reading to or for others, and its subject matter—the physical and characterological features of men born under the influence of each of the seven planets—must have been at once edifying and entertaining.[37]

The diversity of discourse communities, moreover, encountered the text in a variety of contexts, which must imply different *readers* as well as interpretations.[38] As Parkes concludes, there are three types of medieval reader: "the professional reader . . . the cultivated reader . . . [and] the pragmatic reader."[39] Approximately half of the manuscripts containing the Wise Book are largely, or in some cases exclusively, concerned with *materia medica*, ranging in scope from handbooks for bloodletting (such as British Library, Egerton MS 827, which is signed "Welles leche" at fol. 50v, or the professional, university-style codex London, Wellcome Historical Medical Library, MS 564, which contains vernacular copies of the anatomy and surgery of Henri de Mondeville). However, its appeal as a practical text ensures that it has a less narrow context than as a supplement to medical practice. Like the popular lunary texts (frequently found coexisting with the Wise Book), it is preserved in the types of manuscript that suggest a large cross section of society, or what Braswell-Means classifies as six discrete communities: the rural, nonprofessional family; the aristocratic household; the merchant and yeoman families; the domestic staff of large households; ecclesiastical readers, and, of course, professional medical men and women.[40]

The Wise Book, then, finds a wide readership in the miscellanies and commonplace books of the Middle Ages. These books would frequently have had multiple functions, acting as the locus for different types of reading or as a place to remember short recipes, cures, and charms. The books themselves, then, were subject to both general and specific reading, and many of the texts copied into and stored in these volumes may have had to serve multiple purposes. The "Wagstaff Miscellany," owned by John Whittocksmead of Wiltshire, includes, as well as a copy of the *Wise Book*, two spiritual texts: the *De spiritu Guidonis*, and a guide to proper confession. Keiser notes that these texts strongly resemble practical books, being at once didactic and encouraging of devotion.[41] Since the contents of Whittocksmead's miscellany needed to have multiple functions, it is perhaps significant that one of these two spiritual manuals is in Latin; it is not uncommon to discover that such a text would have served a twofold purpose and a dual audience, as both a didactic moral piece and a text that could be used in a schoolroom setting to teach Latin.

Similarly, both the spiritual and practical material found in British Library, MS Add. 12195 is seemingly designed to have more than one function, and a multilayered audience; spiritually, the focus in this manuscript is on carols, which can be read silently or aloud to others, can be sung, or can be used at different times of the year; practically, there are Christmas Day predictions, texts on perilous Mondays, and a *Trotula* gynecological text, the prologue of which recommends that it be read by lettered women to those who could not read and features advice on childbirth and how to choose a nurse.[42] The volume also contains a charm for a difficult childbirth (fol. 142v), a brief prose prayer in Latin about the Virgin's delivery of Jesus, with accompanying instructions in English.[43] Cambridge, Trinity College, MS R.14.51, associated with the Bussell family, has a combination of texts reflecting the utilitarian, literary, and moral concerns of a relatively well-to-do household.[44] The book is topped and tailed by copies of Chaucer's "Gentilesse" and "Lak of Stedfastnesse" (both entitled "balade" in the manuscript)—a moral poem and a complaint about contemporary conditions respectively. This moral and didactic framework, along with charms for difficult childbirth and the devotional aspects of the *Wise Book*, means that sections of the volume might have been suitable for consultation by women. Like John Whittocksmead, who demarcated material of interest within the texts in his book, many readers would not have had the need or the desire to read texts regularly or from beginning to end, or, for that matter, silently.

The companion texts of the *Wise Book* in miscellanies are often such that we can imagine them being read to or for communities of women, children, or the illiterate members of the household. But other reading contexts for the *Wise Book* also need to be considered; Oxford, Bodleian Library, MS Ashmole 189 is a composite manuscript in four parts and, as noted by Ker, has evidence from an inscription that part two was owned by Richard Coscumb, prior of Muchenely Abbey, Somerset.[45] The glut of carols and prayers in the middle of the manuscript, therefore, had a separate existence before being bound into one volume with the *Wise Book* and other astrological materials; however, other parts of the codex have what Taavitsainen terms "a Muchenely connection,"[46] so the *Wise Book* may have continued to circulate in an ecclesiastical setting. Similarly, and as mentioned above, the blend of religious, legal, grammatical, and medical material found in London, British Library, MS Add. 12195 does not immediately obviate its circulation at the house of Augustinian canons at Creake; the volume contains prayers and notes on services for certain times of the year, along with services used by the Carmelites, notices of banns, wills and testaments, and charms and recipes.[47] That a copy of the *Wise Book* found its way, too, into a manuscript of the B-text of *Piers Plowman* in Cambridge, University Library, MS Ll.4.14, may be revealing in terms of alternate uses for our text; Langland, just like the author-compiler of the *Wise Book*, is attuned to the explanation of "complex theological problems";[48] the overall didactic tone of the manuscript (which contains a glossary of difficult words found in *Piers*, a text on the argument of the psalms, and a text of *Mum and the Sothsegger*), both in terms of moral and scientific instruction, may have contributed to its ultimate function as a schoolroom volume.[49]

The multifaceted audience of the *Wise Book* would most likely have used the text in various ways and to different ends, and the nature of the books that preserve the *Wise Book of Philosophy and Astronomy* is such that it is difficult to imagine a narrow, specific community of readers such as alluded to in the prologue. Thus, just as the evidence allows for different readers, so must different readings of the text have occurred. The parallels between devotional and practical material are not immediately clear, but what is apparent is that there are shared elements in both and that aspects of the *Wise Book* remind the reader of a variety of devotional duties and Christian texts. The particular location of the *Wise Book* in miscellany manuscripts, alongside moral and courtesy material and blended with material of a professional interest, must have been "designed to improve the reader's soul, or to multiply his accomplishments and increase his stock of useful, even cultural information."[50]

Moreover, the structure of the *Wise Book* is such that it invites any number of responses from readers, and, textured with reference to devotional material, it can be advisory, didactic, and spiritual as well as utilitarian and scientific. Ultimately, it must challenge some of our assumptions about the nature of reading—particularly with regard to devotional texts—in the later Middle Ages; the evidence provided by the *Wise Book* would suggest that such texts, whether recalled from memory, heard, or privately consulted, were not always approached with devotion in mind.

University College Cork

NOTES

1. All quotations from the Wise Book, unless otherwise noted, are from my edition of the text from New York, Columbia University, MS Plimpton 260, in Carrie Griffin, "'A Good Reder': The Middle English Wise Book of Philosophy and Astronomy, Instruction, Publics, and Manuscripts" (Diss. University College Cork, 2006), 247–263.

2. Ralph Hanna, III, Pursuing History: Middle English Manuscripts and Their Texts (Stanford, CA: Stanford University Press, 1996), 5.

3. George Keiser's important scholarly resource, Works of Science and Information, vol. X of A Manual of the Writings in Middle English (New Haven, CT: Connecticut Academy of Arts and Sciences, 1998), classifies the text as scientific, under the rubric of "Cosmology, Astronomy, Astrology" (3615). Keiser's list of manuscripts is, however, incomplete; see Griffin, 8–10, for a more up-to-date listing.

4. The term "writerly" is from Roland Barthes and is used here to distinguish between the lisible, or "readerly" text, which makes its readers passive consumers, and the "writerly" text, which involves its readers in the production of meaning (Lodge & Wood, 2000, 145–146). I use these terms somewhat cautiously; however, the term "writerly" is useful when describing the nature of the Wise Book and when arguing that it invites different levels of reading and usage from a wide and varied public, and in this sense much of the focus must be on imagined reader response.

5. C. David Benson & L. S. Blanchfield, Manuscripts of Piers Plowman: The B-Text (Cambridge: D. S. Brewer, 1997), 45–48 and passim.

6. Jeanne Krochalis & E. Peters, eds., The World of Piers Plowman (Philadelphia: University of Pennsylvania Press, 1975), xiii, xv.

7. Grothé described and produced a diplomatic transcription of London, Wellcome Historical Medical Library, MS 564, which contains surgical and anatomical tracts attributed to Henri de Mondeville and Lanfranc of Milan; the Wise Book is embedded into the Chirurgie of Henri de Mondeville; Richard Grothé, "Le Ms. Wellcome 564: Deux Traités de Chirurgie en Moyen-Anglais," 2 vols. (Diss. Université de Montréal, 1982), I:152–167.

8. Additionally, Laurel Braswell-Means, "'Ffor as moche as yche man may not haue þe astrolabe': Popular Middle English Variations on the Computus," Speculum 67 (1992): 595–623, 619–620, prints selections from the versions of the Wise Book contained in Cambridge, Trinity College, MS R.14.5 and London, British Library, MS Egerton 2433; and Peter Brown, "The Seven Planets," in Popular Practical Science of Medieval England, ed. L. M. Matheson (East Lansing, MI: Colleagues Press, 1994), 3–21, 9–10, reproduces a section of the physiognomy found as the concluding part of the Wise Book from Cambridge, Trinity College, MS O.10.21.

9. Krochalis and Peters, xvi, 4.

10. Irma Taavitsainen, "Transferring Classical Discourse Conventions into the Vernacular," in *Medical and Scientific Writing in Late Medieval English*, ed. I. Taavitsainen & P. Pahta (Cambridge, UK: Cambridge University Press, 2004), 37–72, 61.

11. It is necessary to distinguish between the terms "audience" and "readership": I read "audience" as the people the text is aimed at, since it cannot be controlled once the text has been disseminated; "readership" refers to those who have physically engaged with a text. I. Taavitsainen & P. Pahta, "Vernacularisation of Scientific and Medical Writing in Its Sociohistorical Context," in *Medical and Scientific Writing in Late Medieval England*, ed. I. Taavitsainen & P. Pahta (Cambridge, UK: Cambridge University Press, 2004), 1–22, 15.

12. The term "discourse community" is David Barton's, who defines it as "a group of people who have texts and practices in common . . . the people a text is aimed at; the set of people who read a text; or . . . the people who participate in a set of discourse practices both by reading and writing. . . ." Claire Jones, "Discourse Communities and Medical Texts," in *Medical and Scientific Writing in Late Medieval English*, ed. I. Taavitsainen & P. Pahta (Cambridge, UK: Cambridge University Press, 2004), 23–36, 25.

13. Jocelyn Wogan-Browne, N. Watson, A. Taylor & R. Evans, eds., *The Idea of the Vernacular: An Anthology of Middle English Literary Theory*, 1280–1520 (Exeter University Press, 1999), 7. Wogan-Browne and colleagues have a thorough discussion of the conventions used in prefaces to medieval texts; ibid., 3–15. I. Taavitsainen, "Middle English Lunaries: A Study of the Genre," *Mémoires de la Société Néophilologique de Helsinki* 47 (1988), 152, quotes Pierre Macherey, A *Theory of Literary Production*, trans. G. Wall (London: Routledge, 1978), 70–73, who notes that an audience is always implied or imagined by the author of a work as a necessary postulate for bringing that work into being.

14. Wogan-Browne et al., xv.

15. Brown, 3.

16. Braswell-Means 1992, 620.

17. Ibid., 602.

18. Ibid.

19. The instruction explicitly states that the penitential psalms and the litany are read and not recited from memory.

20. Grothé, I:157.

21. Braswell-Means 1992, 620; this passage in London, Wellcome Historical Medical Library, MS 564 is variant: "But summe philosophoris puttiþ þe space of an hour as while a foot-man shulde goon a pas in somer .iij. myle, or sumdel lesse; and in wyntir two Mile or a litil lesse"; Grothé, I:156–157.

22. Margaret Connolly, "Practical Reading for the Body and Soul in Some Later Medieval Manuscript Miscellanies," *Journal of the Early Book Society* 10 (2007), 150-151.

23. Monica H. Green, "Masses in Remembrance of 'Seynt Susanne': A Fifteenth-Century Spiritual Regimen," *Notes & Queries* 50.4 (2003), 380–384.

24. Braswell-Means 1992, 621.

25. Silent reading was common from the seventh century onwards, since Isidore of Seville stated a preference for it; M. B. Parkes, *Pause and Effect: An Introduction to the History of Punctuation in the West* (Aldershot, UK: Scolar Press,1992), 1. However, as Joyce Coleman, *Public Reading and the Reading Public in Late Medieval England and France* (Cambridge, UK: Cambridge University Press, 1996), 78, has shown, medieval texts frequently feature "interaction of textual 'reads' and 'hears,'" so reception was dimensioned in both ways. Coleman argues that far from the "technological determinism of the standard orality/literacy model, which assumes that 'orality' became obsolescent as soon as there were enough literate people and enough texts . . . the social experience of literature preserved the popularity of public reading long past the technological watersheds," hence metatextual references to orality can feasibly be taken literally; Coleman, 80.

26. Taavitsainen 1988, 101.

27. I am grateful to Éamonn Ó Carragáin for his suggestions on this matter. Books of Hours frequently feature depictions of astrological signs; see, e.g., the Bedford Hours (London, British Library, MS Add. 18850), which has the symbol and the agricultural activity associated with each month under the litany.

28. Taavitsainen 1988, 28.

29. Genesis 1:27.

30. Transcription mine; see Carrie Griffin and Julianne Nyhan, "Transcending Textual Borders: Digitising a Middle English Lunary from London, British Library, MS Egerton 827, and a Brief Introduction to XML Mark-Up in the Humanities," *Proceedings of Borderlines Interdisciplinary Postgraduate Conference* 2003, http://www.epu.ucc.ie/borderlines/index.

31. Taavitsainen 1988, 104.

32. Ibid., 122; "The Thrytty Daies of the Mone" is found in nine manuscripts, including Oxford, Bodleian Library, MS Digby 88, fols. 64–75, Ashmole 189, fols. 212–215v, and San Marino, Huntington Library, MS HM 64, fols. 84–95 (each of which also contains a copy of the *Wise Book*). See A. J. Minnis, *Medieval Theory of Authorship* (London: Scolar Press, 1984), 201, on *lectoris arbitrium*.

33. J. H. Morey, "Middle English Didactic Literature," *Readings in Medieval Texts: Interpreting Old and Middle English Literature*, ed. D. Johnson & E. Treharne (Oxford: Oxford University Press, 2005), 183.

34. The prologue to the lunary echoes Chaucer's promise to tell "[T]ales of best sentence and moost solas": stories that instruct and please (*General Prologue*, 798).

35. M. B. Parkes, "The Influence of the Concepts of *Ordinatio* and *Compilatio* on the Development of the Book," in *Medieval Literature and Learning: Essays Presented to Richard William Hunt*, ed. J. J. G. Alexander & M. T. Gibson (Oxford: Clarendon, 1976), 115.

36. M. B. Parkes, "The Literacy of the Laity," in *Scripts, Scribes and Readers: Studies in the Communication, Presentation and Dissemination of Medieval Texts* (London: Hambledon, 1991), 296-297.

37. Readings of medieval scientific and utilitarian texts were frequently motivated by *utilitas* and *curiositas*; L. Braswell-Means, "Utilitarian and Scientific Prose," in *Middle English Prose: A Critical Guide to Major Authors and Genres*, ed. A. S. G. Edwards (New Brunswick, NJ: Rutgers University Press, 1984), 337.

38. Similarly, the prologues to lunary texts, according to Taavitsainen, often "name the intended target groups which, however, need not be the same as the actual readership"; Taavitsainen 1988, 152.

39. Parkes 1991, 275. Braswell-Means notes that the readers and users of lunary texts must have come from all three medieval estates: "*Clerus, Miles* and *Cultor*"; L. Braswell-Means, "Popular Lunar Astrology in the Late Middle Ages," *University of Ottawa Quarterly* 48 (1978): 187-194, 190.

40. Ibid., 190–191.

41. George Keiser, "Practical Books for the Gentleman," in *The Cambridge History of the Book in Britain*, vol. III, 1400–1557, eds. L. Hellinga & J. B. Trapp (Cambridge, UK: Cambridge University Press, 1999), 470–494, 474.

42. See Alexandra Barratt, *Women's Writing in Middle English* (London: Longman, 1992), 27-38.

43. Keiser 1998, 3673.

44. Charles Talbot and E. A. Hammond, *The Medical Practitioners in Medieval England: A Biographical Register* (London: Wellcome Historical Medical Library, 1965), 73.

45. Neil R. Ker, *Medieval Manuscripts in British Libraries*, vols 1–3 (Oxford: Clarendon, 1969), I, 73.

46. Taavitsainen 1988, 168.

47. Described by David Thomson, A *Descriptive Catalogue of Middle English Grammatical Texts* (New York & London: Garland, 1979), 193–211.

48. Krochalis and Peters, xii.

49. Benson and Blanchfield, 45.

50. Parkes 1991, 284.

WORKS CITED

Manuscripts

Cambridge, University Library, Ll.4.14
Cambridge, Trinity College Library, O.10.21
Cambridge, Trinity College Library, R.14.51
London, British Library, Add. 12195
London, British Library, Add. 18850
London, British Library, Egerton 827
London, British Library, Egerton 2433
London, Wellcome Historical Medical Library, 411
London, Wellcome Historical Medical Library, 564
New Haven, Yale University, Beinecke 163
New York, Columbia University, Plimpton 260
Oxford, Bodleian Library, Ashmole 189
Oxford, Bodleian Library, Digby 88
San Marino, Huntington Library, HM 64

Secondary Material

Barratt, Alexandra. *Women's Writing in Middle English*. London: Longman, 1992.
Barthes, Roland. "The Death of the Author." In *Modern Criticism and Theory*, Ed. D. Lodge. London: Longman, 2000. 145–150.
Benson, C. David., & L. S. Blanchfield. *Manuscripts of Piers Plowman: The B-Text*. Cambridge: D. S. Brewer, 1997.
Benson, Larry D. (Ed.). *The Riverside Chaucer*. Oxford: Oxford University Press, 1987.
Braswell-Means, Laurel. "'Ffor as moche as yche man may not haue þe astrolabe': Popular Middle English Variations on the Computus." *Speculum* 67 (1992): 595–623.
———. "Utilitarian and Scientific Prose." In *Middle English Prose: A Critical Guide to Major Authors and Genres*. Ed. A. S. G. Edwards. New Brunswick, NJ: Rutgers University Press, 1984. 337–388.
———. "Popular Lunar Astrology in the Late Middle Ages." *University of Ottawa Quarterly* 48 (1978): 187-194.
Brown, Peter. "The Seven Planets." In *Popular Practical Science of Medieval England*. Ed. L. M. Matheson. East Lansing, MI: Colleagues Press, 1994. 3–21.
Coleman, Joyce. *Public Reading and the Reading Public in Late Medieval England and France*. Cambridge, UK: Cambridge University Press, 1996.
Connolly, Margaret. "Practical Reading for the Body and Soul in Some Later Medieval Manuscript Miscellanies." *Journal of the Early Book Society* 10 (2007): 149-169.

Green, Monica H. "Masses in Remembrance of 'Seynt Susanne': A Fifteenth-Century Spiritual Regimen." *Notes & Queries* 50.4 (2003): 380–384.

Griffin, Carrie. "'A Good Reder': The Middle English *Wise Book of Philosophy and Astronomy*, Instruction, Publics, and Manuscripts." Diss. University College Cork, 2006.

———, and Julianne Nyhan "Transcending Textual Borders: Digitising a Middle English Lunary from London, British Library, MS Egerton 827, and a Brief Introduction to XML Mark-Up in the Humanities," *Proceedings of Borderlines Interdisciplinary Postgraduate Conference* 2003, ed. C. Griffin, J. Nyhan and K. Rooney, <http://www.epu.ucc.ie/borderlines/index>.

Grothé, Richard. "Le MS. Wellcome 564: Deux Traités de Chirurgie en Moyen-Anglais." 2 vols. Diss. Université de Montréal, 1982.

Hanna, Ralph, III, *Pursuing History: Middle English Manuscripts and Their Texts*. Stanford, CA: Stanford University Press, 1996.

Jones, Claire. "Discourse Communities and Medical Texts." In *Medical and Scientific Writing in Late Medieval English*. Ed. I. Taavitsainen & P. Pahta. Cambridge, UK: Cambridge University Press, 2004. 23–36.

Keiser, George. "Practical Books for the Gentleman." In *The Cambridge History of the Book in Britain*, Vol. III, 1400–1557. Eds. L. Hellinga & J. B. Trapp. Cambridge, UK: Cambridge University Press, 1999. 470–494.

———. A *Manual of Writings in Middle English* 1050–1500, Vol. 10, *Works of Science and Information*. New Haven, CT: Connecticut Academy of Arts and Sciences, 1998.

Ker, Neil. R. *Medieval Manuscripts in British Libraries*. Vols 1–3. Oxford: Clarendon, 1969.

Krochalis, Jeanne, & E. Peters (Eds.) *The World of Piers Plowman*. Philadelphia: University of Pennsylvania Press, 1975.

Lodge, David, & N. Wood (Eds.) *Modern Criticism and Theory*. London: Longman, 2000.

Macherey, Pierre. A *Theory of Literary Production*. Trans. G. Wall. London: Routledge, 1978.

Minnis, A. J. *Medieval Theory of Authorship*. London: Scolar Press, 1984.

Morey, J. H. "Middle English Didactic Literature." *Readings in Medieval Texts: Interpreting Old and Middle English Literature*. Ed. D. Johnson & E. Treharne. Oxford: Oxford University Press, 2005. 183–197.

Parkes, M. B. *Pause and Effect: An Introduction to the History of Punctuation in the West*. Aldershot, UK: Scolar Press, 1992.

———. "The Literacy of the Laity." In *Scripts, Scribes and Readers: Studies in the Communication, Presentation and Dissemination of Medieval Texts*. London: Hambledon, 1991. 275–297.

————. "The Influence of the Concepts of *Ordinatio* and *Compilatio* on the Development of the Book." In *Medieval Literature and Learning: Essays Presented to Richard William Hunt*. Ed. J. J. G. Alexander and M. T. Gibson. Oxford: Clarendon, 1976. 115–141.

Taavitsainen, Irma. "Transferring Classical Discourse Conventions into the Vernacular." In *Medical and Scientific Writing in Late Medieval English*. Ed. I. Taavitsainen & P. Pahta. Cambridge, UK: Cambridge University Press, 2004. 37–72.

————. "Middle English Lunaries: A Study of the Genre." *Mémoires de la Société Néophilologique de Helsinki* 47 (1988).

————, and P. Pahta. "Vernacularisation of Scientific and Medical Writing in Its Sociohistorical Context." In *Medical and Scientific Writing in Late Medieval England*. Ed. I. Taavitsainen & P. Pahta. Cambridge, UK: Cambridge University Press, 2004. 1–22.

Talbot, Charles and E. A. Hammond. *The Medical Practitioners in Medieval England: A Biographical Register*. London: Wellcome Historical Medical Library, 1965.

Thomson, David. *A Descriptive Catalogue of Middle English Grammatical Texts*. New York & London: Garland, 1979.

Wogan-Browne, Jocelyn, N. Watson, A. Taylor & R. Evans (Eds.). *The Idea of the Vernacular: An Anthology of Middle English Literary Theory, 1280–1520*. Exeter: Exeter University Press, 1999.

Providing for the Learned Cleric: Schemas and Diagrams in *Sacerdos Parochialis* in British Library MS Burney 356

NIAMH PATTWELL

Devotional manuscripts and medical manuscripts are primarily books of instruction designed to share knowledge or in some cases to assist in the process of recalling previously acquired knowledge. As books of instruction, they need to be authoritative and user-friendly, as much for the novice or less-well-educated reader as for the professional reader. Carrie Griffin illustrates how these qualities are worked out in the wise book tradition in her article, "'A Good Reder and a Deuout': Instruction, Reading, and Devotion in the *Wise Book of Philosophy and Astronomy*," in this volume. Provision for more than one type of reader was of particular relevance to religious writing in England in the late Middle Ages. Not only were the laity seeking access to religious material despite the restrictions imposed by the Church, but there were also significant differences in levels of knowledge among the clergy. In this paper, I illustrate how one simple, vernacular manual of religious instruction, *Sacerdos parochialis*, is adapted to meet the needs of a more theologically sophisticated reader through the inclusion of schemas and diagrams.

Sacerdos parochialis is a late-fourteenth- or early-fifteenth-century manual of religious instruction written to assist the clergy in the instruction of the laity four times a year on the six principles of faith deemed necessary for the laity to know in order to avoid heresy.[1] It contains tracts on the credo or fourteen articles of the faith, Ten Commandments, seven deadly sins, seven sacraments, seven virtues, and the seven works of mercy. The structure of *Sacerdos parochialis* is based on the 1281 Lambeth Constitutions of Archbishop Pecham, but much of the material is translated from William Pagula's *Oculus sacerdotis*.[2] According to the opening rubric of *Sacerdos parochialis*, the cleric was to preach in the vernacular without subtlety in order to prevent confusion, error, or heresy among the laity:

> Quilibet sacerdos parochialis siue curatus tenetur parochianos suos predicare et docere in lingua materna quater in anno videlicet: In primis septem peticiones in oratione dominica, salutacionem beate et gloriose virginis marie, duodecim articulos fidei et simbolo contentos, decem precepta decalogi, septem mortalia peccata, septem opera misericordie, septem virtutes cardinales, duo precepta euangelij, septem sacramenta ecclesie, excommunicaciones.

> [Every parish priest or curate is obliged to preach and teach to his parishioners in the native language four times a year as follows: first the seven petitions of the Our Father, the Hail Mary, the twelve articles of faith and their significance, the ten Gospel commandments, the seven deadly sins, the seven works of mercy, the seven cardinal virtues, the evangelical commandments, the seven sacraments of the church, the excommunications.][3]

The 1281 Lambeth Constitutions of Archbishop Pecham provide authority as well as the structure and outline of what is to be covered, although much of the material is translated from William Pagula's *Oculus sacerdotis*.[4] The opening rubric lends authority to the text, just as the prologue of the *Wise Book* derives its authority from belonging to a philosophical tradition that originated in Greece.[5] The question of authority was particularly important for religious writings in an era in which the authorities viewed vernacular religious material with suspicion.[6] Pecham's statute, also known as "Ignorancia sacerdotum" from its opening words, seems to have been a regular feature in English manuals of religious instruction throughout the late Middle Ages, even when those manuals offered more than the rubric outlined. The sixteenth-century *Exornatorium curatorum*, for example, opens with Pecham's statute "Ignorancia sacerdotum," but includes material on the examination of conscience and on preparing for death. *Sacerdos parochialis*, in most of the manuscripts, follows the outline of contents in Pecham's statute "Ignorancia sacerdotum"; it includes the *minimum* that the laity ought to know as well as a short tract on the Pater Noster and Ave Maria.[7] It would have been a useful compendium for a cleric not well versed in Latin who was working in a parish in late-medieval England.

The manuscripts in which *Sacerdos parochialis* occurs suggest a clerical audience. They are plain and unadorned. Decoration consists of nothing more than red or blue paraph marks and the occasional pen flourishes on a capital letter; the script varies from tract to tract or every two or three tracts so that subdivisions within a manuscript are apparent. Most were the personal notebooks or commonplace books of diocesan clergy. For example, British Library MS Harley 4172 bears a number of names, none of which can be identified with certainty, but a license for temporalities on one of the final folios and a set of marriage banns on folio 107v are indicative of clerical ownership.[8] An inscription in Cambridge, University Library MS Dd.12.69, folio 2v, links that manuscript to the parish of Shermansbury.[9] Both British Library MS Additional 10053 and Cambridge, Pembroke College MS 285 are linked to Augustinian canons; the former to Aldgate in London, and the latter to Ossyth in Essex.[10] Durham, University Library MS Cosin V.iv.2 was written and owned by a Carmelite anchorite in Norwich.[11] Oxford, Bodleian Library MS Bodley 110 was owned by at least one cleric working in the parish of Cliffe-at-Hoo, Kent. According to a note on folio 1r, the manuscript was purchased from a London stationer, J. Pyle, on August 10, 1463, by the rector of a parish in Cliffe-at-Hoo in Kent: "hunc librum emit W.C. de J. Pyle stacioner London, 2v die Augusta a W. Ed. iiij tercio coram Rob. paling."[12] On folio 182v, another note indicates that William Cleve gave this manuscript to William Camyl, chaplain of his chantry, and to Camyl's successors:[13]

> Hunc librum libere contulit Willelmus Cleve nuper Rector ecclesie de Clyve Kant Domino Willelmo Camyl huius Cantarie capellano et successoribus suis perpetuis hic deuotius Deo confiteatur.

On folio 128v, in another hand of the late-fifteenth century, is a note by a Johannes Huntt of Beverley.

The contents of most of the manuscripts can be described as middle-of-the-road theology such as *Speculum ecclesie*, *A Short Form of Living*, various forms of confession, or the *Stimulus Conscience* to name but a few. Nearly all of the manuscripts give the sense of collection: that the manuscript is a personal gathering of tracts or treatises that were compiled either by the owner or by a later archivist. In the case of Oxford, Bodleian Library MS Bodley 110, it may have been the gathering of several clergy, the original notebook being passed down from cleric to cleric within the one parish. In the case of Oxford, Bodleian Library MS Rawlinson D913, *Sacerdos parochialis* forms part of a large body of material gathered by a sixteenth-century antiquarian, a truly eclectic collection of romances, theological writings, poetry, and medical recipes in Middle Dutch, Anglo-Norman, Latin, and Middle English.

Sacerdos parochialis presents a practical and basic knowledge of the principles of faith, suitable for a priest working in a parish. Even on its own *Sacerdos parochialis* would have provided enough material for the less-well-educated parish priest if, as Leonard Boyle claims, all that was required of the priest working in the parish "was simply a knowledge of what his parishioner, by the law of the church, should believe and observe."[14] The manuscripts of *Sacerdos parochialis*, in their completed form, would have provided ample material for preaching or for the private devotion of a parish curate. They resemble the gatherings of a curate over an entire life.

British Library MS Burney 356 differs from the other *Sacerdos parochialis* manuscripts in that it is not a loose collection of theological tracts bound together by unknown circumstances. Instead it is a manuscript bespeaking intention and purpose. While it does not display an internal framework as obvious as that visible in *Orchard of Syon* or *Contemplations on the Dread and Love of God*, one could argue that there is a movement from a legalistic sense of right and wrong to a more personal relationship based on meditation and contemplation.[15] BL MS Burney 356 opens with books addressing the fundamental, basic principles of religious faith such as *Templum domini* by Grossteste and *Directorium sacerdotum simplicium*. The latter part of the manuscript contains primarily meditative and reflective pieces such as *De miseria humane condicionis* and reflections by St. Bernard of Clairvaux, Anselm, and Augustine. The contents reflect accurately the index found at the beginning of the manuscript, although the final book has been lost, so only twenty-two of the original twenty-three books remain.[16]

BL MS Burney 356 is a more lavish and careful production than the other *Sacerdos parochialis* manuscripts. The initial letters of each text are gold surrounded by mauve and azure decoration, and the script is a uniform anglicana formata throughout. There is little evidence of provenance, but, taking into consideration the contents, decoration, and layout, it is probably safe to assume that it was produced in a monastery for a particularly well-educated cleric or clergy.

The scribe of BL MS Burney 356 was not content with the simple outline of the faith provided in *Sacerdos parochialis* and included a number of extra items, such as short verse schemas and diagrams that would demand more of its reader.[17] These extra items occur only in BL MS Burney 356 and in poorly replicated form in Oxford, Trinity College MS 7.

At a first glance, it is tempting to assume that these diagrams are but summaries of detail included in the book, much as one would find in a school textbook today. However, this is rarely the case. More often than not, the material in the diagrams, while composed of standard theological material, is far more detailed and more sophisticated than that found in the main body of the text. Schema 5 in the appendix is an outline of the twelve articles of faith which are linked to the Apostles and to lines from the Old Testament. It is a version of a diagram found in the psalter of Robert de Lisle,[18] although it originally comes from *Speculum theologiae* or the *Orchard of Consolation*, which is a collection of diagrams or pictures composed by the Franciscan friar Johann de Metz in the early thirteenth century.[19] Schema 7, which follows it, in which the Ten Commandments are listed as remedies to the Ten Plagues of Israel, is also derived from the de Lisle psalter, although in the Robert de Lisle psalter schemas 5 and 7 of our manuscript appear as a single diagram. The diagrams contain more information than that found in the main body of *Sacerdos parochialis*; therefore the scribe in BL MS Burney 356 is not merely summarizing material but is in fact expanding the tract. For example, the tract on the Credo in *Sacerdos parochialis* is just a list of the articles cited in Latin, translated into Middle English, and followed by a brief explanation in Middle English:

> *Credo in deum patrem omnipotentem.* Ych by-leue in god, fader almy3ty.
> In þes wordes beþ vnderstonde fowre artycles of þe ry3tbyleue þat
> longeþ to þe godhede. ¶The furst ys þat whe shul by-leue in o god
> and þre persones in trinite. ¶An-oþer ys þat þe fadyr ys verey god
> wyþ-þout by-gynnygge, neuer y-bore, neuer y-makyd of any-þyng.

The Ten Commandments follow a similar pattern. The commandment is given in Latin, translated into Middle English, and followed by a brief explanation:

> Þe .iij. *preceptio, Sabbata sanctifices.* Þou shalt halwe þy holy day. By þys
> hest alle crystene men beþ y-holde to be as busy in god hys seruice
> euerech holy day as hy beþ in wordlyche workys oþer dayes.

Schema 8 on the seven deadly sins, in which each of the head sins is grouped with its "soldiers," or vices, is similar to the *Psychomachia* and its many derivations.[20] However, the material itself is less puzzling than the manner in which the material is brought together. There are many inconsistencies in the grammar where different tenses and different forms of a word are deployed throughout. It is as if the scribe plucked various bits of text from a number of different sources and yoked them together here without due regard for concordance or consistency.

The diagrams and schemas dispersed throughout *Sacerdos parochialis* in BL MS Burney 356, on the other hand, draw upon a larger and fuller tradition in which the Credo was linked to the Apostles, and the Ten Commandments to the ten plagues.[21] Therefore the scribe is not making links for the first time but is drawing upon a long tradition of associating these biblical events. Furthermore, the diagrams, composed of disjointed fragments of text, assume a certain amount of knowledge on the part of the reader. He or she must understand the simple three words *"in plaga egypti"* and know the story behind *"rubens vnda"* before making sense of the layout of the schema. The material on the page would be inaccessible without some prior knowledge on the part of the reader.

Much of the extra material in the BL MS Burney 356 *Sacerdos parochialis* is amplification of material that is otherwise basic and rudimentary and therefore might be considered useful for a preacher. Yet it also provides for a profound private reading experience. For example, immediately following a short poem celebrating Mary as intercessor, there is a two-columned schema based on the words of the Ave Maria (schema 2). The prayer is written in Latin on the left and translated into Middle English on the right. The two columns are linked by three words in a central column "þorw þys word." It reveals a translator choosing words in Middle English less for their grammatical accuracy in the translated form and more for their closeness to the original Latin form and for their neatness or ability to complete the symmetry of the diagram. In the fourth line, for example, a word has been coined to complete the pattern of the other lines. The suffix "nesse" has been added to "þral" to form "þralnesse," a word not found in the Middle English Dictionary, although there is a word "þrallesse," meaning "female slave or menial."[22]

The neatness, balance, and symmetry seem to be integral to the schema or diagram. Avril Henry talks about the "synthesis" or "wholeness" of the Vernon *Pater Noster* table, a far more elaborate, more colorful, and more intricate diagram than any found in BL MS Burney 356.[23] She suggests that "the structure of (the Vernon diagram) derives ultimately from classical attempts to systematize experience, and immediately from the methods of scholastic philosophy." But she goes on to talk about the achievement of meaning through "purely visual means": "The image's interwoven balance of tones and colours communicates a profound sense of the inter-relatedness of all the concepts it embodies—a sense far deeper than can be given by an unadorned diagram or simple list."[24]

I would challenge her views on "unadorned diagrams," that is, the type of diagram that we find in the Burney *Sacerdos parochialis*. Their visual impact, although much less colorful and less nuanced than the Vernon table, is suggestive of interconnectedness and wholeness. Patterns and stories are being completed. The Ten Commandments complete the ten plagues. The Apostles of the New Testament and their twelve statements of faith complete the statements of the Patriarchs and Prophets of the Old Testament.

The diagrams are more than lists or, as I mention above, synopses or syntheses of material in the text. They are also tools for meditation. They demand an active engagement with the material, an ability to make connections and perceive unspoken or unarticulated theological truths. In schema 4, which is written completely in Latin, each of the actions necessary for the rearing of Christ by Mary is linked to some important quality in the Church. Mary has been elevated, almost as if she were part of the Trinity, to be celebrated for her part in the act of redemption. Again we note the neatness and completeness of the diagram. The key words from the prayer are on the far-left column. In the next column, in ascending order or rank, are the people who are blessed because of Mary's actions. Women, despite the fact that Mary is a woman, are at the top or least position. In these schemas or diagrams, as in the previous schemas discussed, the reader is being offered more than a tool for memory. There is a mental challenge or enigma that invites the reader to ponder the mysteries being explained there. The spaces between the words are as fundamental as the words themselves. They leave room for private engagement, for filling with meditation or contemplation so that understanding is complete.

Mary Carruthers explores these schemas in *The Book of Memory*. She suggests that we need to move away from a distinction between "oral culture" and "literate culture" and argues that memory (long associated with oral culture) continues to play an important role in a literate culture (defining "literate," after Eric Havelock, as "book-acquiring public"). In her view, books are tools to accessing a text as it exists in the mind of the reader: "Rather books are themselves memorial cues and aids, and memory is most like a book, a written page or a wax tablet upon which something is written. . . . In none of the evidence I have discovered is the act of writing itself regarded as a supplanter of memory."[25]

It is possible to argue, therefore, that these schemas, divided into three, five, or seven key points, were aids to preaching. In *The Book of Memory*, Carruthers does suggest that preachers were encouraged to recall from such schemas *"sententiae"* rather than *"verbaliter"*; the sense being more important than the exact words.[26] However, the schemas become prosaic or wooden when one attempts to explain or expand them. Their value or impact rests in their visual shape on the page, and they are therefore more likely aids to devotion rather than instruction. They are aimed at the religious specialist rather than the ignorant who know little more than the Creed. BL MS Burney 356 is directing *Sacerdos parochialis* toward a sophisticated audience. Even if the schemas were intended for use as sermon material, the Burney 356 scribe is still employing a method not found in the other manuscripts, in which sermons are written out in full.[27] Like the *Wise Book* discussed by Griffin, *Sacerdos parochialis* is adapted to meet the needs of more than one type of reader.[28]

I want to look at one final schema, schema 9, because it draws attention in a very particular way to the overlap between devotional manuscripts and medical manuscripts. The schema is comparable to a particular type of lyric founded on the number of wounds of Christ's Passion and set up to counteract the sins of the five senses or the seven deadly sins.[29] Woolf suggests that most of these lyrics are "didactic rather than meditative, in that the suffering is recalled as a reproach or antidote to sin rather than as an appeal for love."[30] In BL MS Burney 356, the schema occurs before the tract on the seven deadly sins and is not a poem but simply links each of the wounds of Christ with one of the seven deadly sins. The schema follows the pattern of collections of medical recipes, in which the ailments and their remedies are presented not in alphabetical order but in order from head to feet.[31] The body, here specifically Christ's body, provides an ideal prompt for anyone attempting to memorize the sins and their effects.

I suggest that the diagrams and schemas integrated into *Sacerdos parochialis* in BL MS Burney 356 were designed specifically for the purpose of memory retrieval. They are there not to help the reader remember the rather rudimentary material written in full in the book but to supplement this basic material with more sophisticated theological or devotional material acquired elsewhere. These extras were a mixture of verse, interlinked columns, Latin and Middle English (macaronic), associating or mapping abstract concepts onto physical representations. Some of the schemas were complete in themselves, while others pointed towards more extensive material.

If the schemas were designed to assist memory retrieval, and I think that this is the case, then BL MS Burney 356 provides access to more material than the twenty-three items listed in its opening index and provides for more than one type of audience. There is much about the manuscript to suggest a display book—the careful writing, ornate lettering, index—a book to be consulted by a well-educated cleric, probably monastically trained. *Sacerdos parochialis* provides a basic manual of instruction, possibly demanded by the bishop of a particular diocese, written in full and without space (literally and figuratively) for further reflection. Yet in the Latin diagrams that accompany the text, there is invitation to ponder, meditate, recall, or recollect more abstract, abstruse material for the more sophisticated or literate reader.

In this way, BL MS Burney 356 is quite different from the others in the *Sacerdos parochialis* tradition, each of which seems to have belonged or have been in the possession (possibly private) of one type of reader, the simple pastor with responsibility for the cure of souls. These were "notebooks" or "personal libraries" into which were gathered, over time, other sermons and devotional texts. Perhaps we witness in these manuscripts the beginning of books as we have them today, books to be read and to be returned to for the purposes of consultation, but which were never dependent for sense on the prior knowledge of the reader. In BL MS Burney 356, the original compiler or scribe provides for more sophisticated readers. In other words, material intended for the amateur or occasional reader is adapted to provide for the professional and more theologically astute reader.

University College Dublin

Appendix: Transcript of Schemas and Diagrams in Order of Appearance in British Library MS Burney 356

1.
Man þat art in care y-brow3t, to Marie þou clype and grede,
Sette styfly on heere þy þow3t, þy nedes for to spede,
And sey "Mercy ych haue myswro3t, Lady þou me rede."
Hee ys a frend þat fayleth now3t, synful men at nede.
[fol. 44r]

2.

Ave excludit penalitatem		Ave ys out pult al hardnesse
Gracia excludit iniquitatem		Gracia ys out pult al wykkednesse
Plena excludit vacuitatem	þorw	Plena ys out pult al barnesse
Dominus excludit servilitatem	þys	Dominus ys out pult al þralnesse
Tecum includit societatem	word	Tecum ys clyped al holy felaw-nesse
Benedicta includit sanctitatem		Benedicta ys clyped al holynesse
Tu includit singularitatem		Tu ys vnderstonde al soþnesse [fol. 44r]

3.

		hee ys moder of clennesse	
In þre þynges	videlicet	hee ys mayd of meknesse	Maria
		And of mercy þe maystresse	[fol. 44r]

4.

Bene	Mulieres		Fecunditatem quia virgo concepit et peperit
dicta	Homines		Dignitatem prelacie quia mater dei fuit
mari	Angelos	propter	Oficii sedulitatem quia Christum lactauit
a super	Terras		Fructus vtilitatem quia prima fruges habuit
omnes	Celos		Capacitatem immensitate quia quod totus mundus

capere non poterat illa digna fuit pepere habere et lactare dominum nostrum Ihesum Christum qui omnia habet omnia condidit et omnia gubernat in saecula saeculorum. [fol. 44r]

	Credo in deum patrem		Patrem inuocabis	
Deus pater	omnipotentem cr[e]ato-	Petrus	qui terram fecit	Iheremiah
	rem celi et terre		et condidit celos	

	Et in Ihesum Christum fili-		Dixit dominus ad	
Ihesu Christo	ium eius vnicum	Andreas	me filius	David
	dominum nostrum		meus es tu	

	Qui conceptus		Ecce virgo con-	
Nativitas	est de spirito sancto natum	Jacobus maior	cipiet et pa-	Ysaia
	ex maria virgine		riet filium.	

	Passus sub poncio		Aspicient om-	
Passio	pilato cruci-fixus	Iohannes	nes ad me quem	Bacaris
	mortuus et sepultus		crucifixerunt	

	Descendit ad in		mors ero	
Resurectio	ferna tercia die re	Thomas	mors tua	Osee
	surrexit a mor-tuis		et cetera.	

	Ascendit ad ce-		Qui edifica-	
Ascensio	los sedet ad dex-	Iacobus minor	vit in celo as-	Amos
	teram domini patris omnipotentis		censionem suam	

	Inde venturus		Accedam ad vos	
Aduentus ad iudicare	est iudicare vi-	Philippus	in iudicio et e-	Saphonias
	uos et mor-tuos		ro testis velox.	

	Credo in		Effundam de spi-	
Spiritus sanc-tus missio	spiritum	Bartholomeus	ritu meo su-	Iohel
	sanctum		per omnem carnem.	

	Sanctam eccle-siam		Inuocabunt omnes	
Ecclesiam cum sancti	catholicam sancto-	Matheus	nomen domini et	Micheas
	rum commu-nionem		seruient ei.	

	Remissi-		Deponet do-	
ve[*]iam crim-inium	onem pec-	Symon	minus omnes	Malachias
	catorum		iniquitates nostras.	

	Carnis		Educam vos	
[***]cicacione m omni	resurrec-	Thadeus	de sepulcris	
	cionem		populus meus.	

	Et vitam		Euigilabunt omnes	
vitam eternam	eternam.	Mathias	alii ad vitam alii	E3echiel
	Amen		ad obprobium.	[fols. 44v-45r]

7.

	Prima rubens vnda	Quia in deum non crediderunt	
	Ranarum plena secunda	Quia nomen dei blasfemauerunt	
	Inde culex tristis	Quia sabbata con-tempserunt	
	Post musca recen-ciorum istis	Quia parentibus non obedierunt	
Decem pla[ge]	Quinta pecus strauit	Quia sanctos occiderunt	Causae
Egyptii	Vesicas sexta creavit	Quia furtis inten-derunt	
	Pene subit grando	Quia fornicacioni vacauerunt	
	Post bructum dente nephando	Quia iniquia testimonia pro-tulerunt	
	Nona tegit solem	Quia adulteria commiserunt	
	Primam necit ultima plebs	Quia auariciam tulerunt	[fol. 45r]

8. *De septem mortalibus peccatis sive capitalibus*
Superbia, Inuidia, Ira, Accidia, Avaricia, Gula et luxuria. Et / quodlibet eorum habet sub se quatuor milites. Milites superbie.

Iactancia impietatis	
Simulacio scientatis	Milites superbie sunt hec:
Presumpcio elacionis	Iacta, te simula, presume, resiste superbe.
Resistencia correccionis	

Detraccio bonitatis	Milites inuidie sunt hec:	
Odium prosperitatis		
Susurracio malignitatis	Inuide, detractor, odio, sussuro, sinistra.	
Sinistracio pietatis		

Rixa contencionis		
Conuicium maledictionis	Milites ire sunt hec:	
Inclinacio blasphemie	Rixas, conuicio, blasphemat, prouocat ira.	
Prouocacio occisionis		

Furtum prodicionis		
Fallacia periuracionis	Milites accidie sunt hec:	
Duricia obstinacionis	Prodigus, et fallax periurus, duris, auaris.	
Auaricia retencionis		

Laborem in querendo		
Timorem in possidendo	Milites auaricie sunt hec:	
Horror in distribuendo	laborat, timet, horret, dolet omnis auaris.	
Dolor in amittendo		

Loquacitas infeccionis		
Inmundicia diuersacionis	Milites gule sunt hec:	
Ebetudo in sensibus	Loquax inmundus, ebes, fetens quod gulosus.	
Fetorum in naribus		

Excecacio corporal		
Illaqueacio infernal		Milites luxure sunt hec:
Eneruacio visceral	Excecat, illaqueat, eneruat, precipitatque	
Precipitacio temporal		[fol. 46r-v]

9.

Coronam in capite	superbiam	vult s[*]re s[*]rius super capit
Lanceam in latere	inuidiam	corpus et cor affligit
Flagellum in corpore	luxuriam	oritur ex carnis voluptate
Spongeam in ore vicit	gulam que	oritur ex gustis dulcer et oris sui
Clauum in manu dextra	iram	parata est ad percussum ¶auitis
Clauum in sinistra	auariciam	parata est ad recipien-dum
Clauum in pedibus	accidiam	sentina est omni vicio-rum [fol. 46v]

NOTES

1. On the production of manuals for the clergy and laity in the late Middle Ages, see Leonard E. Boyle, "The Fourth Lateran Council and Manuals of Popular Theology," in Thomas J. Heffernan, ed., *The Popular Literature of the Medieval England* (Knoxville: University of Tennessee Press, 1985), 30–43. See also W. A. Pantin, *The English Church in the Fourteenth Century* (Cambridge, 1955), 189–243.

2. The ninth chapter of Pecham's 1281 statutes is a complete compendium or catechism of religious instruction. Pecham's catechism is often cited as the source for many manuals of religious instruction intended for either the clergy or the laity. It outlines the minimum deemed necessary for the laity to know following the Fourth Lateran Council of 1215. For a copy of the statute, see F. M. Powicke and C. R. Cheney, *Councils and Synods with Other Documents relating to the English Church* A.D. 1205–1313, vol. 2 (Oxford: Clarendon Press, 1964), 900–901. William Pagula (d. 1332) was vicar of Winkfield when he was issued with a *Cum ex eo* license in 1314, freeing him from his parochial duties to attend university at Oxford for approximately seven years. The following five works are attributed to him: *Summa summarum, Speculum praelatorum, Speculum religiosorum, Epistola ad regem angliae Edwardum III,* and the *Oculus sacerdotis.* To the best of my knowledge, there are no available editions of Pagula's works; however, for a study of William Pagula and his works, see Leonard Boyle, "A Study of the Works Attributed to William Pagula with Special Reference to *Oculus Sacerdotis* and *Summa Summarum,*" (D. Phil. dissertation, Oxford, 1956). Leonard Boyle, "The *Oculus Sacerdotis* and some other works of William Pagula," repr. in *Pastoral Care, Clerical Education and Canon Law, 1200–1400,* Collected Studies 135 (London: Variorum Reprints, 1981), pt. IV.

3. Transcription and translation mine. More detailed discussion on *Sacerdos parochialis* and its manuscripts can be found in Niamh Pattwell, "*Sacerdos Parochialis* Edited from British Library MS Burney 356 and *Exornatorium Curatorum* edited from Cambridge Corpus Christi Sp. 335.2" Ph.D. dissertation, Trinity College, Dublin, 2004.

4. For detail on the closeness of the two texts see Pattwell, "*Sacerdos Parochialis* Edited from British Library MS Burney 356," xxxii–xxxv.

5. See Griffin, "'A Good Reder and a Deuout': Instruction, Reading, and Devotion in the *Wise Book of Philosophy and Astronomy,*" in this volume.

6. For a comprehensive discussion on the effects of Arundel's 1409 Constitutions, which limited the circulation of vernacular material among the laity, see Nicholas Watson, "Censorship and Cultural Change in Late Medieval England: Vernacular Theology, the Oxford Translation Debate and Arundel's Constitutions of 1409," *Speculum* 70 (1995): 822–864.

7. Arguably, in the fifteenth century, this was the *maximum* that the laity was supposed to know. "Any suggestion that the Constitutions are simply reviving the force of earlier archiepiscopal legislation ignores a crucial difference: that here Pecham's *minimum* necessary for the laity to know if they are to be saved has to be redefined as the *maximum* they may hear, read or even discuss. This revisionist version of the Syllabus shows how much seemed, to Arundel in 1409, to have changed since 1281. No longer was it the ignorance of the laity and their priests (*ignorancia sacerdotum*) that was a matter for concern; it was the laity's too eager pursuit of knowledge"; Watson, "Censorship and Cultural Change in Late Medieval England," 828.

8. The two signatures are Thomas Buckley (fol. 94r) and John Buckley (fol. 106v). See also Pattwell, "*Sacerdos Parochialis* Edited from British Library MS Burney 356," 42–45, for attempts to identify some of the names in the marriage banns.

9. "This present boke ys gevyn to the paryshe chyrche of Shermanbury by the handes of John Haynes. In nomine dei. Amen" (fol. 2v).

10. An inscription in British Library Additional MS 10053, fol. 83v, reads: "Orate *per anima dominum* iohannis pery canonici ecclesie *sancte* trinitatis london infra algate qui hunc librum fieri fecit cuius anime propicieter deus. Amen." Entries on fols. 69v and 72v in Cambridge, Pembroke College MS 285 link the book to "Raffe Mainarde." It has not been possible to identify Raffe Mainarde with certainty, although Mainarde was the name of a well-to-do family in the Essex area (Pattwell, "*Sacerdos Parochialis* Edited from British Library MS Burney 356," 61). Moreover, A. I. Doyle notes that Cambridge, Pembroke College MS 285 had associations with the Augustinian Priory in Ossyth, Essex; A. I. Doyle "A Survey of the Origins and Circulation of Theological Writings in English in the 14th, 15th and Early 16th Centuries, with Special Consideration of the Part of the Clergy Therein," Ph.D. dissertation, Cambridge, 1953, 11.

11. On fol. 116v the name and date of the scribe are given: "Anno domini 1477 12 die mensis Iuli per Thomas Olyphaunntt Capellano." The year and name of Olyphaunt is also noted on fol. 89v of the manuscript. Thomas Olyphaunt was a Carmelite anchorite in Norwich at the end of the fifteenth century. Veronica O'Mara, *A Study and Edition of Selected Middle English Sermons*, Leeds Studies in English (Leeds: University of Leeds, 1994), offers a comprehensive description of this manuscript.

12. A note in British Library Royal MS 5 C.III identifies Pyle as the seller of another book; Helen Forshaw, ed., *Speculum Ecclesie and Speculum Religiosorum* (London: Oxford University Press, 1973), 8–9. Cleve can also be linked to another book, a Bible, now Oxford, Bodleian Library MS Auct. D.3.6; Pattwell, "*Sacerdos Parochialis* Edited from British Library MS Burney 356," 20–21.

13. A. B. Emden, *Biographical Register of the University of Oxford to* 1500 (Oxford: Clarendon Press, 1957–1959), 437. See also A. I. Doyle "A Survey of the Origins and Circulation of Theological Writings," n. xxiv, 272.

14. Leonard Boyle, "Aspects of Clerical Education in Fourteenth-Century England," repr. in *Pastoral Care, Clerical Education and Canon Law* 1200–1400, Collected Studies 135 (London: Variorum Reprints, 1981), pt. IX.

15. See Margaret Connolly, "Practical Reading for Body and Soul in Some Later Medieval Manuscript Miscellanies," in this volume.

16. For unknown reasons, British Library MS Burney 356 has two identical indices.

17. See appendix to this article for transcripts of the schemas and diagrams.

18. Lucy Freeman Sandler, *The Psalter of Robert de Lille in the British Library* (London: Oxford University Press for Harvey Miller, 1983).

19. Carruthers, commenting on these "late medieval diagram-encyclopedias," observes "that the group was called the '*Speculum theologiae*' or, in England, the '*Orchard of Consolation*,' names which suggest both the encyclopedic intention of their maker and their contemplative purpose." Mary Carruthers, *The Book of Memory: A Study of Memory in Medieval Culture* (Cambridge: Cambridge University Press, 1990), 254.

20. For a fuller discussion on the influence of the *Psychomachia*, see Mary Carruthers, *The Craft of Thought: Meditation, Rhetoric, and the Making of Images,* 400–1200 (Cambridge: Cambridge University Press, 1998), 143–150.

21. Curt Bühler, "The Apostles and the Creed," *Speculum* 28 (1953): 335–339. The Ten Commandments and ten plagues are linked in J. H. L. Kengen, ed., *Memoriale Credencium: A Late Middle English Manual of Theology for Lay People Edited from Bodley MS Tanner 201* (Nijmegen, Netherlands: Nijmegen University, 1979).

22. C.f. *thrallinge* or *þralunge* in Robert E. Lewis, ed., *Middle English Dictionary* (Ann Arbor: University of Michigan Press, 1986).

23. Avril Henry, "'The Pater Noster in a Table Ypeynted' and Some Other Presentations of Doctrine in the Vernon Manuscript," in Derek Pearsall, ed., *Studies in the Vernon Manuscript* (Cambridge: D. S. Brewer, 1990), 101–102.

24. Ibid., 102.

25. Carruthers, *Book of Memory*, 16.

26. Ibid., 90.

27. See, e.g., Oxford, Bodleian Library MS Bodley 110 or Cambridge, Pembroke College MS 285.

28. Griffin, "'A Good Reder and a Deuout,'" 1.

29. Rosemary Woolf, *The English Religious Lyric in the Middle Ages* (Oxford: Clarendon Press, 1968), 219–229.

30. Ibid., 220.

31. See, e.g., Dublin, Trinity College MS 158, fol. 83r, and Kari Ann Rand Schmidt, "The Index of Middle English Prose and Late Medieval English Recipes," English Studies 75:5 (1994): 423–429.

WORKS CITED

PRIMARY SOURCES
Cambridge, University Library, MS Dd.12.69
Cambridge, Pembroke College, MS 285
Dublin, Trinity College, MS 158
Durham, University Library, MS Cosin V.iv.2
London, British Library, MS Additional 10053
London, British Library, MS Burney 356
London, British Library, MS Harley 4172
Oxford, Bodley Library, MS Bodley 110
Oxford, Bodley Library, MS Rawlinson D913
Oxford, Trinity College MS 7

SECONDARY SOURCES
Boyle, Leonard E. "A Study of the Works Attributed to William Pagula with Special Reference to Oculus Sacerdotis and Summa Summarum." D.Ph. dissertation, Oxford, 1956.
———. "The Oculus Sacerdotis and Some Other Works of William Pagula." Repr. in Pastoral Care, Clerical Education and Canon Law, 1200–1400. Collected Studies 135. London: Variorum Reprints, 1981.
———. "Aspects of Clerical Education in Fourteenth-Century England." Repr. in Pastoral Care, Clerical Education and Canon Law 1200–1400. Collected Studies 135. London: Variorum Reprints, 1981.
———. "The Fourth Lateran Council and Manuals of Popular Theology." In The Popular Literature of the Medieval England. Ed. Thos. J. Heffernan. Tennessee Studies in Literature 28. Knoxville: University of Tennessee Press, 1985. 30-43.
Bühler, Curt. "The Apostles and the Creed." Speculum 28 (1953): 335–339.
Carruthers, Mary. The Book of Memory: A Study of Memory in Medieval Culture. Cambridge: Cambridge University Press, 1990.
———. The Craft of Thought: Meditation, Rhetoric, and the Making of Images, 400–1200. Cambridge: Cambridge University Press, 1998.
Connolly, Margaret. "Practical Reading for Body and Soul in Some Later Medieval Manuscript Miscellanies." Journal of the Early Book Society (2007): 149-171.
Doyle, A. I. "A Survey of the Origins and Circulation of Theological Writings in English in the 14th, 15th and Early 16th Centuries, with Special

Consideration of the Part of the Clergy Therein." 2 vols. Unpublished Ph.D. dissertation, Cambridge University, 1953.

Emden, A. B. *Biographical Register of the University of Oxford to 1500*. Oxford: Clarendon Press, 1957–1959.

Forshaw, Helen (Ed.) *Speculum Ecclesie and Speculum Religiosorum*. London: Oxford University Press, 1973.

Griffin, C. "'A Good Reder and a Deuout': Instruction, Reading, and Devotion in the *Wise Book of Philosophy and Astronomy*." *Journal of the Early Book Society* (2007): 105-125.

Henry, Avril. "'The Pater Noster in a Table Ypeynted' and Some Other Presentations of Doctrine in the Vernon Manuscript." In *Studies in the Vernon Manuscript*. Ed. Derek Pearsall. Cambridge, UK: D. S. Brewer, 1990. 101–102.

Kengen, J. H. L. (Ed.) *Memoriale Credencium: A Late Middle English Manual of Theology for Lay People Edited from Bodley MS Tanner 201*. Nijmegen, Netherlands: Nijmegen University, 1979.

Lewis, Robert E. (Ed.) *Middle English Dictionary*. Ann Arbor: University of Michigan Press, 1986.

O'Mara, Veronica. *A Study and Edition of Selected Middle English Sermons*. Leeds Studies in English. n.s. 13. Leeds, UK: University of Leeds, 1994.

Pantin, W. A. *The English Church in the Fourteenth Century*. Cambridge: Cambridge University Press, 1955.

Pattwell, N. "*Sacerdos Parochialis* Edited from British Library Burney MS 356 and *Exornatorium Curatorum* Edited from Cambridge Corpus Christi Sp. 335.2." Ph.D. Dissertation, Trinity College, Dublin. 2004.

Powicke, F. M., and Cheney, C. R. *Councils and Synods with Other Documents relating to the English Church* A.D. 1205–1313. Vol. 2, pt. 2 Oxford: Clarendon Press, 1964.

Rand Schmidt, Kari Ann. "The *Index of Middle English Prose* and Late Medieval English Recipes." *English Studies* 75.5 (1994): 423–429.

Sandler, Lucy Freeman. *The Psalter of Robert de Lille*. London: Oxford University Press for Harvey Miller, 1983.

Watson, Nicholas. "Censorship and Cultural Change in Late Medieval England: Vernacular Theology, the Oxford Translation Debate and Arundel's Constitutions of 1409." *Speculum* 70 (1995): 822–864.

Woolf, Rosemary. *The English Religious Lyric in the Middle Ages*. Oxford: Clarendon Press, 1968.

Practical Reading for Body and Soul in Some Later Medieval Manuscript Miscellanies

MARGARET CONNOLLY

> Take a sawge lief þat is not perced and write þer on with a penne
> with ynke: *in principio principio erat verbum angelus nunciat*, and þanne 3if
> hit þe seke to ete. And let þe seke seye first v pater noster in þe wor-
> shippe of þe v woundes of our lord iesu criste criste [*sic*], and v
> aueys in þe worship of þe v ioyes of oure lady and þanne in þe
> secunde day take anoþer lef and write þeron *et verbum erat apud deum
> iohannes iohannes predicat* and seye þe prayers forseyde and þe þridde
> day take anoþer lef and write þeron *et deus erat verbum cristus tonat* and
> 3if hit þe seke. A[nd] let hym seye þe prayers forseyde and by
> goddis grace he shal be hole.

To modern eyes the mixture of medical and devotional formulae in medieval
charms such as this may appear hopelessly unscientific and necessarily
superstitious: how could such prescriptions be taken seriously and believed
to be effective? The manuscript volumes in which such texts frequently survive can seem similarly haphazard, since they jumble together medical and
veterinary recipes and charms, plague texts, dietary regimens, uroscopies,
prognostications, and astrological material. Such volumes are very often the
products of many different hands, showing evidence of the accretion of fur-

ther texts over time; dirty and worn with use, they defy easy attempts at classification beyond the broadest catchall category of "practical miscellany," a term that, with its connotations of the unique and individual, tends to frustrate more detailed investigation. Although longer texts are sometimes extracted for separate consideration, miscellany volumes in general have been rather under-investigated. The following discussion will suggest that this lack of investigation has left us unappreciative of the similarities between devotional and practical texts and their contexts, and in the responses that they elicited from contemporary readers.

The sage-leaf charm cited above is recommended in two of its various manuscript versions as "a medicyn for þe axes" (ague or fever) and "for the feuere a souereyne medcyne provyd."[1] Its prescribed elements aptly demonstrate the way in which medieval medical practitioners happily combined medical and devotional elements in the pursuit of healing. The herb sage, *salvia officinalis*, is now most frequently encountered in the context of cooking, with sage-and-onion stuffing being one of the most traditional accompaniments to roast poultry or pork in British cuisine. Previously sage was also valued for its therapeutic properties, as indicated by its Latin name *salvia*, "the healing plant," and an infusion of its leaves could be used as a slight stimulant or to treat disorders of the stomach. In the context of the charm, however, the intrinsic therapeutic properties of sage are augmented by the power of the written word. The leaf of the plant is to mimic the role of the leaves of a book—the more usual location for writing—in becoming the vehicle for a medicinal script which invokes both the mystery of Latinate diction (a powerful, impenetrable language to many of the charm's recipients) and the authority of the Bible. The sick person is to be given the leaf to eat, following the usual practice of ingesting drugs or herbal compounds but also parodying the administration of the Sacrament, where the wafer or bread is transformed into the Body of Christ by the words of the priest. Belief in the power of words continues to be manifest, as the sick person is then advised to effect his or her own cure by repeating well-known prayers (the Pater Noster and Ave), according to particular multiples that reflect aspects of Christian devotion (Christ's five wounds, the five joys of Mary). This ensures that while the herb works to cure the body, the mind is focused on spiritual nourishment.

This mixing together of medicinal, devotional, and lexical elements is typical of many charms, as may be seen from some other examples that survive in the same manuscript, Cambridge University Library Dd.4.44, a fifteenth-century remedy book that contains recipes and charms for both human and equine ailments. On folio 31v is a multipurpose remedy "for al maner yveles in hors" which involves a mixture of Latin and English holy words (*"in nomine patris et filij et spiritus sancti amen* oure lord was bore and honged on þe rode as wisly as hit ys soth be þaw hors hole amen"), to be spoken into the horse's right ear while making the sign of the cross on his head; the charm is to be repeated three times, along with three pater nosters; the medicinal element, hen's eggs, to be eaten raw, is mentioned almost as an afterthought. On the same folio is another charm which, in addition to the familiar prayers, invokes "seynt epolit" (St. Hypolitus) and directs that the horse eat oats that have been blessed and mixed with holy water and wax from a holy candle.

Although most veterinary charms seem to involve spoken rather than written words, two charms in this manuscript advocate the power of script. One, to be used when shoeing horses, relies on six special words, punctuated in manuscript by crosses and other signs, which are to be written in lead and set in the horse's hood.[2] (See Figure 1.) Another, a "charme for þe fassine" on folio 28v, invokes St. Nicasius and advises the writing of certain magical words that are to be bound "in þe right ere of an hors in þe saturday afore sonne goynge downe and lat hit abyde stille tille þe mounday afore sonne risynge," a three-day period reminiscent of the duration of Christ's death and resurrection.[3] Similar elements are found elsewhere in charms intended for human consumption, such as the "Maria peperit cristum" charm for a difficult childbirth, which details a Latin text that is to be written on parchment and tied to or around the woman's stomach.[4] The Magi charm, effective against epilepsy, combines the power of the names of the biblical wise men, which are to be written on parchment and hung about the neck, with a charade of bloodletting and finally a parody of the mass: "in a maser wiþ þe blode and wash þe maser wyth ale or wiþ mylk and let þe chyld drynk yt and he shall be hole."[5]

Such charms are frequently found among collections of medical recipes, as in CUL Ll.1.18, where the Magi charm on folio 76v is immediately preceded by a plague recipe and (on fols 75v–76v) by a dietary regimen against pestilence which also incorporates various medical recipes; this manuscript also contains texts on the care of horses and hawks as well as dietary advice and culinary recipes. CUL Dd.5.76, a leechbook with short texts on wounds and urine, contains a collection of ninety medical recipes followed by a shorter collection of twenty recipes and charms. In CUL Dd.4.44 the sage-leaf charm keeps company on folio 29r with a straightforward medical recipe for hemorrhoids and another recipe for some kind of paint, while overleaf on folio 29v is a small collection of six recipes for dyeing cloth.[6] Before this is a text on the care of horses, with the heading on folio 19r, "þis is þe marchalcie of Piers Mori3 good and trewe," which incorporates various veterinary remedies to which others have been added, along with the charms in Latin and English for shoeing horses and curing the *farsi*.

The *Marchalcie* relies mostly on mundane elements in its prescriptions: boar's grease, beans, sheep's tallow, salt, and garlic, as do other isolated recipes in this early part of the manuscript: so, on folio 18v, a recipe for swelling of the neck, which has been added by a contemporary hand, recommends barley "and none oþer prouender," failing which, a concoction of badger's grease, incense, milk and honey, pork fat, and red nettle is to be used. However, another remedy promises that a horse will be cured "of wormes botes and schurf of skyn by þe offryng of þes candels in þe worschip of seint firmyn" (St. Firmin).[7]

The amalgamation of devotional and medical elements in medieval charms may strike us as bizarre, suggestive of both medical ignorance and the power of the Church as well as the strength of popular superstition in the pre-modern era. If this blending of devotional and practical were confined to the narrow context of charms, it might be more easily dismissed, but in fact such juxtapositions may be observed elsewhere in collections of recipes. For example, the first part of CUL Dd.5.76, a composite fifteenth-century volume, contains approximately 140 recipes (including some charms).[8] The first English prescription (fols. 6r–v) is for a wonder-cure herbal drink which promises to heal and cleanse wounds and be effective against many other ills such as cancer, fistula, and "scabbe." The next series of twenty-eight recipes, on folios 7r–12v, describes substances related to bookmaking (black and colored inks, glue, and gilt), after which the focus becomes medical again, with "a boke of gode medicines" on folios 12v–22r that consists of ninety recipes, followed on folios 22v–25r by a further group of twenty recipes and herbal charms that may be used to determine whether a sick person will live or die.

This grouping together of sets of recipes for different purposes is itself an interesting juxtaposition, perhaps indicative that the interests of the compiler may have been more those of an apothecary than a healer, but more relevant to the present discussion is the inclusion of two Latin prayers that occur on folios 6v–7r, after the prescription for the tonic but before the bulk of the recipes. The English rubrics to these prayers clearly specify the occasions for their use. The first, on folio 6v, is to be used when concocting remedies: "Here begynnes a gode orysoun for to say when þou makes a medicyne to giffe or to do to any creature þat god has wrought and þus it begynnes"; the second, on folio 7r, is to be used when treating the patient: "And when þou gefes any man or woman or any creature any medycine say to þam on þis wise." The whole of the act of healing, from the initial choice and blending of ingredients for the prescription right through to its administration, is framed within the context of prayer, with such devotions to be used when treating animals ("any creature") as well as sentient human subjects.

Similarly, while medical recipes against plague were common, prayers and devotion were believed to be equally efficacious. A collection of advisory texts on the topic of plague occurs at what is now the beginning of CUL Ll.1.18. A fragment from the very end of the short version of John of Burgundy's plague tract is followed by recipes and dietary advice against plague, advice on healthy living in times of pestilence, and more recipes. Punctuating this collection of more practical material is a short advisory text (on fols. 3r–v) that advocates the use of "gostly remedye" against pestilence, specifying this to consist of repentance of heart, shrift, penance, prayer, fasting, almsgiving, and so on, and prescribes Latin prayers and anthems that may be used in this respect.[9]

Another "goode prayer ayenste þe pestelence" is found in a more strictly devotional context at the end of CUL Dd.6.1, a fifteenth-century book of hours. Here a different hand from that of the main scribe has added a series of English verses on folios 138v–142v: "And ye will please god gretly / Use preuey penaunce discretly" (IMEV 317), and a number of Latin prayers with English rubrics, culminating in the popular prayer to the "good angel" ("Angele qui meus es custos pietate superna"), and a prayer to the Virgin. The pestilence prayer has an English rubric (on fol. 143r) but is otherwise in Latin, ending with the Pater Noster, Ave, and Credo, and the further English instruction (on fol. 143v): "Sey this iij tymes." This prayer for medical assistance is sandwiched between two other Latin prayers that focus on spiritual relief; the first of these, also on folio 143r, promises that the Virgin will come to the aid of "whosum euyr is in any heuynesse wiþouten cownsell and counfort," while the second, on folio 144r, offers remission from damnation and purgatory. As a later addition to the manuscript, this miniature collection is somewhat unlike the other contexts discussed above, but its combination of prayers for spiritual and bodily health demonstrates a similar sense of ease with the contiguity of such material.

Individually such instances of the mixing of different types of material might be dismissed as mere jumbles. Mixed anthologies such as CUL Dd.4.44 that combine medical and veterinary prescriptions with charms, prayers, non-medical recipes, and short texts on the virtues of specific herbs such as rosemary and betony can be regarded as eclectic individual compilations, assembled initially by a single person and retained for the use of successive generations of the same family or household. But collectively the survival of many such volumes demonstrates that in the fifteenth century, and for a considerable time afterward, there was a general willingness to tolerate the mixing together of what are now regarded as generically distinct materials.[10] Evidence of the comfortable accommodation of such juxtapositions may be found not only in the association of disparate texts but within texts themselves. For example, The Thyrtty Days of the Mone, a fifteenth-century poem on which many prose lunaries are based, associates each day with a biblical character or event and then discusses nativities, bloodletting, and dreaming, among other matters.[11] A similar mixture of contents characterizes *The Wise Book of Philosophy and Astronomy*, a Middle English prose text extant in thirty-three manuscripts. It advocates a method for determining the length of a planet's reign, which is equated with the length of time it would take to read twice through the seven penitential psalms.[12] In fact, although as modern scholars we are used to dividing devotional and practical texts into different generic categories, they are more similar than our categorization allows, with a crisscrossing of contents and shared patterns of internal and external organization.

Further evidence that generic distinctions were not rigidly demarcated may be derived from some consideration of the way in which different kinds of miscellanies were shaped by their compilers. Although dealing with materials of a different nature, compilers of devotional and medical miscellanies clearly found the same forms of *ordinatio* to be useful and appropriate when assembling their collections. One basic organizational technique that is frequently found in both contexts is the use of numbers to control material and elucidate information. The quantifying of important elements is a device used extensively in fourteenth- and fifteenth-century devotional manuals, which typically enumerate the ten commandments, seven sins, seven works of mercy (bodily and spiritual), seven principal virtues, five wits (bodily and spiritual), and so on. This methodology is employed in devotional collections from the most basic, such as the simple lists found in CUL Nn.4.12, folios 39r–40r, and on a single leaf, folio 109r, in CUL Hh.3.13, to manuals that offer more exposition, such as CUL Ii.4.9 and Ii.6.43.

Medical, alchemical, and other types of practical anthologies of the same period also rely on enumeration as a method of organization and to explain the properties and functions of things. Their equivalents to the devotional catalogue are lists and short texts that quantify the four humors or complexions, the four seasons, the seven days of the week, the seven planets, and the twelve months and zodiacal signs. CUL Dd.10.44, a fifteenth-century leechbook, contains a range of such texts among its many medical recipes. The four humors which govern the body (heat, cold, moisture, dryness) are enumerated in a treatise on urine (fols. 114r–17v) and in a note (f. 143r), while another short diagnostic text (on fols. 132r–133r) outlines "þe 4 partyes of man in which euery man comonly is moste and rathest agreuyd wyth euyll" (namely, the head, breast, womb, and bladder). Another urine text on folios 144r–v is headed "To know þe 4 complexions of man by the vrine at euery tyme," and a brief note on folio 139v, probably an extract from a longer text, outlines the three quantities of urine. Twenty is another favored number, especially in the context of uroscopies; in this manuscript, the twenty contents of a woman's urine are enumerated on folios 144v–145v, with the twenty colors of urine listed shortly before this on folios 140r–143r (as also in CUL

Dd.6.29 fols. 26r–30r and CUL Ee.1.13 fols. 97r–100v); elsewhere we find lists of twenty medicinal waters or distillations (CUL Ee.1.15 fols. 79v–80v, embedded within an extensive collection of medical recipes).

The numbers used for textual organization in both devotional and practical contexts are often those to which a biblical or doctrinal significance could be attributed. Frequently occurring numbers are three, four, five, seven, ten, and twelve, reminiscent of the Trinity, the three temptations, and the three days before Christ's resurrection; the four evangelists and gospels; the five wounds of Christ, and the joys and sorrows of Mary; the seven days of creation; the ten commandments; and the twelve apostles, or tribes of Israel. In at least one instance, the power and significance of the number seven seems to have led to its employment in an inappropriate context: a short tract on the various operations of alchemy, known from its incipit as the "Seven Terms" ("Ther ben 7 termes or keys"), proves on closer examination to contain *eight* terms.[13] The use of such spiritually resonant numbers in the context of practical as well as devotional collections is a reminder of the way in which religious significance and meaning pervaded all aspects of everyday life in the Middle Ages.

The compilers of both types of miscellanies also used numbers to achieve a sense of overall organization through the provision of tables of contents. One very striking example of this in a devotional context is CUL Hh.1.12, a collection of short works of spiritual guidance that follows a typical progression from brief expositions of the basics of faith to more complex discussions of the abstract concept of the love of God. The volume is distinguished by its kalendar on folios 2r–3v in which the book's contents are enumerated (see Figure 2). The kalendar was drawn up after the main work of compilation was finished and is written by a slightly later hand than that of the main scribe; this later hand apparently also added the marginal rubric chapter numbers which occur within the main body of the manuscript. A clear effort has been made here to help the reader(s) negotiate the contents of the volume and to facilitate different modes of reading.

The provision of this type of *accessus* was by no means unique, nor was it confined to devotional miscellanies. Another such table of contents, titled "The kalender of this present booke," prefaces CUL Mm.3.29 (fols. 4r–6v), a fifteenth-century collection of statutes and other historical material, in this instance listing seventy-three entries. A fragment of another survives at the beginning of CUL Kk.1.6, the collection of devotional poetry and prose owned and partly written by Richard Fox, steward of St. Albans, in the mid-fifteenth century. Here, due to the loss of the opening leaves of the manuscript, only what was originally the final entry of the table, "How seynt gregory saued his moderes sowle by his preyere," now survives on folio 2r, followed by the note "thus endeth the contentus of this booke quod rychard ffox."[14]

Perhaps the best-known such tables are the versified examples created by John Shirley to preface two of his three major anthologies of poetry and prose, MSS BL Additional 16165 and Cambridge, Trinity College R.3.20, though in the case of the latter, the list of contents is now detached from the volume and exists only in the form of a sixteenth-century copy made by John Stow.[15] The fragmentary survival of these latter examples is a reminder that such kalendars were intensely vulnerable due to their position at the head of large collections, perhaps (since they were usually composed at a late stage of the volume's construction) also copied onto singletons which were trickier to bind successfully; their use may have been much more widespread than is now apparent.

Collections of recipes are frequently accompanied by lists of contents, though the lists do not always match the actual contents precisely. The collection of culinary recipes in MS BL Additional 5467, a manuscript derived from one or more lost exemplars written by John Shirley, has its contents itemized in *two* lists; the one that precedes the collection gives its contents only partially, while the one that follows attempts a complete listing.[16] There is an intrinsic difficulty in achieving accuracy in such indexes, but in the case of recipe collections this is intensified by their accumulative nature. These collections were naturally augmented by successive practitioners keen to record additional remedies or variants on original recipes found to be effective through personal experience. In addition, finding lists and indexes may not always have been integral features of the texts they accompany. The collection of recipes in CUL Dd.6.29, folios 34r–106r, is indexed a few leaves earlier by a different hand; the table of contents lists 231 entries, the last five of these relating to recipes on folio 106r which have been added to the main collection by a later hand. In the table not all rubricated initials have been supplied, though in some cases the guide-letters are still visible, which makes it difficult to see at a glance how many separate recipes are indexed. A more user-friendly feature is the use of red ink, which links groups of recipes to a series of numbers running from ij to clxv, corresponding to similar numbers that have been added to the top margins of folios 34v–106r; this makes it easier to find particular recipes within the volume (see Figure 3).

In the context of miscellany volumes, where many short items are brought together, numbers and numbered tables of contents were obviously helpful to readers. But the usefulness of the tabular format was not confined to a means of *accessus*. In both devotional and practical collections, tables were included for other purposes, in particular for computation. Many aspects of spiritual observance required some form of calculation. In the specific context of the Wycliffite Bible, the kalendar or table was used as quick reference to the correct biblical readings for Sundays and festivals throughout the Church year. A feature that occurs more generally among devotional collections is the provision of tables that allow the date of the moveable feast of Easter to be worked out (a feature still included in the Church of England prayer book). Short texts in both verse and prose that explain these calculations are also common, such as that which has been added by a later hand to CUL Ff.6.8, folio 3v, beginning: "Accompt x dayes aftre the furst prime folowing aftre the epiphanie and the nexte sonday"; this is followed by another short text that explains how to calculate ember days from Wednesdays.[17] Other short texts identify and quantify particular days when religious observances such as fasting might be required, as in "The xij fridays to fast seynt barnardis fast."[18]

The conjunction of certain days of the week with important religious occasions was also believed to carry meaning for the future: the weekday on which Christmas Day or New Year's Day fell was taken as indicative of the social, political, and meteorological conditions which would ensue in the following year.[19] Even certain weather conditions could be used as the basis for such prognostication, as in the series of verses "When thonder comeþ in Janeuere" (NIMEV 4053), which is introduced in CUL Ff.5.48 with the following note: "Here sueth a tabulle of diuerse monethe in the 3ere if thondur be herd in theym what it betokenethe aftur her seyng that ar holdyn wyse men of soth thyngiis" (fol. 9v).[20]

Prognostication and knowledge of auspicious days were also regarded as of utmost importance for the successful outcome of medical treatment, hence the proliferation among medical miscellanies of *Perilous Days* tracts, which detail those days on which one should not undertake bloodletting or surgery, nor even eat certain types of food. A typical example occurs in CUL Kk.6.33, Part 2, folios 11r–v, beginning: "A wise man and gode leche seyþe that in þe monþe of januarij whit wyn is gode to drynk fastyng erly and blode letyng forbere for þer beþe vij dayes of perel þe furst þe ij þe iiij þe v þe x þe xv þe xix in þe moneþ of februari ete no potage of lekis."[21] Other similar texts relate perilous or evil days to the phases of the moon.[22] Lunar kalendars, containing the information necessary to compute the daily variations in the moon's cycle (again important for medical treatment), occur in practical volumes of all types. The one that occurs in CUL Dd.3.52, a late-fifteenth-century copy of Guy de Chauliac's *Chirurgia magna*, consists of a table of figures in red and black which is preceded by useful step-by-step instructions for the novice user:

> For to knowe motus diei of þe moune and þe very meuyng in euery hour of the day and of þe ny3tte firste looke how many grees þe moune remeueth in a day and be þe allmynake þen tak þees greese in þe hede of þe table þat her folewth and þe next nombre vnderneth is þe meuyng of a hour and so eny hour after oþer item take þe forseyde meuyng in a day be þe allmynake and tak þat in þe

hede of þe tables þat here foloweth þen loke in þe allmynake howe
many greese þer remayneth of þat sygne and þer þat remaynethe of
þat sygne take it and loke yt derectly vnder þe hede of þe greese þat
he remeneth in a day þen looke þyn hours in þe rede lyne and þus
in þe mettyng tak þe cumyng in of þe next sygne in þat hour. (fol.
262r)

With a little effort it is possible to detect numerous similarities in the
contents, presentation, and organization of later medieval manuscript miscellanies of different types, and further work could be done to investigate the
ways in which the compilers of such volumes selected, extracted, and
reshaped the texts they were anthologizing.[23] The question remains as to why
these similarities are present. It might be objected that the features that are
highlighted above as common factors are no more than commonsense solu-
tions that might be devised independently by individual compilers.
Compilations that seek to inform and instruct, as both types of anthology do,
obviously require structures that facilitate easy reference; perhaps, then, what
have been identified as common factors may be no more than the products
of independent invention in different spheres. Historical reasons may also
account for the simple resemblances between these types of volumes. In the
early Middle Ages, before the rise of the universities, when monastic book
production was the norm, all types of volumes were assembled in the scriptorium. When scribes accustomed to preparing Bibles and commentaries prepared a lapidary or herbal, they would naturally employ the same techniques
of presentation and organization, transferring skills learned in one context to
another.

By the time manuscript production outside the monasteries became
widespread, monastic techniques had become firmly entrenched as norms of
book construction, and secular scribes naturally followed these available
models, in much the same way the early printers aped the appearance of
manuscripts when preparing printed books.[24] The common factors shared
between these types of anthologies would not seem so surprising if they
could be shown to have scribes in common, too. As our knowledge of the circumstances of later medieval book production extends, it is becoming
increasingly clear that copyists did not confine themselves to particular types
of writing work, nor was their working environment subject to rigid boundaries. Research by literary scholars in documentary archives is leading to
spectacular advances, such as Linne Mooney's celebrated discovery of the
real Adam Scriveyn.[25] As yet I know of no instance where the hand that compiled a devotional anthology can also be found in a leechbook, but it should
be remembered that the "Hammond scribe" was responsible for copying a
medical miscellany as well as several literary ones and that Doyle and
Parkes's "Scribe Delta" copied both devotional and medical material, albeit in

the form of longer texts (Love's *Mirror* and the *Chirurgia* of Guy de Chauliac).[26] More palaeographical attention to both categories of manuscripts and more investigation of professionally produced documents might uncover some such connections, especially if we had a database of scribal hands at our disposal.

The main focus of this discussion is on matters of production rather than consumption, but it is also important to remember the context of reading. It should not be imagined that medical compilations were used only by medical professionals, any more than religious anthologies were used only by clerics. Parish priests frequently practiced healing, though they were prohibited from doing so, and would thus have had need of both types of book. We also have evidence of "lay" use in both instances. The owner or reader of a devotional anthology such as CUL Hh.1.12 might easily have also been the owner or reader of a remedy book such as CUL Dd.4.44; each volume would be valuable within the household as a manual for self-healing and a means of promoting family health, whether in spiritual or physical terms. Both contemporary and later fifteenth- and sixteenth-century readers seem to have treated such volumes in similar fashion, and it is not surprising to find different contemporary or later hands adding material to such anthologies. There are many examples, too numerous to mention, of the inscription of individual recipes or prayers, added by rough hands keen to preserve bodily or spiritual remedies which were believed to be especially efficacious. English prayers find their way into Latin books of hours, psalters, and missals, as in CUL Dd.6.1 or in Dd.10.21, where a different hand from that of the main scribe has written a prayer to the heart of Jesus ("O most glorious and precyous herte of iesu cryst let thy peyne habounde in me") on folio 155r, after the psalter, canticles, and litany, and before a series of Latin hymns for the different Hours. The contents of practical anthologies in particular are naturally accretive, and recipe collections are frequently swelled by contemporary and later additions.

In these layers of augmentation, rigid generic distinctions are often not maintained or even recognized. Successive contributors to CUL Dd.4.44 saw nothing anomalous in assembling on a single leaf (fol. 34v) four recipes and a charm, as follows: a cure for headaches (in humans, it seems), a powder to treat eye complaints in horses, a Job charm to cure worms in horses, an eyewash "to clere a manys sy3t," and a cure for gout attributed to St. Cuthbert. (See Figure 1.) In general, later readers and annotators, at least in the fifteenth and sixteenth centuries, seem unperturbed by generic distinctions, adding prayers to recipe collections and recipes to devotional anthologies. In CUL Ii.6.43, a fifteenth-century devotional anthology described by A. I. Doyle as "a priest's private book," a later rough hand has added ten medical recipes to the back of the book, working backwards and upside down from the back of the manuscript.[27] Similarly, CUL Hh.1.3, a late-fourteenth- or early fifteenth-century Latin vulgate and missal, has various later additions, including a recipe for ink on folio 387r and a mnemonic of the seven works of spiritual mercy noted in the margin of folio 400r.

Later users also used both types of volumes to record important transactions, receipts, and memoranda, including family records.[28] Medieval Vulgate Bibles seem to be largely free of such annotation, but other religious manuscripts, typically books of hours, were regularly used in this way. The calendar of CUL Gg.6.25, a fifteenth-century Latin hours, has a number of English annotations in its margins, recording the marriage of Thomas Derham and Isabell Pagnell and the births and deaths of their children and other members of the Pagnell family, relating to the period 1485–1540. Members of the Roberts family made similar use of CUL Ii.6.2, a religious anthology with texts in Latin and English, also during the first half of the sixteenth century. The use of the family Bible as a repository of family record survived into the twentieth century, but there are sixteenth-century examples that show that this practice formerly extended to other non-religious volumes too. In the alchemical anthology CUL Kk.6.30, a table on folio 49r that has the names of the months in English set down the left-hand side has had six notes of birth dates added to it in the early sixteenth century. The table is otherwise blank, so it is hard to be sure of its original purpose, but the function that has later been assigned to it is clearly that of a log of significant personal dates. Similarly CUL Dd.10.44, an anthology of practical texts, has a note of the birth in 1561 of "An Thorowgood," first daughter to William Thorowgood, added to an otherwise blank leaf, folio 102v. These cases may signify little more than a scarcity of suitable writing paper for permanent record, but they might also be taken as indicative of the regard in which these old books were held by their later owners. In the sixteenth-century at least, family remedy books and other practical anthologies seem to have been esteemed as highly valued resources that were consulted as frequently and preserved as carefully as Bibles and prayer books, and used in similar ways.

It is difficult to determine at what stage this respect diminished. At some point (presumably *prior* to the point when the manuscript entered the Cambridge University Library collection), five leaves have been excised from the collection of remedies in Dd.6.29, folios 34r–106r.[29] The contents of the missing leaves can be identified from entries in the preceding table of contents, which otherwise matches the collection closely, and it is interesting to note that in all cases the vandalism seems to have been prompted by the presence of charms on the relevant leaves. Thus folio 51 formerly contained a charm "for þe hawe in a manis i3e" as well as a recipe for "sore i3en" (detailed in the contents list on fol. 22r);[30] folio 53 had recipes for the eyes and for toothache and a charm for toothache (detailed in the contents list on fol. 22r);

folio 59 contained a charm for the bloody flux, a remedy for nosebleeds, and a recipe for "costifnes" (detailed in the contents list on fol. 22v); folio 61 had a recipe for hemorrhoids and a charm or charms to staunch blood (probably in Latin, since the one surviving on fol. 62r is headed "here is a fair charme on englisse"; the contents list on fol. 22v signals more of the same type of thing by using the additional term "item"); and folio 102 had a recipe for fever in the stomach (the contents list on fol. 24v indicates there should be three, but only two are now present) and "a charme for wickiid wy3tis" (in Latin), of which only the end now survives on folio 103r.

Leaves are sometimes removed from manuscripts because of their rich illumination or other decoration, but that was clearly not a consideration in this case; nor do these losses seem merely serendipitous, since the volume is otherwise in a reasonable condition. Instead, it seems that a former reader wished to remove one particular type of textual material, probably because charms were no longer valued as remedies and no longer felt to be appropriate among a collection of medical recipes. In just the same way the modern medical establishment insists upon drawing a firm line between its own, scientifically tested methods based on surgery and licensed drugs, and other approaches such as holistic or homeopathic treatments, aromatherapy, and so on. The modern church, except in its more extreme expressions, is also suspicious of alternative therapies and faith healing.

Such entrenched attitudes naturally lead us to view the inclusion of charms among collections of medieval medical recipes as merely superstitious and unscientific. However, as the preceding discussion has sought to emphasize, our failure to recognize points of contact between devotional and practical texts and anthologies can lead us to reinforce false divisions. Ostensibly the idea that the simple repetition of certain words might be therapeutically efficacious may seem unlikely, yet belief in the power of words seems much less odd when considered in the context of a medieval spirituality in which pardons and indulgences were institutionally promoted. Spiritual health, specifically the well-being of the soul after death, could be improved by certain practices such as the saying of particular prayers, and Latin prayers with English rubrics that promise that the speaker will see Our Lady before he dies or gain many days of pardon are common in contemporary manuscripts. A frequently occurring feature is an emphasis on the Holy Name of Jesus, as in this popular series of indulgences:

> Whoso seyth in the ende of aue maria iesu shall haue xl days of pardoun. Whoso knelyth or deuoutely inclyneth when he heryth the name of iesu shall haue xl dayes of pardoun. Whoso at thre tyllynges of the bell sayth thre aue maria shal haue xl dayes of pardon. Whoso devoutely inclyneth whyll *gloria patri et filio et spiritu sancto* ys in seyng shall haue xl days of pardon. Whoso in the masse at *gra-*

cias agamus domino deo nostro devoutely knelyth shall haue a hundred
dayes of pardon. Whoso in te deum at this holy verse *te go- quis-* knelyth shall haue xx dayes of pardon. Whoso in the masse *credo in vnum
deum* knelyth at thys verse *et homo factus esse* shall haue xl dayes of
pardon. Whoso in takyng holy water sayth this prayer *huius aque
aspersio sit domini peccatorum meorum remissio in nomine patris et filij et spiritus sancti amen* shall haue x dayes of pardon. Whoso deuoutly sayth
or heryth the holy gospell of Seynt John *in principio erat verbum* and in
the ende when it ys seyd *verbum caro factum est et habitant in nobis* knelyth and kyssyth the grownde or the wall or the forme shall haue
oon yere and xl dayes of pardon grauntyd of pope clement þe vth.

In manuscript this prescription is invested with various types of
authority. The reader is assured that the text of the pardon is physically
inscribed on the walls of a church in Rome, and its efficacy is vouched for by
the authority of several popes.[31] The intrinsic power of the Holy Name of
Jesus was also stressed through many devotional texts, among them the *Pore
Caitif* and Rolle's *Form of Living*, and promoted through dedicated fraternities
such as the one associated in the fifteenth century with the Jesus Chapel at
St. Paul's, London, which flourished until the Dissolution. If merely saying the
name of Jesus at the end of the Ave Maria could gain the soul remission from
purgatory, surely saying the same name, and other holy words, when in need
of physical healing would be effective? Viewed in this context it is clear that
charms sought merely to harness the power of prayer to achieve healing in
this life. In the Middle Ages, as now, what was desired for the body was simply
a remedy that would work, which might be labeled "probatum est" and
recorded and preserved for future generations; the means to this end might
be either practical or spiritual but would necessarily involve in either case
recourse to prayer and the power of God.

University of St. Andrews

NOTES

1. The charm is quoted from Cambridge University Library Dd.4.44, fol. 29r;
the ends of some words at the extreme right edge of the page have been lost
to cropping. For the second copy, which differs in some aspects, see CUL
Ee.1.15, fol. 16v: "Take a sauge leff and wrtye theronn *christus tonat* and gyff hit
the syke to ete, and charge hym to sey a pater noster and aue maria wiþ a
credo. The secunde daye take another sawge leff and wryte ther on *angelus nun-
ciat* and gyf hit hym to ete and lete hym sey ij pater nosteris ij aue maria and
ij credys. The thyrde daye take another sawge leff and wryte ther on *johannes
predicat* and gyff hit hym to ete, and lete hym sey iij pater nostris iij aue maria
and iij credys and he shall be hole. Charge hym to here a masse of the holy

gost, another of seynt mychell, and the thyrde of seint john baptiste, and whan þou heryst any man speke of the feuer lete hem blysse hym and sey and aue maria saron and saron and saracion bere thyse iij namys abowte 3ow are gode for the feuer here 3ow mass when 3e be hole etc." Wells Rev. 10:3869 [338] notes twelve copies of this sage-leaf charm (against fever). The charm is edited (not from this MS) by F. Heinrich, *Ein Mittelenglisches Medizinbuch* (Halle: M. Niemeyer 1896), 186; and Gottfried Müller, *Aus mittelenglischen Medizintexten: Die Prosarezepte der stockholmer Miszellankodex X.90*, Kölner anglistische Arbeiten, X (Leipzig: 1929); and there are extracts in George Stephens, "Extracts in Prose and Verse from an Old English Medical Manuscript, Preserved in the Royal Library at Stockholm," *Archaeologia* 30 (1843): 349–418; and F. Holthausen, "Rezepte, Segen und Zaubersprüche aus zwei Stockholmer Handschriften," *Anglia* 19 (1897): 75–86, 78.

2. "Thes wordys scold be wrete in lede and sette hyt in þe hors hod," followed by six words: "3aron 3eronen 3eronem betonent astra lubia." There are two copies of this charm on fol. 35r, and the same magical words have also been written on fol. 33r.

3. "fassine," MED farsi(n *n.* (a) a disease of horses and other animals characterized by swollen lymphatics, small tumors, and sores.

4. See Margaret Ogden, *Liber de Diversis Medicinis*, EETS os 207 (London: Oxford University Press, 1938), 57. Wells Rev. 10:3873 [347] lists twenty-five MS copies of this charm.

5. Quoted from CUL Ll.1.18, fol. 76v. Other copies are edited in Ogden, *Liber de Diversis Medicinis*, 42; and C. F. Bühler, "Three Middle English Prose Charms from MS Harley 2389," *Notes and Queries* 207 (1962): 48. Wells Rev. 10:3868–3869 [336] lists twenty-five MSS that contain Magi charms for different purposes, some of which contain multiple versions; this copy in Ll.1.18 is not listed.

6. This may be the fragment of a larger collection as fol. 30 is now missing.

7. On fol. 19r, immediately preceding the beginning of Þe Marchalcie of Piers Mori3.

8. The table of contents on fols 2r–3v lists only 104 of these.

9. The text also occurs in Cambridge, Fitzwilliam Museum 261, fols. 27r–29r; see *Index of Middle English Prose* (IMEP) 18, 89–90 [A21], and the discussion in Kari Anne Rand, "A Previously Unnoticed Fragment of John of Burgundy's Plague Tract and Some Connected Pest Regimens," *Notes and Queries* 251 (2006): 295–297.

10. Evidence of the existence of many such mixed volumes is emerging gradually as the work of the IMEP progresses. Two other examples from the Cambridge University Library collection are Ee.1.15 and Ll.1.18. The majority of examples cited in this article are from manuscripts in the University Library that I have examined in the preparation of IMEP Handlist 19.

11. NIMEV 970, 1991, 3341. See the discussion by Irma Taavitsainen, *Middle English Lunaries: A Study of the Genre. Mémoires de la Société Néophilologique de Helsinki* 47 (Helsinki: Société Néophilologique, 1988): 65–69.

12. For discussion of this text, see Carrie Griffin, "'A Good Reder and a Deuout': Instruction, Reading, and Devotion in the *Wise Book of Philosophy and Astronomy*," *Journal of the Early Book Society* 10 (2007): 105-125; and her more extensive analysis in Griffin, "'A Good Reder': The Middle English *Wise Book of Philosophy and Astronomy*, Instruction, Publics, and Manuscripts," unpublished Ph.D. thesis, University College Cork, 2006.

13. As noted by Linne Mooney, IMEP 11, Trinity College O.5.31 [7]; the text also survives in CUL Kk.6.30, fols. 37v–38v. The error might also have arisen from inaccurate transcription of "viii" as "vii" at an earlier stage in the text's history.

14. The entry relates to "The Trental of Saint Gregory" which occurs on fols. 242v–245v.

15. In MS BL Additional 29729, fols. 177v–179r. The briefer list of contents which prefaces Shirley's third anthology, MS Bodley Ashmole 59, fol. iir, is not by Shirley's hand and does not relate to the contents of the volume; it may indicate a missing Shirley codex, see Margaret Connolly, *John Shirley: Book Production and the Noble Household in Fifteenth-Century England* (Aldershot, UK: Ashgate, 1998), 171–172.

16. In BL Additional 5467, the lists of recipes occur on fol. 23r and fols. 65r–66v.

17. Calculation of Easter and the Moveable Feasts by Primes. Cf. Wells Rev. 10:3771–3772 [73, 74]. See the edition by Laurel Means, "'Ffor as Moche as Yche Man May Not Haue þe Astrolabe': Popular Middle English Variations on the Computus," *Speculum* 67 (1992): 595–623, esp. 611–614; she also notes five similar texts.

18. Extant in CUL Ee.1.14, fol. 139r and at least three other copies; see the edition by Linne R. Mooney, "Practical Didactic Works in Middle English: Edition and Analysis of the Class of Short Middle English Works Containing Useful Information," unpublished Ph.D. thesis, University of Toronto, 1981, 395–397.

19. As in the prognostications edited in J. Y. Downing, "An Unpublished Weather Prognostic in Camb. Univ. MS Ff.5.48," *English Language Notes* 8 (1970–1971): 87; and Mooney, "Practical Didactic Works in Middle English," 319–320.

20. Max Förster, "Beiträge zur mittelalterlichen Volkskunde VII: 10: Mittelenglische Donnerbücher," *Archiv fur das Studium der Neuren Sprachen und Literaturen* 128 (1912): 285–291; Janay Young Downing, "A Critical Edition of Cambridge University MS Ff.5.48," PhD diss. U of Washington, 1969; facsimile published by University Microfilms, 1980, pp. 19-21, notes pp. 346-47 .

21. See the edition and discussion in Linne R. Mooney, "Diet and Bloodletting: Monthly Instructions," in *Practical and Popular Science and Medicine of Medieval England*, ed. Lister M. Matheson (Ann Arbor: Colleagues Press, 1994), 245–262.

22. For some examples, see CUL Ee.1.15, fols. 6r—v, and CUL Kk.6.33, fol. 37r.

23. I hope to discuss these aspects in a separate article.

24. The classic study of this process is Malcolm Parkes, "The Influence of the Concepts of *Ordinatio* and *Compilatio* on the Development of the Book," in *Medieval Learning and Literature: Essays Presented to* R.W. Hunt, ed. J. J. G. Alexander and M. T. Gibson (Oxford: Clarendon Press, 1976), 115–141.

25. Announced at the New Chaucer Society Congress at the University of Glasgow, July 2004, and subsequently published in Linne R. Mooney, "Chaucer's Scribe," *Speculum* 81 (2006): 97–138.

26. On the Hammond scribe, see Linne R. Mooney "More Manuscripts Written by a Chaucer Scribe," *Chaucer Review* 30 (1996): 401–407; and Mooney, "A Middle English Text on the Seven Liberal Arts," *Speculum* 68 (1993): 1027–1052. On Scribe Delta, see A. I. Doyle and M. B. Parkes, "The Production of Copies of the *Canterbury Tales* and the *Confessio Amantis* in the Early Fifteenth Century," in *Medieval Scribes, Manuscripts and Libraries: Essays Presented to* N. R. Ker, ed. M. B. Parkes and A. G. Watson (London: Scolar Press, 1978), 163–210; and Linda Ehrsam Voigts, "Scientific and Medical Books," in *Book Production and Publishing in Britain* 1375–1475, ed. Jeremy Griffiths and Derek Pearsall (Cambridge: Cambridge University Press, 1989), 345–402 (384).

27. A. I. Doyle, "A Survey of the Origins and Circulation of Theological Writings in English in the Fourteenth, Fifteenth and Early Sixteenth Centuries with Special Consideration of the Part of the Clergy Therein," unpublished Ph.D. thesis, University of Cambridge, 1953, 2 vols, I.47.

28. For an example, see CUL Kk.1.3, Part 22, fol. 12v where a later fifteenth-century hand has added a note of receipt at the end of the devotional manual.

29. The missing leaves are fols. 51, 53, 59, 61, and 102.

30. Probably the St. Tobias charm, see Wells Rev. 10:3881 [376b].

31. The text is quoted from CUL Ff.6.33, fols. 26r–v, where the rubric ascribes the indulgences to John XXII (1316–1334), though Clement V (1305–1314) is cited at the end of the text. The text's physical display in a church dedicated to Our Lady in Rome is noted both here and in the copy in CUL Ff.1.14, fols. 212v–213r. In CUL Dd.14.26, fols. 37v–38r, where, as in Ff.1.14, the indulgence occurs with the *Speculum Christiani*, John XXII is also mentioned. The same pope, wrongly cited as John XII, is linked to the text in Trinity College Cambridge R.3.21, fol. 216v, for which see IMEP 11, R.3.21 [28]. In CUL Dd.12.69, however, where the indulgence appears on fol. 25v as part of the *Sacerdos Parochialis*, the authority cited is that of Urban IV (1261–1264). According to Niamh Pattwell (personal communication) all of the manu-

scripts of the *Sacerdos Parochialis* that refer to the Jesus-name blessing mention Urban IV, except Bodley Rawlinson D.913, which attributes it, erroneously, to Urban I.

32. See Elizabeth New, "The Cult of the Holy Name of Jesus in Late Medieval England, with Special Reference to the Fraternity in St. Paul's Cathedral, London, c. 1450–1558," unpublished Ph.D. thesis, University of London (Royal Holloway and Bedford College), 1999.

WORKS CITED

Primary Sources
Cambridge, Fitzwilliam Museum, MS 261
Cambridge, Trinity College, MS O.5.31
Cambridge, Trinity College, MS R.3.20
Cambridge, Trinity College, MS R.3.21
Cambridge, University Library, MS Dd.3.52
Cambridge, University Library, MS Dd.4.44
Cambridge, University Library, MS Dd.5.76
Cambridge, University Library, MS Dd.6.1
Cambridge, University Library, MS Dd.6.29
Cambridge, University Library, MS Dd.10.21
Cambridge, University Library, MS Dd.10.44
Cambridge, University Library, MS Dd.12.69
Cambridge, University Library, MS Dd.14.26
Cambridge, University Library, MS Ee.1.13
Cambridge, University Library, MS Ee.1.14
Cambridge, University Library, MS Ee.1.15
Cambridge, University Library, MS Ff.1.14
Cambridge, University Library, MS Ff.5.48
Cambridge, University Library, MS Ff.6.8
Cambridge, University Library, MS Ff.6.33
Cambridge, University Library, MS Gg.6.25
Cambridge, University Library, MS Hh.1.3
Cambridge, University Library, MS Hh.1.12
Cambridge, University Library, MS Hh.3.13
Cambridge, University Library, MS Ii.4.9
Cambridge, University Library, MS Ii.6.2
Cambridge, University Library, MS Ii.6.43
Cambridge, University Library, MS Kk.1.3
Cambridge, University Library, MS Kk.1.6
Cambridge, University Library, MS Kk.6.30

Cambridge, University Library, MS Kk.6.33
Cambridge, University Library, MS Ll.1.18
Cambridge, University Library, MS Mm.3.29
Cambridge, University Library, MS Nn.4.12
London, British Library, MS Additional 5467
London, British Library, MS Additional 16165
London, British Library, MS Additional 29729
Oxford, Bodleian Library, MS Ashmole 59
Oxford, Bodleian Library, MS Rawlinson D.913

Secondary Sources
Boffey, Julia and A.S.G. Edwards. A New Index of Middle English Verse. London: British Library, 2005.
Bühler, C. F. "Three Middle English Prose Charms from MS Harley 2389." Notes and Queries 207 (1962): 48.
Connolly, Margaret. John Shirley: Book Production and the Noble Household in Fifteenth-Century England. Aldershot, UK: Ashgate, 1998.
Downing, Janay Young. "A Critical Edition of Cambridge University Library MS Ff.5.48." PhD diss. U. of Washington, 1969; facsimile published by University Microfilms, 1980.
Downing, J. Y. "An Unpublished Weather Prognostic in Camb. Univ. MS Ff.5.48." English Language Notes 8 (1970–1971): 87.
Doyle, A. I. "A Survey of the Origins and Circulation of Theological Writings in English in the Fourteenth, Fifteenth and Early Sixteenth Centuries with Special Consideration of the Part of the Clergy Therein." Unpublished Ph.D. thesis, University of Cambridge, 1953. 2 vols.
Doyle, A. I., and M. B. Parkes, "The Production of Copies of the Canterbury Tales and the Confessio Amantis in the Early Fifteenth Century." In Medieval Scribes, Manuscripts and Libraries: Essays Presented to N. R. Ker. Ed. M. B. Parkes and A. G. Watson. London: Scolar Press, 1978. 163–210.
Förster, Max. "Beiträge zur mittelalterlichen Volkskunde VII: 10: Mittelenglische Donnerbücher." Archiv fur das Studium der Neueren Sprachen und Literaturen 128 (1912): 285–291.
Griffin, Carrie. "'A Good Reder': The Middle English Wise Book of Philosophy and Astronomy, Instruction, Publics, and Manuscripts." Unpublished Ph.D. thesis, University College Cork, 2006.
———. "'A Good Reder and a Deuout': Instruction, Reading, and Devotion in the Wise Book of Philosophy and Astronomy." Journal of the Early Book Society 10 (2007): 105-125.
Heinrich, F. Ein Mittelenglisches Medizinbuch. Halle: M. Niemeyer 1896.
Holthausen, F. "Rezepte, Segen und Zaubersprüche aus zwei Stockholmer Handschriften." Anglia 19 (1897): 75–86.

Keiser, George R. XXV. *Works of Science and Information.* Vol 10 of *A Manual of the Writings in Middle English 1050–1500.* New Haven, CT: Connecticut Academy of Arts and Sciences, 1998.

Means, Laurel. "'Ffor as Moche as Yche Man May Not Haue þe Astrolabe': Popular Middle English Variations on the Computus." *Speculum* 67 (1992): 595–623.

Mooney, Linne R. "Chaucer's Scribe." *Speculum* 81 (2006): 97–138.

———. "Diet and Bloodletting: Monthly Instructions." In *Practical and Popular Science and Medicine of Medieval England.* Ed. Lister M. Matheson. Ann Arbor, MI: Colleagues Press, 1994. 245–262.

Index of Middle English Prose Handlist 11: Manuscripts in the Library of Trinity College, Cambridge. Woodbridge: D.S. Brewer, 1995.

———. "A Middle English Text on the Seven Liberal Arts." *Speculum* 68 (1993): 1027–1052.

———. "More Manuscripts Written by a Chaucer Scribe." *Chaucer Review* 30 (1996): 401–407.

———. "Practical Didactic Works in Middle English: Edition and Analysis of the Class of Short Middle English Works Containing Useful Information." Unpublished Ph.D. thesis, University of Toronto, 1981.

Müller, Gottfried. *Aus mittelenglischen Medizintexten. Die Prosarezepte der stockholmer Miszellankodex X.90.* Kölner anglistische Arbeiten, X. Leipzig, 1929.

New, Elizabeth. "The Cult of the Holy Name of Jesus in Late Medieval England, with Special Reference to the Fraternity in St. Paul's Cathedral, London, c. 1450–1558." Unpublished Ph.D. thesis, University of London (Royal Holloway and Bedford College), 1999.

Ogden, M.S. (Ed.) *Liber de Diversis Medicinis.* EETS os 207. London: Oxford University Press, 1938.

Parkes, Malcolm B. "The Influence of the Concepts of *Ordinatio* and *Compilatio* on the Development of the Book." In *Medieval Learning and Literature: Essays Presented to R.W. Hunt.* Ed. J. J. G. Alexander and M. T. Gibson. Oxford: Clarendon Press, 1976. 115–141.

Rand, Kari Anne. *Index of Middle English Prose Handlist 18: Manuscripts in the Library of Pembroke College, Cambridge, and the Fitzwilliam Museum.* Woodbridge: D.S. Brewer, 2006.

Rand, Kari Anne. "A Previously Unnoticed Fragment of John of Burgundy's Plague Tract and Some Connected Pest Regimens." *Notes and Queries* 251 (2006): 295–297.

Stephens, George. "Extracts in Prose and Verse from an Old English Medical Manuscript, Preserved in the Royal Library at Stockholm." *Archaeologia* 30 (1843): 349–418.

Taavitsainen, Irma. *Middle English Lunaries: A Study of the Genre.* Mémoires de la
    Société Néo-philologique de Helsinki 47. Helsinki: Société
    Néophilologique, 1988.
Voigts, Linda Ehrsam. "Scientific and Medical Books." In *Book Production and
    Publishing in Britain 1375–1475.* Ed. Jeremy Griffiths and Derek
    Pearsall. Cambridge: Cambridge University Press, 1989. 345–402
    (384).

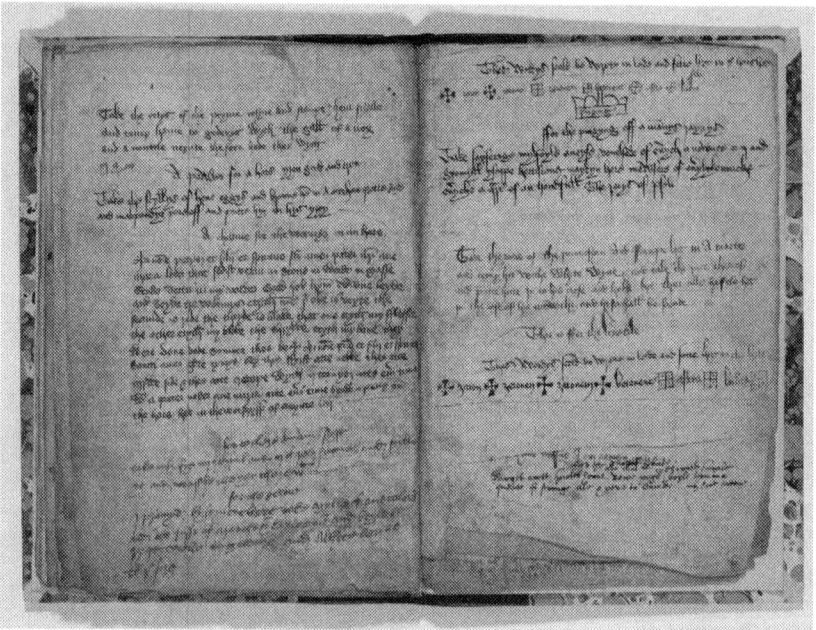

Figure 1 Four recipes and a charm for horses on the verso, with two copies of another charm for horses and three recipes, the last incomplete, on the recto, with crown (drawing). Cambridge University Library Dd.4.44 fols. 34v-35r.. Reproduced by kind permission of the Syndics of Cambridge University Library.

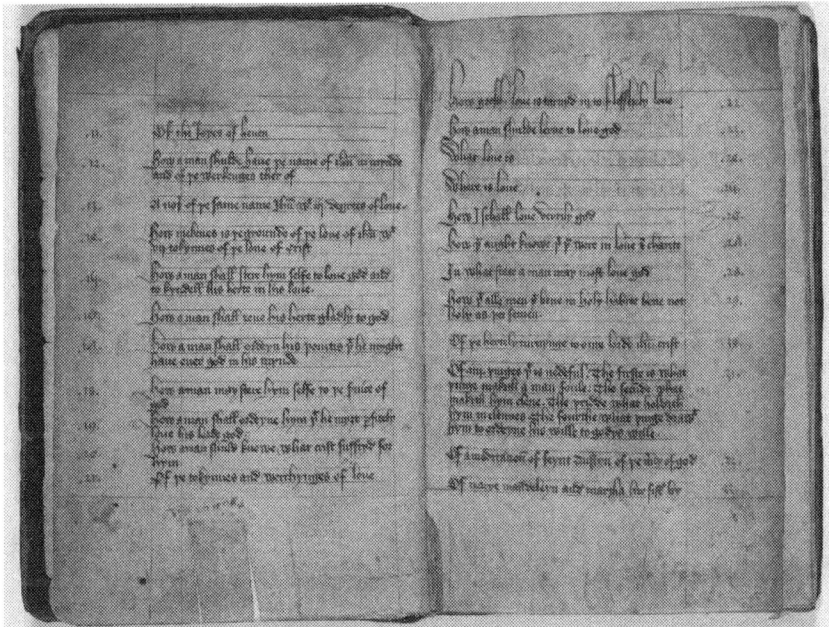

Figure 2 Part of the volume's list of contents with marginal numbers in red ink. Cambridge University Library Hh.1.12 fols. 2v–3r. Reproduced by kind permission of the Syndics of Cambridge University Library.

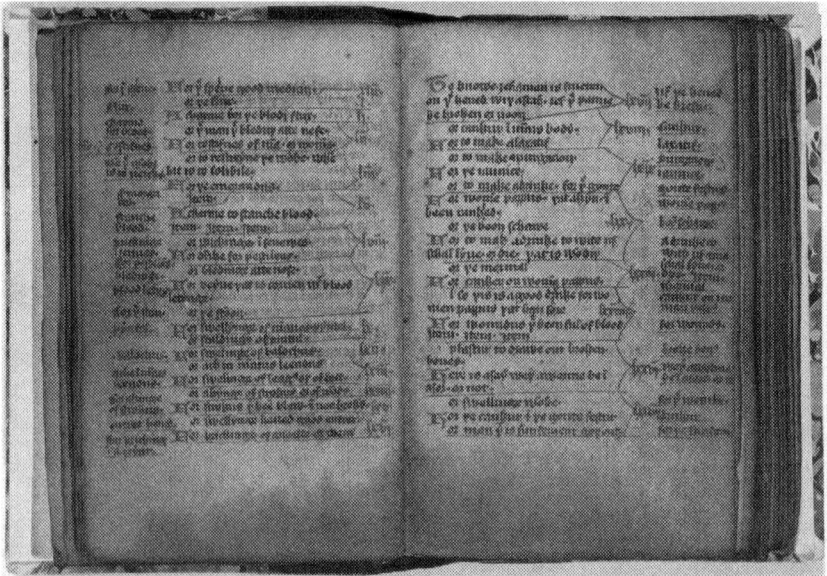

Figure 3 Part of the list of contents, with entries in red and black ink, corresponding to the collection of c. 230 recipes and charms on fols. 34r-106r. Cambridge University Library Dd.6.29 fols. 22v–23r. Reproduced by kind permission of the Syndics of Cambridge University Library.

Nota Bene: Brief Notes on Manuscripts and Early Printed Books

highlighting little-known or recently uncovered items or related issues

Profitable Devotions: Bodley MS 423, Guildhall MS 7114, and a Sixteenth-Century London Pewterer

NICOLE R. RICE

Oxford, Bodleian Library MS Bodley 423 is a much-studied fifteenth-century Middle English devotional anthology; London Guildhall MS 7114 is a relatively little-known manuscript, a guild book compiled over the fifteenth and sixteenth centuries to collect statutes, oaths, and obit provisions. These two volumes appear to have little in common, but both are linked to the London craft of pewterers: two sections of Bodley 423 came into the possession of an early-sixteenth-century member, and Guildhall 7114 has been the property of the pewterers from its donation in 1463 up to the present day. This circumstantial connection enables us to envision these two volumes as participating in complementary ways, perhaps concurrently, in the late-medieval nexis that Carole Meale has called "mercantile literary culture,"[1] offering a valuable glimpse into this culture in practice. One of the hallmarks of mercantile literary culture was an interest in religious subjects, as evidenced by merchants' frequent ownership of devotional collections.[2] In this case, I shall suggest, the religious anthology and the guild book provide complementary literary and performative techniques for living and dying in a well-regulated lay community, in which material prosperity is continuously converted into common spiritual profit.

MS Bodley 423 is today a composite of four separate manuscripts bound together in the seventeenth century.[3] Sections B and C, the only two parts that originated together and that are relevant to my discussion, were copied in the middle to late fifteenth century by a single scribe, the Carthusian monk Stephen Dodesham.[4] The physical condition of the sections shows that while B circulated for some time unbound, C was designed to be appended to B and always circulated together with it.[5] These two sections of the manuscript contain a long series of Middle English devotional works.

Some of B's contents include the long spiritual guide *Fervor amoris*, two short excerpts from the *Revelations* of St. Bridget of Sweden, five sections of the multi-tract devotional work *The Poor Caitiff*, and the Middle English translation of Aelred of Rievaulx's anchoritic rule. Section C contains as its major work the English *Ars moriendi*, followed by extracts from *Fervor amoris* and Richard Rolle's anchoritic guide the *Form of Living*.[6]

We do not know who was originally envisioned as the reader for this collection, but its contents, particularly the anchoritic rule, suggest that it may have been intended for a professed religious reader, perhaps a woman.[7] Although the book's fifteenth-century history remains obscure, an ownership note at the end of Section B indicates that by the sixteenth century the book had entered the world of the London livery companies. On folio 227r (the last leaf of Section B), a two-line ownership note reads, "Ego sum bonus puer quem deus amatt / Per me Alin Kyes Pewterarius of London."[8] Then follows another set of names, reading "Master Robertt Cuttynge master gouernor of ?SG; Peter Pungyarnard."[9] Alin Kyes is recorded as a pewterer in the guild's records: first as an apprentice in 1503 to 1504, later as a member paying quarterage in 1520 to 1521 and 1529 to 1530.[10] I have not been able to identify the other two individuals.[11] It seems likely from the primacy of his note that Kyes was at one time the owner of the manuscript; perhaps the other two were witnesses to his signature or associates who shared the use of the devotional collection.

As a second- or third-generation owner of the Bodley collection, Alin Kyes was an unanticipated reader, but this apparently pious craftsman would have been an appropriate user for the devotional volume. Its vernacular contents include several works designed for lay readers as well as professed religious (*Fervor amoris*, *The Poor Caitiff*, the English *Ars moriendi*). Moreover, some of these works overlap with those typically found in "common-profit" books, collections of devotional material whose copying was financed by the estate of a mercantile donor.[12] These books were passed on, often to fellow guild members, with the understanding that recipients would use the volumes to pray for the donor's soul.[13] As one well-known common-profit inscription reads, "This booke was made of þe goodis of John Collopp for a comyn profite, that þat persoone þat hath þis booke committid to him off þe persoone þat haþ power to committe it haue þe vse þerof þe teerme of his lijf prayng for þe soule of þe seid John."[14] Thus "profit" accrues to the dead and the living alike: as the dead receive intercessory benefits, the living receive spiritual credit for performing acts of pious reading and prayer. As I will suggest further, the Bodley collection offers a set of self-disciplinary and meditative texts that emphasize the possibility for a spiritually profitable life and death in a communal context.

Guildhall 7114, the "Jury Book" belonging to London's Worshipful Company of Pewterers,[15] suggests an institutional framework for the forms of self-regulation and prayer that the Bodley devotional collection would have made available to Alin Kyes, the sixteenth-century pewterer. The Jury Book is so called because it contains the oaths to be sworn by members at their induction into the craft. It also contains a variety of texts related to the group's regulation and practice: ordinances, obit provisions, and lists of saints' days to be observed by members.[16] The texts were copied in a variety of fifteenth- and sixteenth-century hands, and the book features a striking full-page illumination of the Virgin Mary, the pewterers' patron saint.

Despite its somewhat miscellaneous appearance and the difficulty of dating many of its texts, the Jury Book attests quite consistently to the guild's goal of making spiritual and financial profit compatible with each other and of sharing this profit among all members. The volume was presented to the pewterers by an illustrious member, Robert Chamberlayn, in 1463: the note on folio 9v describes the spiritual motives behind this gift and draws attention to the craft's religious affiliations.[17] The note reads in part, "Be hit had in mynde that Robert Chamburlayn, citezen and peuterer of London, and Ceale his wife, 3afe þis boke in to þe crafte of peuterers in the worschep of God and þe Assumpcion of Oure Lady, to be prayed fore euer perpetualli. ¶The xj day of August in the 3ere of Oure Lorde mcccclxiij."[18] The note also records the gift of decorative garlands for the guild's wardens: one garland was "garnishit with syluer and þe armes of þe craft þer on." The gifts of the book, with its sumptuous picture of the Virgin, and of this luxurious headgear, the mark of administrative distinction, enlist these markers of material prosperity in the service of common profit: intercession for Robert and Cecily, and communal devotion by all participating members.

Alin Kyes was a member of the pewterers' craft during the time that the Jury Book was being compiled and when it was likely in frequent use. Given the value that the pewterers attached to the volume[19] and given the need to employ it every time a new member was sworn in, most members were probably aware of the book, if not intimately familiar with all of its contents. Several oath formulae were copied into the book over the period of its use; these initiatory texts consistently mandate communal obedience, piety, and cooperation.[20] The formula that may have been in use during Alin Kyes' career refers summarily to the guild's regulations (covering such topics as quality control, supervision of apprentices, and sales), casting obedience to these rules as an act of devotion to the community and to God. Every member must:

be good in aberynge [enduring] and obedyent to all laufull comaundementes of the master and wardens of the felyschep of pewterars for the tyme beinge, and theire successours, master, and wardens. . . . ¶And shalbe contributor to all charges within the said crafte nowe accustomed or here to fore hath bene. ¶You shall aide and socoure the poore brotheren of the saide crafte to youre poure. ¶In all thes thynges above rehersed, and in all other that to the same crafte belonges well and truly for the welle and worschep of the same crafte, you schall behaue you and kepe you, soo God you helpe and all sayntis &c.[21]

According to the formula's logic, individual obedience to the group's leaders and "comaundementes" will produce communal "welle and worschep." Membership in the craft requires affective and financial contributions in due measure: willingness to pay "all charges," whether in money, service, or prayer.

The early sixteenth-century ordinances[22] recorded later in the Jury Book further specify cases in which individual advantage must cede to common profit. In response to certain members making "vnlaufull bargaynes . . . for their singuler profyte and aduauntage which neither regarded the honestie of the saide crafte nor . . . the highe displeasure of allmyghtye God," the ordinances prohibit such self-serving "bargaynes," making them punishable by fines to be paid "halfe to thuse of the said wardeyns and comynaltie of peauterers" and half to those wronged by the particular transactions (fol. 15r-v). The desire for "synguler profyte" has no place in the regulated world of the craft, in which common material and spiritual benefit are inseparable from each other.

In view of this sort of communal rhetoric, it seems possible to imagine the pewterer Alin Kyes using his devotional collection as a more personal set of rules within the larger context of the "laufull comaundementes of the . . . felyschep of pewterars." In the Bodley collection, common profit also comes to the fore as a central ideal in the conduct of spiritual life. The first and longest text in Bodley's section B is *Fervor amoris*, a work written at the end of the fourteenth or beginning of the fifteenth century for readers seeking guidance in "how þei schul loue God, and in what maner þei schul liue to his plesaunce for his endles goodnes."[23] *Fervor amoris*, like better-known lay guides *The Abbey of the Holy Ghost* and *The Charter of the Holy Ghost*, adapts monastic techniques of regulation, meditation, and prayer into the language of the world, promoting the virtues of active charity and the safe collective contemplation of the suffering Christ while deferring the promise of individual mystical union.

Fervor amoris is visually organized to resemble a rule, laid out in a series of chapters generally subtitled A-Z in extant manuscripts. (Most extant manuscripts contain a table of contents, which is, however, missing from the Bodley text.) *Fervor amoris* offers directives on how to love God in a regulated

and controlled way, how to resist sin, and how to orient this love of God outward toward service of neighbor rather than inward toward cultivation of mystical experience.

This lay spiritual rule encourages readers to understand love of God
as a form of productive work, always profitable to self and others if undertaken in the correct spirit. As the chapter treating "What is charite and how
and why thou shalt loue God," explains, "if þou loue God, thou wilt gladly
trauayle and suffre for the loue of God. . . . Ffor who that loueth treuly and
sadly, he loueth as wel in aduersite as in prosperite, for what God sendith vs,
it is for our profit" (fol. 130r–v). Moreover, individual spiritual progress must
always take account of "other men"; in the chapter entitled "how thou shalt
love thy neighbor," the text explains:

> Whan thou forsakist a singuler profit for the loue of thy neighbor,
> than thou louest thi neighbor. ¶Also thou louest thi neighbor as
> thiself whan thou doost him no harme, but desirest the same
> godenes and profyt gostly to him that thou desirest to thiself. (fol.
> 132v)

The concept of demonstrating love of God and neighbor through
hard work and obedience would fit quite neatly within Alin Kyes's wider urban
disciplinary milieu. Avoiding "singuler profit," the very phrase seen previously
in the pewterers' ordinances, was already a familiar goal for the sixteenth-
century craftsman. The spiritual guide complements the pewterers' concern
for collective keeping of the rules that bind them together as a craft, offering
reinforcement for the notion of worship as profit predicated on obedient participation.

Just as both the Jury Book and the devotional anthology offer strate-
gies for the joint production of spiritual and material profit during life, so they
express strongly the desire to further "common profit" after death. Some of
the first texts recorded in the Jury Book concern themselves with the proper
obituary commemoration of deceased members. These memorials, which
usually included the performance of masses and the lighting of candles on
specified days,[24] would, like prayer over a "common-profit" volume, generate
individual benefit for the deceased person while testifying to the collective
generosity and charity of the guild. In the Jury Book, some obituary notes tes-
tify quite explicitly to the interrelation of spiritual and material profit, threatening members with financial sanctions if they fail to carry out these pious
requirements. For example, the obit provisions of William Smalwood, master
of the pewterers' craft in 1469, 1477, 1481, and 1486, read as follows:

> William Smalwod citesyn and peauterer of London deceased the
> xxliJth day of May the iiiJth yere of Kyng Harry the viJth, and his

obite shalbe kepid betwixt the ffyft and xijth day of May in the
parish chirch of Saynt Mary Wolmor in Lumbardstrete of London
yerely during vj yeres next folowyng after the said ffyft day of May
the vijth yer aforesaid, by the maister, wardeynes, and craft of
peautrers of London, upon payne of forfat of an obligacon of xl.s.
(fol. 1v)

In this atmosphere of brotherly obligation seasoned with the occasional threat to collective wealth and morale, one can see the appeal, for a
member of the craft, of a text that explains the proper actions to be taken at
another member's death. Turning to section C of Bodley 423, we find one such
work, situated at the head of a series of texts treating practical and spiritual
preparation for death. This section of the manuscript is palpably concerned
with last things, including as its first and longest work the Middle English Ars
moriendi, "the boke of the crafte of dyeng" (fol. 228r). Appropriately enough for
its eventual mercantile owner, the work promotes knowledge of how to die
well as a communal skill, constructing the supervision of the dying as a "craft"
shared by religious and secular alike: "allas ther ben ful fewe, not only
amonge seculers, but also in dyuerse religiouse, that han the konnynge of this
crafte, and wyl be nye, and assiste to hem that ben in poynt of deeth" (fol.
239r–v). The final chapter gives instructions for saying communal prayers over
either a dying "religious" or a dying "secular." For the secular, "let these
prayers be sayde, as the deuocyoun and dispocioun and the profyt of hem and
other that ben aboute hem asken and requiren, and as þe tyme woll suffre"
(fol. 239r). These prayers are said in the spirit of common profit, ensuring a
spiritual benefit to be shared by the dying person and the surrounding community, whether joined together by monastic vows or by craft ordinances.
    Although the "boke of the crafte of dyeng" describes a communal
endeavor, it is striking that the compiler concludes section C of the Bodley
collection by juxtaposing an individual Passion meditation extracted from
Fervor amoris with a section taken from Rolle's Form of Living, entitled "four profitable things," the last of which is an exhortation to reflect on the joys that
await those who love God, and on the "fyre of helle" awaiting those who have
foolishly placed their "lust and lykyng of thys lyf" above love of God. The
movement outward from consideration of the Passion to concern for the fate
of souls suggests the necessity for nurturing personal spiritual ambition
within a collective disciplinary framework.
    Thus the Bodley 423 collection, though almost certainly not intended
for a mercantile audience, unfolds according to a logic that might well have
seemed useful to a sixteenth-century pewterer. By considering the fifteenth-
century devotional volume within the pewterers' system of regulation and
practice, as described in their communal volume, the Jury Book, we may be
able to imagine more comprehensively how texts combined with practice to

contribute to the accumulation of "common profit" in sixteenth-century London.

Yale University

ACKNOWLEDGMENTS

For assistance in obtaining necessary materials and permissions, I would like to thank B. J. N. Coombes, Stacey Gee, Carolyn E. Jacobs-Booker, Susanne Roberts, and Paddy Watson. Many thanks to Marlene Hennessy for reading the article in draft and to Jessica Brantley for help with paleographic questions. I also thank Caroline Barron and David Grummit for their helpful responses to my London-related research questions.

NOTES

1. Carole Meale, "The Libelle of Englysshe Polycye and Mercantile Literary Culture in Late-Medieval London," in Julia Boffey and Pamela King, eds., London and Europe in the Later Middle Ages (London: Queen Mary and Westfield College, 1995), 181–227.

2. Meale notes Bodley 423 as one example of a devotional collection owned by a member of the mercantile class; Meale, "The Libelle of English Polycye," 190–192. Also see Wendy Scase, "Reginald Pecock, John Carpenter and John Colop's 'Common-Profit' Books: Aspects of Book Ownership and Circulation in Fifteenth-Century London," Medium Aevum 61.2 (1992): 261–274.

3. See John Ayto and Alexandra Barratt, eds., Aelred of Rievaulx's "De Inclusione Inclusarum": Two English Versions, EETS OS 287 (Oxford: Oxford University Press, 1984), xix.

4. For comprehensive discussion of Dodesham's career, see A. I. Doyle, "Stephen Dodesham of Witham and Sheen," in P. R. Robinson and Rivkah Zim, eds., Of the Making of Books: Medieval Manuscripts, Their Scribes and Readers: Essays Presented to M. B. Parkes (Aldershot, UK: Scolar Press, 1997), 94–115 (103 for details on Bodley 423).

5. Ayto and Barratt, Aelred of Rievaulx's "De Inclusione Inclusarum," xx.

6. For a full description of the contents of sections B and C, see Ayto and Barratt, Aelred of Rievaulx's "De Inclusione Inclusarum," xxi–xxvi. A brief list also appears in Alexandra Barratt, ed., "The Book of Tribulation," ed. from MS Bodley 423, Middle English Texts 19 (Heidelberg: Carl Winter, 1983), 7–9.

7. See Meale, "The Libelle of English Polycye," 192; likewise, Doyle suggests that the volume may have been intended for a "devout and possibly a female reader" ("Stephen Dodesham of Witham and Sheen," 103).

8. This formula is a familiar one from schoolboys' exercise books but was not used exclusively by children. Nicholas Orme notes, "A phrase such as 'Ego sum bonus puer quem deus amat' ('I am a good boy whom God loves') may

look like a schoolboy's own attempt at expressing himself in Latin, but it occurs in several manuscripts and was evidently a well-known phrase"; Orme, "The Culture of Children in Medieval England," *Past and Present* 148 (August 1995): 76. For a similar phrase in a schoolboy's book, see Roger Bowers, Andrew Wathey, and Susan Rankin, "New Sources of English Fourteenth- and Fifteenth-Century Polyphony," *Early Music History* 3 (1983): 171, n. 52. In this case, a page from a late-fifteenth- or early-sixteenth-century school text was added as a flyleaf in a musical manuscript; this scrap contains the phrase "Ego sum bonus puer quem zelat altissimus."

9. The final name is not fully legible. There is a short prayer in another hand on fol. 228v. Ayto and Barratt imply that all three names are written by the same hand, remarking "a note of ownership and a prayer in two later (sixteenth century) hands"; Ayto and Barratt, *Aelred of Rievaulx's "De Inclusione Inclusarum,"* xx. Margaret Connolly notes, "B has references on F. 227r to Alin Kyes, a pewterer of London, Robert Cuttyng, master governor, and Peter Pungyarnar—(the last unclear)." See Margaret Connolly, ed., *Contemplations of the Dread and Love of God*, EETS OS 303 (Oxford: Oxford University Press, 1993), xvi, n. 5.

10. See the Pewterers' Audit Book I (Guildhall MS 7086), fol. 147r (a record of dues paid by William Richmond for his apprentice Alin Kyes); fol. 191r for the 1520–1521 quarterage list; fol. 215r for Alin Kyes listed among the "yongmen" paying quarterage in 1529–1530.

11. I would like to thank Caroline Barron and David Grummit for their help in the search for these two elusive individuals.

12. For example, BL MS Harley 2336, a common-profit book made from the goods of John Gamalin, contains the complete *Poor Caitiff* (Scase, "Reginald Pecock, John Carpenter and John Colop's 'Common-Profit' Books," 261).

13. As Scase notes, in the case of a devotional book, "The charity was therefore identical with the means to repay it through prayer. Every time a book was used, its purpose was being fulfilled"; ibid., 263.

14. This inscription appears in Cambridge University Library MS Ff.vi.31, fol. 100r. Transcription from Scase, "Reginald Pecock, John Carpenter and John Colop's 'Common-Profit' Books," 261.

15. The title "Company," which the Pewterers use today, was formally adopted in 1569–1570. Charles Welch notes that the older "style or title 'Craft of Pewterers' was retained (as it appears from the headings of the annual audits) until 1528–9, when it was altered to 'Craft or Mystery.' In 1546–7, the 'Mystery' usurps the place of the 'Craft,' the style being 'Master of the Mistery of the Pewterers and Wardens of the same Craft or Mystery.'" By 1611–1612, the terms "Mystery" and "Craft" had ceased to be used, and the style "Company of Pewterers" was favored. Because I am treating texts that refer to the organization as "craft," I will use that designation or the term "guild" in my discus-

sion. See Charles Welch, *History of the Worshipful Company of Pewterers of the City of London* (London: Blades, East & Blades, 1902), vol. 1, 5.

16. In a recent Guildhall guide, MS 7114 is called the "Oath bk 15th–16th cent" and is listed as containing the following categories of contents: charters, ordinances, memorandum books. See *City Livery Companies and Related Organisations: A guide to their archives in Guildhall Library* (London: Guildhall Library, 1989), 87–88. This volume, with its ornate illumination of the Virgin Mary and its injunction, appearing after the text of the oaths, to "kis the boke," is briefly mentioned in C. R. H. Cooper, "The Archives of the City of London Livery Companies and Related Organisations," *Archives* 16.72 (1984): 331.

17. As Caroline Barron notes in her study of London's parish fraternities, "every craft association in London, as elsewhere, had at its core a fraternity or religious brotherhood dedicated to the worship and promotion of a particular saint." See "The Parish Fraternities of Medieval London," in Caroline M. Barron and Christopher Harper-Bill, eds., *The Church in Pre-Reformation Society: Essays in Honour of F. R. H. Du Boulay* (Woodbridge, UK: Boydell Press, 1985), 14.

18. In my transcriptions, I have silently expanded abbreviation and modernized punctuation and capitalization.

19. An inventory of 1489–1490 indicates that the Jury Book was kept in a locked box with other precious documents. See Welch, *History of the Worshipful Company of Pewterers*, vol. 1, 69.

Caxton's Printing of Christine de Pisan's *Fayttes of Armes and of Chyualrye*

SANAE IKEDA

In 1489 William Caxton printed the *editio princeps* of *The Book of Fayttes of Armes and of Chyualrye* by Christine de Pisan (STC 7269, 2^0: $[\Pi]^2$ A-R^8 S^6), many of the copies of which contain a number of set-offs on their pages.[1] A close examination of the eleven extant copies of the edition shows that set-offs are found on more than 15 percent of the total number of pages of each copy. These set-offs[2] are not merely the accidental stains, smudges, or blots of ink that occur through printing, but rather imposed impressions, as if they have been printed as an exact copy of their respective pages. They have been transferred in reverse, like mirror images, and they are clearly legible, as shown in figures 1 to 3. The impression made by the set-offs varies in thickness from page to page and also varies in quantity from the majority of the page to only a single letter. Identifying the sources of the set-offs has been very difficult. Previous scholars who examined set-offs tried to find models in books other than the volumes in which the set-offs occurred, but through my research on Wynkyn de Worde I found that set-offs could be transferred within the same volume. This prior research enabled me to identify all of the set-offs in the *Fayttes* as coming from pages within the volume itself. Close examination of the set-offs helps to elucidate the processes of operation in Caxton's printing house, as this paper will further explain.

In the epilogue of the *Fayttes*, Caxton states that he was commissioned by King Henry VII to translate the work into English and publish it.[3]

This was two years before his death, by which time he would have had command of the art of printing through continuous experience dating back to his first printing of the *Recuyell of the Histories of Troy* in 1473 or 1474 at the press in Bruges. Although he would have been able to operate the press effectively, the *Fayttes* retains set-offs, which would normally have been entirely undesirable to printers. The fact that Caxton had important patrons and clients of such high rank as kings and nobles tells us that his press was already renowned for its mastery of printing. It seems unusual that Caxton's press presented the king with a printed book in which a considerable number of set-offs remained.

Lotte Hellinga's study of the set-offs in the Winchester Manuscript, (British Library MS Additional 59678) is one of the pioneering studies in this field and proves that the manuscript was held at Caxton's press at the time.[4] Likewise, Peter W. M. Blayney, who studied the set-offs in Elizabethan playbooks[5] and Shakespeare's First Folio,[6] has verified the first evidence of concurrent printing in Renaissance print shops. In the case of the *Fayttes*, William Blades first pointed out the existence of the set-offs without evidence and description;[7] Seymour de Ricci, in his *Census of Caxtons*,[8] and A. T. P. Byles, in the EETS edition,[9] also refer to their existence. Since the set-offs that appear on quire II in the *Fayttes*, at the first unsigned quire, are clearly visible, these scholars devoted their attention to analysis of these set-offs. Curt Bühler discusses them in connection with Caxton's bindings while objecting to Blades's idea that printed sheets went straight to the hands of the binder,[10] but he stopped short of providing a further explanation of their causes. Since then the study of set-offs remained a scarcely cultivated field.

It has not yet been satisfactorily determined how the printing press was actually operated at the time of Caxton as few practical discussions of the process of printing survive from that period. However, the set-offs that remain in the *Fayttes* are themselves evidence of the workings of Caxton's press. A detailed study of this matter will provide clues to help to clarify the nature of the printing process. Further study of the set-offs in the *Fayttes* will uncover what happened to the leaves after they were printed. In this paper, then, I analyze what the existence of set-offs shows us and discuss what new light this sheds on the continuity of the book-production process.

Examination of the Set-offs in the *Fayttes*

The present research involves first-hand analysis of eleven of the twenty-five extant copies, and analysis of an additional nine copies listed in Appendix 1 with the assistance of the libraries that own them.[11] The first task was to determine the nature of the set-offs, and the following checklist proved useful:

1. Do the letters appear in reverse, not in reverse, or upside down?
2. In what part of the page are they located?
3. From where/what page has each set-off been transferred?
4. Are the letters legible or not, and is the ink/impression thick or not?
5. Which quire set-offs remain in the book?

These questions generated answers as follows:

1. The transferred letters are not upside down but seen in reverse, as if through a looking glass.
2. Some set-offs of an entire page appear on the facing page, whereas quite a number of others are concentrated in the margins, frequently appearing in the head, foot, and outer margins. The position of a set-off is actually a major clue in determining why and how the set-off arose.
3. The set-offs all appear in the same quire. There are two possible explanations for this: (a) the first page may have been transferred to the last page in the same quire, or equally the last page may have been transferred to the first page in the same quire; (b) many of the set-off pages correspond to those on each respective facing page. The locations of set-offs provide clues about how they happened; for instance, if set-offs are caused during printing, they never appear on facing pages.
4. The letters are legible, and the set-offs in one copy commonly appear on the same page in the other copies. One other significant point in this category is that if a thick impression appears on one page, then such a thick impression is not seen on its facing page.
5. An overview of one copy as a whole shows that fewer set-offs appear in the earlier pages of the copy, but comparatively more appear in the latter pages.

Causes of Set-offs

We have an approximate idea of the process by which set-offs occur. The very first quire of the edition, quire Π, has four pages formed out of one sheet; it is the quire on which the table of contents appears and is hence the last quire to have been printed. The very simplicity of this quire renders it significant in revealing the process by which set-offs occurred. Strongly impressed set-offs arise on the facing pages Π1v and Π2r, and it can readily be imagined that this kind of set-off would occur when the paper was folded inwardly and the ink had not yet dried (fig. 3). On the outer form, the impression of Π1r was transferred onto the blank page of Π2v.

The results of the analysis of the set-offs are shown in Appendices 2 and 3. The set-offs in the *Fayttes* are divided into two groups according to the pages from which they were originally transferred. The first group is shown in Appendix 2 and includes those appearing on facing pages. Appendix 2 shows how many set-off pages are detected in each copy per total number of pages, with the percentage rate also calculated. The average for the eleven copies is 16.2 percent; if the Ox3 copy is excluded, the average works out at 16.7 percent. The second group is shown in Appendix 3 and includes set-offs derived from a distant page within the same quire, that is, where the first page of the quire is transferred to the last page of the quire, and vice versa.

The first page of quire P, P1r, for instance, is transferred to the last page of the same quire, P8v. This means that the other set of quire P was piled up on the first page of the quire P. The first page of the quire was transferred to the very last page of the same quire when the quires were piled up. This phenomenon indicates that each quire was bundled, in other words, that the same quires were put in piles together. Quire Π was no exception. This process contrasts with the practice outlined in the oldest English printing manual, Joseph Moxon's *Mechanick Exercises* (1677–1683), which says that printed papers were gathered with "all the single *Signatures* on each Sheet orderly and successively on one another."[12] Caxton, in contrast, gathered each signature separately; that is, each signature was separately piled up one at a time. This is clearly indicated by the set-offs in the *Fayttes*.

Ink and Press

Following the discovery of the set-off ink from Caxton's press in the Winchester Manuscript, Hellinga mentions that "a typographical identification would not only prove that the smudges were caused by printing ink, but would also establish *whose* printing ink caused them."[13] She correctly points out one aspect of the set-offs that occurred at the printing press.[14]

It is necessary here to focus the attention on the meaning of "dry." There is a time difference between the paper drying and the ink drying.[15] For printing incunabula and other books with movable types using a hand press, dampening the paper with water before printing was regarded at that time as an essential process. Wetting the paper in advance was necessary to facilitate the fixing of printing ink on rag paper, as Philip Gaskell indicates: "Paper had to be wetted in order to secure a good colour on the printed sheet, for there was not enough power available in the common press to force the fibres of dry rag paper to take ink evenly and fully."[16]

Printing ink, on the other hand, was usually elaborately prepared by mixing pigments such as lampblack with linseed oil.[17] Pigment particles were covered with oil; the ink slowly set through the oxidization and polymerization of the oil and was then fixed onto the filaments of the paper. The time required for ink to dry naturally varied, depending upon the kinds of oil used, its characteristics, the mix proportions, and the room temperature and humidity.[18]

Research Results

My bibliographical research leads to the following three inferences about Pisan's *Fayttes*. The first inference is that the set-offs are not those that occur through simple contact between papers. The second inference is that at Caxton's press the printed papers *were folded by quires* and *piled up not in book form* but in respective quires before the ink dried. This point contradicts Moxon's description of printed papers being gathered in book form by taking one quire each in the order of quires: "Having *Gathered, Colationed* and *Folded* these *Books*."[19] Most of the set-offs in the *Fayttes* can be identified through tracking the transference of signatures, as shown in Appendix 3. I presented the evidence for this finding at the Conference of the Early Book Society in July 2005.[20]

According to my firsthand examination of the eleven copies, all the set-off pages conform to the following regular pattern, although the printed signatures were often transferred in the following regular way. For instance, in quire A, consisting of four leaves, the signatures Ai, Aii, Aiii, and Aiiii transfer in an orderly way to signatures A8v, A1v, A2v, and A3v. As explained earlier, two groups of set-offs in the *Fayttes* were indicated: the set-offs from the facing pages and those from distant pages. These two groups of set-offs actually occurred at the same time by the folding of each quire and the piling up of those quires, which then received a strong, even force all at once. There are no other kinds of set-offs among all the examined copies. This could be due to the manner in which the set-offs occurred in the *Fayttes*. Moreover, the set-offs identified in the data of Appendix 2 involve 476 pages out of a total of 2,854 pages in ten copies (excluding Ox3, Bodleian Library Douce 180, because of the large quantity of missing pages).

These findings do not necessarily mean that Caxton caused these effects intentionally but rather suggest that they were the result of the printing process at Caxton's press; the process is revealed by the set-offs. Other editions from Caxton's press might not necessarily reveal the process because the ink dried well and so set-offs did not occur. The results of the examination suggest that printed papers were kept for a while in piles, not in book form but in one pile per quire. A concrete example exists where quire E of one book was mistakenly replaced by quire E of another book, both of which were printed by Caxton.[21]

My third inference is that some sort of force was applied to the papers at the press. It is not clear whether set-offs were caused by the weight of the paper itself or by the application of force to the papers. However, the weight of the papers alone, even large numbers of them, is unlikely to have generated legible set-offs, and most set-off letters in the *Fayttes* are clearly legible. My research analysis leads me to conclude that the printed papers of the *Fayttes* were pressed by some sort of mechanical equipment, because set-offs appear in quire Π of every one of the ten copies examined firsthand. It is possible that the papers were pressed before they were fully dry to ensure that they were flat. While there is no description of this procedure in scholarly discussions of Caxton's printing process, this conjecture is supported by the fact that the clearest set-offs appear in the margins, where the weight of the paper itself would have been lightest. Moxon describes the standing press in his manual, and the set-offs in the *Fayttes* suggest the possibility that papers were pressed by such a piece of equipment.

A more detailed explanation of the standing press will help to illustrate this possibility. As both sides of the dampened paper were printed, once the paper was fully dry, the shrinkage or wrinkles could not be completely removed. It was necessary to press the papers with an even, strong, mechanical force in order to produce a smooth surface; such a force was necessarily applied to half-dried papers. This process is described by Moxon who mentions the job of the warehouse man, who hung the papers out to dry quire by quire. After the papers were mostly dry (note that the ink would not be dry by this point), he took them down and piled them on the desk, gathering them into quires and then placing one quire on top of the other in order to complete the book. After collating them:

> he puts them into the *Standing Press*, placing in it so many *Books* as the *Press* will hold, both in width and Heighth; observing to set in every *Pile* he puts Range by Range into the *Press*, an equal number of *Books*, that each *Pile* may equally feel the force of the Screw. Then with a strong Iron Bar he turns about the *Spindle* as oft as he can, . . . and Press the Books as close and tight as he can together: and so lets them stand in Press about a Day and a Night.[22]

Though no evidence has been found as to whether Caxton owned such a standing press in his printing house, if he did, it would have been used to press the printed sheets immediately after printing, and consequently set-offs might have occurred. Even if this particular machine was not used, set-offs with such evenly pressed impressions could not have occurred without the use of some kind of mechanical force.

Binding work begins by piling up printed papers in the form of a book, but as far as I have observed, the extant set-offs are in reality, without exception, all those that occurred by heaping the printed papers quire by quire. If one were to gather paper into the form of a book, one would pile quire A onto quire Π2v. If this were the case, the set-offs of quire A1r would have been transferred to the quire Π2v. However, no such set-offs occur in the *Fayttes*, and therefore, it is highly unlikely that the papers were heaped in a form of a book. This contrasts with the earlier description of the process by Moxon.

Finally, it could be assumed that Caxton was not aware that set-offs would occur at the time of the printing of Pisan's *Fayttes* at his press. The fact that he was commissioned to print the book by the king suggests that Caxton would have liked to finish it without set-offs. My conjecture is that the surface of the ink looked as though it had already dried up; he would therefore have folded, piled up, and stacked the heaped papers after pressing them. Moxon's following description depicts one aspect of the state of printing ink at that time:

> Before the *Press-man* goes to Work, he Rubs out his *Inck*. If the *Inck* have lain long on the *Inck-block* since it was *Rubbed out*, the Superficies of it generally is dryed and hardened into a Film or Skin, wherefore the *Press-man* carefully takes this Film quite off with the *Slice* before he disturb the Body of the *Inck*:[23]

The study of printing ink may help to assess the possibility that it might have taken some days for the ink to dry. Its surface might have looked comparatively dry after printing, and it may have seemed that the ink would no longer cause a stain. As this drying out occurred only on the surface of the ink, however, if some force was applied to the impression, the ink might well have leaked, as it was not solidified when pressed. Though Caxton is regarded as having had a thorough knowledge of printing technique, this possibility provides a reasonable explanation for the set-offs found in the *Fayttes*.

Moxon's printing manual was written in 1683, nearly two hundred years after Caxton's era, but Moxon's book is the first we have to depict the workings of the printing house in some detail. In the case of Caxton's edition, it could be assumed that set-offs were attributable to the press. If printed papers were still half-wet, an even pressure would produce a fine book consisting of flat-surfaced paper. The set-off examples in figures 1 to 3 demonstrate that strong pressure might have caused legible impressions, or the standing press might have caused set-offs if the printed paper was not fully dry. There is no evidence as to whether Caxton owned or employed such a standing press. However, the extant copies of Caxton editions would be the evidence in themselves of the probability of using such a press machine. Even if this kind of machine was not used, such set-offs with evenly pressed impressions could not have occurred without the use of some kind of mechanical force. Moreover, the data from my investigation suggest that in Caxton's printing house printed materials were pressed not in a book form but in stacks consisting of identical quires. Successive quires were pressed in sequence to be set aside for collation and binding.

To conclude, the bibliographical evidence suggests the following sequence of events. At Caxton's press, papers were printed, folded by quires before the ink dried, piled up in quires, pressed by some sort of mechanical force, and then stacked in quires. It should be emphasized that the phenomenon of the set-offs in the *Fayttes* provides us with clues as to the continuity of the book production process after printing in the printing house run by Caxton. Further study is required of the processes that were employed after the actual printing of incunabula if this area is to become clearer, although the following two findings have been made: (1) a "standing press" or other similar compression device appears to have been used; (2) at Caxton's press the printed materials were pressed in bundles consisting of quires with the same signature.

Caxton supposedly implemented working processes in his printing house that included not only the work of printing on paper itself but also those processes necessary for the completed publication of books. From this viewpoint we can see that the extant set-offs give us clues as to the printing process implemented at Caxton's printing house. In combination with other studies on Caxton and his printing house to date, the examination will lead to a new understanding of his printing processes. Although the set-offs have been treated as a rather minor phenomenon in the study of incunabula, they are in fact important evidence that remains in the extant copies and should not be overlooked.

Keio University, Tokyo

ACKNOWLEDGMENTS

This essay is based on my paper, "Some Examples of Set-offs in English Incunabula: Pisan's *Fayttes of Armes* in Caxton's Printing House," read at the Ninth Biennial Conference of the Early Book Society at Queen's University, Belfast, on July 5, 2005. I am very grateful to Lotte Hellinga of the British Library for reading the original version of this paper and giving her stimulating comments and advice, and to Toshiyuki Takamiya of Keio University for encouraging me to work on this topic. John Goldfinch, British Library, inspired me during discussions. My thanks also to Jeremy Lowe for his help in checking the language of my draft. I am also indebted to the following librarians for their assistance in examining nine of the extant copies of the *Fayttes*: Julie Ramwell, John Rylands Library; Timothy James Cutts, National Library of Wales; Stephen Tabor, Huntington Library; Daniel De Simone, Library of Congress; John Bidwell, Pierpont Morgan Library; Stephen Ferguson, Princeton University Library; Robert Babcock, Yale University Library; Elisabeth Fairman, Yale University, Centre for British Art; Consuelo W. Dutschke, Columbia University; Lotte Hellinga, British Library (the former Longleat copy).

NOTES

1. For basic information on the book, see A. T. P. Byles, *The Book of Fayttes of Armes and of Chyualrye*, Early English Text Society, 189 (London: Oxford University Press, 1932, repr. New York: Kraus, 1971).

2. The OED defines "set-off" as the "transference of ink from one page to another," and as "an impression transferred" (OED, 2nd ed., vol. 15, 77). "Set-off" and "offset" have the same meaning. The transference from a back page is often called "show-through" or "see-through," according to the situation. A "show-through" is sometime used to mean that printed ink on the back page is visible through the paper. This type of set-off should not be included in the category of set-off, in order to establish an appropriate set of data. In this paper I therefore focus on the examination of set-offs after the exclusion of examples of show-through and the like. For an example to qualify as a set-off, it is required that ink or an impression is transferred from one page to another.

3. Norman F. Blake, *Caxton's Own Prose* (London: Andre Deutsch, 1973), 81–83.

4. Lotte Hellinga, "The Malory Manuscript and Caxton," in Toshiyuki Takamiya and Derek Brewer, eds., *Aspects of Malory* (Cambridge: D. S. Brewer, 1981). Also see Lotte Hellinga, *Caxton in Focus: The Beginning of Printing in England* (London: British Library, 1982), 44–47. In an e-mail correspondence, after Dr. Hellinga kindly read the draft of the present paper in November 2006, she told me that she had also arrived independently at the same conclusion as expressed in this paper; she has outlined her thinking in the final version of her draft for a forthcoming publication in volume XI of the *Catalogue of Books Printed in the XVth Century Now in the British Library*. The present paper was given in July 2005, at the EBS Conference, one and a half years earlier than my e-mail correspondence with Dr. Hellinga.

5. For concurrent perfecting, see Peter W. M. Blayney, *The Texts of "King Lear" and Their Origins*, vol. 1 (Cambridge: Cambridge University Press, 1982), 43–46.

6. William Shakespeare's First Folio (STC 22273) contains two set-offs, both of which come from André Favyn, *The Theater of Honour and Knight-hood* (STC 10717). The set-offs occurred by "concurrent perfecting" at the Jaggard printing house. For details, see Peter W. M. Blayney, *The First Folio of Shakespeare*

(Washington, DC: Folger Library, 1991), 7, and Anthony James West, *The Shakespeare First Folio: The History of the Book* (Oxford: Oxford University Press, 2001–2003), II: 186 and 197. I am grateful to Chiaki Hanabusa, Keio University, for the suggestion that inspired my research on the First Folio.

7. William Blades, *The Life and Typography of William Caxton, England's First Printer, with Evidence of His Typographical Connection with Colard Mansion, the Printer at Bruges*, 2 vols. (London, 1861–1863). Blades first mentions in his book the existence of the set-offs in quire Π, but without any evidence.

8. Seymour de Ricci, *A Census of Caxtons* (Oxford: Oxford University Press, 1909), 31–35.

9. See Byles, *The Book of Fayttes of Armes and of Chyualrye*.

10. Curt F. Bühler, "The Binding of Books Printed by William Caxton," in *Early Books and Manuscripts: Forty Years of Research* (New York: Pierpont Morgan Library, 1973), 74–80.

11. The list of the extant copies is in Appendix 1.

12. Joseph Moxon, *Mechanick Exercises on the Whole Art of Printing*, ed. Herbert Davis and Harry Carter, 2nd ed. (Began January 1, 1677, and intended to be continued monthly, then compiled and published in 1683; repr. London: Oxford University Press, 1958), 315.

13. Hellinga, "The Malory Manuscript and Caxton," 129–130.

14. Hellinga uses the word "off-set" in her article, and it has the same meaning as "set-off" in this paper. Peter Blayney, who revealed the existence of concurrent printing through the analysis of set-offs, uses the term "set-off."

15. I am indebted to James Mosley (University of Reading) for his advice on the technical aspects of early printing practices.

16. Philip Gaskell, *A New Introduction to Bibliography* (Oxford: Oxford University Press, 1972), 125.

17. The most authoritative reference to the printing ink of the time is C. H. Bloy, *A History of Printing Ink: Balls & Rollers 1440–1850* (London: Evelyn Adams & MacKay Limited, 1967). For experimental research on the time it takes for ink to dry, see Holbein Industrial Technology Ltd., *Science of Paints* (Tokyo: Chuo-Koron Art Publication, 1994) [in Japanese].

18. I am indebted to Yuko Hayashi, Tokyo Institute of Technology, for the information on printing ink.

19. Moxon, *Mechanick Exercises on the Whole Art of Printing*, 318.

20. See Acknowledgments; the program of the EBS Conference in July 2005 is available at http://www.nyu.edu/projects/EBS/ProgBelf05.pdf.

21. Among Caxton's printed editions, quire E of *Life of Our Lady*, written by J. Lydgate [Westminster,] (W. Caxton,) [1484](STC17023), held in Yale University Library, is misbound in *The Pilgremage of the Sowle* by Guillaume de Deguileville (westmestre, W. Caxton, 1483) (STC 6474), held in the Beinecke Rare Book and

Manuscript Library, Yale University. For details, see Bühler, "The Binding of Books Printed by William Caxton," 78.

22. Moxon, *Mechanick Exercises on the Whole Art of Printing*, 318.

23. Ibid., 278.

Appendix 1

List of the Original Copies Examined

Twenty-five extant copies: first eleven examined firsthand, latter nine examined by librarians on request, one mentioned in the catalogue, four unexamined.

1. BL1	British Library (IB55131)
2. BL2	British Library (G10546)
3. BL3	British Library (C.10.b.11)
4. Ox1	Bodleian Library, Oxford (S.Seld.D.13)
5. Ox2	Bodleian Library, Oxford (Douce 180)
6. Ox3	Bodleian Library, Oxford (Arch.G.d.16)
7. Q	Queen's College, Oxford (Sel. a. 113)
8. CUL	Cambridge University Library (Inc. 3. J. 1. 1 [3524])
9. Pepys	Magdalene College, Cambridge (PL 1938 [1])
10. W	Windsor Royal Library (RCIN 1057893)
11. Mei	Meisei University Library, Tokyo (MR 3841)

12. John Rylands Library (10810)

13. The National Library of Wales (IL West 89)

14. Huntington Library (59139)

15. Library of Congress (R570)

16. Pierpont Morgan Library (PML 781)

17. Princeton University Library (Kane Incunabula 1489 Christine)

18. Yale University Library (Zi +9677)

19. Yale University, Center for British Art (U101 P5 1489+)

20. Columbia University (Incunabula Goff C472)

21. The former Longleat copy, Christie's London, June 13, 2002, lot 19

Appendix 2
Set-offs in Pisan's *Fayettes*

Quire	BL1	BL2	BL3	Ox1	Ox2	Ox3	Q	CUL	Pepys	W	Mei
Π	3/4	3/4	2/2*	3/4	3/4	want-ing	3/4	3/4	3/4	3/4	3/4
A	0/16	0	0	0	0	0/10	0	0	0	0	0
B	0/16	0	0	0	0	0/16	0	0	1	0	0
C	0/16	0	0	0	0	1/16	0	0	0	1	1
D	0/16	0	0	0	0	0/16	1	0	0	0	0
E	1/16	0	0	0	0	0/16	0	1	1	1	0
F	0/16	0	0	0	1	0/12	0	1	1	1	0
G	1/16	0	0	0	0		0	0	1	2	0
H	0/16	5	1	1	0		0	0	1	2	0
I	1/16	0	0	0	0		0	0	0	1	0
K	1/16	0	0	0	0		0	2	1	0	0
L	2/16	1	1	1	0		2	0	1	5	3
M	2/16	4	7	3	3	want-ing	2	3	6	8	2
N	8/16	3	7	15	8	ing	4	12	6	4	8
O	2/16	14	9	2	4		7	5	6	3	8
P	5/16	2	6	2	1		3	7	9	5	7
Q	5/16	4	9	5	0		4	5	9	5	1
R	10/16	5	6	5	4		4	9	10	7	3
S	7/12	7/10	6/10	3/10	6/10		10/12	6/10	9/10	want-ing	8/12
Setoffs/ total pages	48/ 288	48/ 286	54/ 284	40/ 286	30/ 286	1/86	40/ 288	59/ 286	65/ 286	48/ 276	44/ 288
Setoffs (%)	16.7	16.8	19.0	14.0	10.5	1.2	13.9	20.6	22.7	17.4	15.3

Average of the eleven copies: 16.2%; average if Ox3 is excluded: 16.7%
*In BL3, the set-offs are visible on both extant pages of Π2r and Π2v, although Π1r and Π1v are facsimiles.

Appendix 3
List of Set-offs Transferred from a Distant Page

Quire			Set-offs	Total
Π	First Page	Π1r	(As the last page of this quire is a blank page, no set-off occurred on it.)	-
	Last Page	Π2v	BL1, BL2, Ox1, Ox2, Q, CUL, Pepys, W, Mei	9/10
N	First Page	N1r	CUL	1/10
	Last Page	N8v	Ox1, Ox2, CUL, W	4/10
O	First Page	O1r	BL3	1/10
	Last Page	O8v	BL2, BL3, Mei	3/10
P	First Page	P1r	Q, CUL, Pepys	3/10
	Last Page	P8v	BL1, BL3, Ox1, Pepys, Mei	5/10
Q	First Page	Q1r	BL3, Ox1, CUL	3/10
	Last Page	Q8v	BL1, BL3, Ox1, Pepys	4/10
R	First Page	R1r	(none)	0/10
	Last Page	R8v	BL1, Pepys	2/10
S	First Page	S1r	(As the last page of this quire is a blank page, no set-off occured on it.)	-
	Last Page	S6v	BL1, Q (There are only three complete copies.)	2/3

There are no set-offs signatures on the first and the last pages in quire A through quire M.

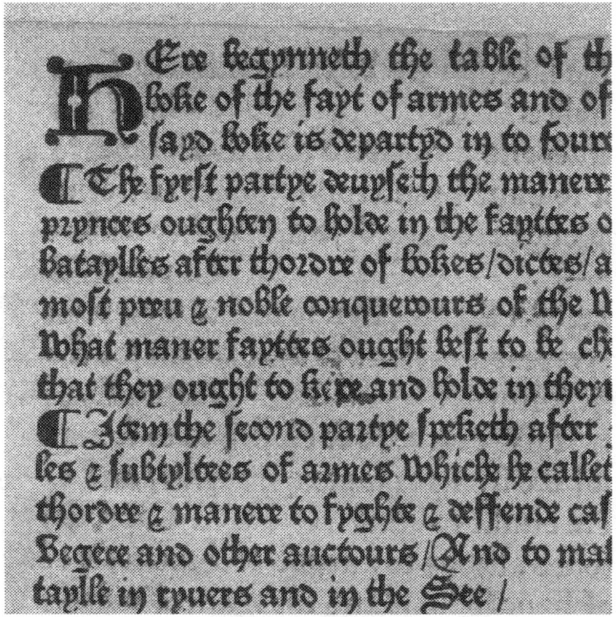

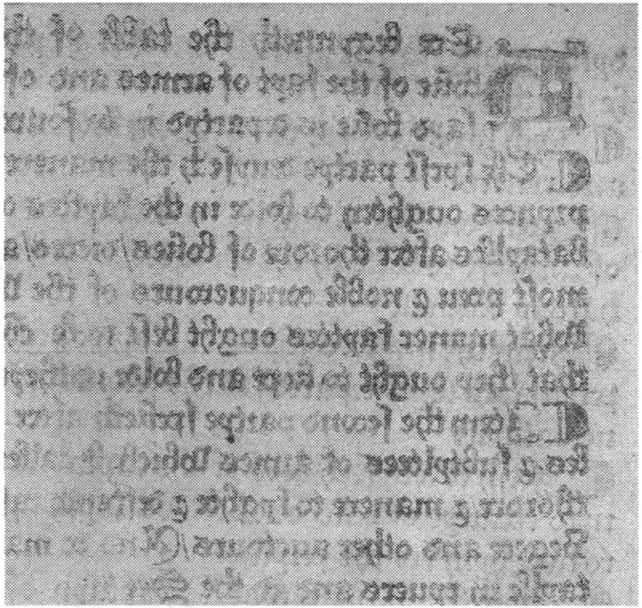

Figure 2: *The Book of Fayttes of Armes & of Chyualrye*, sig. II2v (Westminster: Caxton, 1489), British Library IB55131. The impressions of III r are transferred onto II2v, which is a blank page. Reproduced by permission of the British Library.

Figure 1: *The Book of Fayttes of Armes & of Chyualrye*, sig. II1r (Westminster: Caxton, 1489), STC 7269, British Library IB55131. Reproduced by permission of the British Library.

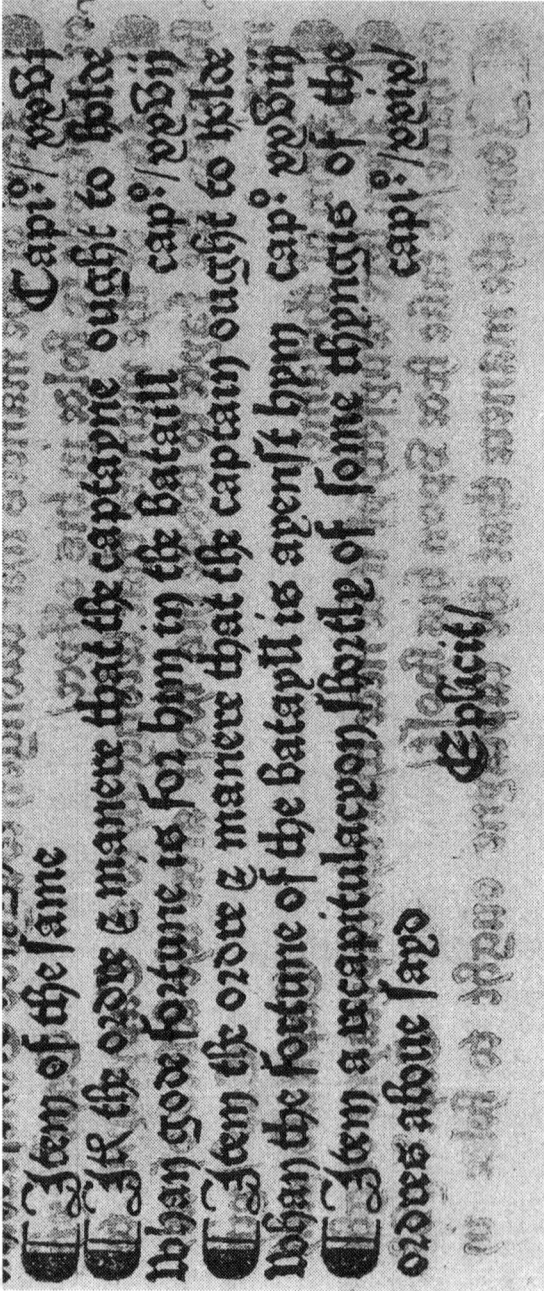

Figure 3: *The Book of Faytes of Armes & of Chyualrye*, sig. II2r (Westminster: Caxton, 1489), British Library IB55131. The impressions of II1v are transferred onto II2r. Reproduced by permission of the British Library.

Ars Imitationis: The Ellis Manuscript of Ovid's Metamorphoses and the Venice edition of 1584

STEPHANIE PRYOR

During the Middle Ages and the Renaissance, the stories and myths from Ovid's *Metamorphoses* were illustrated in the miniatures of manuscripts and books.[1] Ovid, one of the great poets of the Augustan age, wrote the *Metamorphoses* sometime before his exile to Tomi in C.E. 8. Consisting of fifteen books, Ovid's poems weave together mythological stories from the Near East, Greece and Rome. The *Metamorphoses* survived the fall of the Roman empire and the rise of Christianity to become popular in the later Middle Ages and Renaissance, especially once the moralized versions appeared in the fourteenth century.[2] These moralized versions of Ovid sought to synthesize Christian moral doctrine and the pagan stories of the *Metamorphoses*.[3] In the Renaissance, Ovid continued to be important, especially in the circle of the Lorenzo di Medici,[4] and his stories were re-allegorized, but this time in humanistic and Neo-Platonic terms.[5]

This paper explores a relatively unknown sixteenth-century manuscript of Ovid's *Metamorphoses* in the Special Collections of Ellis Library at the University of Missouri-Columbia.[6] I will refer to this manuscript as the Ellis Ovid and will discuss its relationship to a Venetian edition of the

Metamorphoses published in 1584. The edition of 1584 was illustrated by Giacomo Franco, a Venetian artist.[7] The illustrations in this printed book and those in the manuscript are nearly identical, suggesting that either Franco's frontispieces were based on the manuscript or vice versa.

The Ellis Ovid is a manuscript on paper. The text, which is in Latin,[8] is written in script characteristic of the sixteenth century (Fig. 1).[9] A decorated initial begins each book. The scribe has written the text in one column and has included catchwords at the bottom of each page. The wide spacing used for this manuscript was clearly intentional because there is an interlinear Italian translation until folio 24v. The wide spacing made the manuscript a total of 602 folios in length (or 1,204 pages). Because the manuscript was written on paper and not vellum, the patron could afford to have such wide spacing, as paper was less expensive than vellum.

Six watermarks appear in the volume. The watermark on the first leaf, which has no pagination, is (upside down) an image of Christ with a halo and the number 1399 below him. On the last page, which also has no pagination, there is a representation of a hand. These two sheets of paper are not original to the manuscript as both exhibit evidence of rebinding.[10] Four other watermarks also appear in the text block of the manuscript. While one of these watermarks is similar to watermark Briquet 3246, which was produced in Genoa in the late sixteenth century, I have been unable to find examples similar to the other three.[11]

The manuscript contains fifteen pen and ink miniatures, each of which opens a book of the manuscript (Fig. 2). Each miniature depicts the stories from that book in a composite scene. The miniatures vary in size, but generally a third of the page is given over to each one. For example, the miniature from Book One measures 14.61cm x 10.80cm and the illustration at the beginning of Book Ten is larger, measuring 15.88cm x 12.70cm. The scenes are drawn in pen and are monochromatic. The figures are labeled in Italian, making it easier for the reader to identify each scene.

Each of the miniatures illustrates the major stories from its book. Table 1 records the scenes from each book that are depicted. These composite scenes follow the text very closely, combining and condensing the stories from each book into one image. Because there are only fifteen miniatures to illustrate the fifteen books, the artist or patron had to exclude some stories from the depiction. For example, there are no scenes from the Ages of Man included in Book One's miniature. In other printed versions, such as the woodcut of 1563 in Frankfort and the engraving of 1591 in Antwerp, the Golden and Silver Ages are given their own scenes.[12]

Earlier medieval manuscripts of the *Metamorphoses* tended to depict individual scenes interspersed throughout the text or had historiated initials.[13] Many of the earliest printed books of the *Metamorphoses* followed the manuscript tradition and depicted individual scenes scattered throughout the text.[14] The Venice edition of 1584, which was a translation of the *Metamorphoses* into Italian, contains fifteen full-page frontispieces illustrating the various stories of the fifteen books. Like the Ellis manuscript, they are composite illustrations that combine the different stories from each book into one scene.

The miniatures of Book One from the Ellis Ovid and the Venetian Edition of 1584 share the same composition and scenes (Figs 2, 3). The Gigantomachy, or war of the giants, and creation are represented in the same manner. On the left side of each miniature, the giants are shown throwing large rocks at Zeus as he hurls thunderbolts at them. In the foreground, the creation by God is clearly visible, described by Ovid as "the animals of the kingdom of earth appear ... within the weed-grown swamps left by the flood."[15] The small scenes in the middle ground depict the same stories of Pyrrha and Deucalion, Apollo slaying the Python, Apollo and Daphne, Io, and Argos and Mercury in nearly an identical manner. The illustrations to Book Two in the Ellis Ovid and Venice edition of 1584 are also similar in composition and include the same scenes (Figs 4, 5). Phaethon is shown asking for permission to drive solar *quadriga* in the upper-right corner, and the Fall of Phaethon appears dramatically at the center.

These similarities continue throughout the remainder of the miniatures and frontispieces. While there are some additional details in the Venice edition of 1584, such as in Book Five where Franco's illustration includes more details of architecture and landscape, they are nonetheless strikingly similar and are clearly related (compare Figs 6 and 7).

One possible explanation for the similarities between the Ellis Ovid and the Venice edition of 1584 is that Franco saw the Ellis Ovid and drew the iconography for his engravings from the images in the manuscript. Manuscripts commonly served as models for images in printed books. However, if Franco copied the Ellis Ovid, one would expect to find the images of the Venice edition inverted, because in the process of copying an image the engraving becomes reversed. For example, later copies of Franco's plates are all inverted; compare, for example, the illustration in the 1617 Paris edition (see Figs 5, 8).

While Franco may have used the Ellis Ovid as an exemplar, he was probably not the artist of the Ellis Ovid. Stylistically the manuscript and the printed book are different. Giacomo Franco is clearly a better draughtsman than the artist of the Ellis Ovid's miniatures. For example, in Book One the lion in the right hand lower corner of the Ellis Ovid is more clumsily rendered than the one in Franco's illustration (compare Figs 2, 3). In Book One, Franco's depiction of a camel is more successful than the one drawn by the artist of the Ellis Ovid. All of this suggests that the artist of the Ellis Ovid must have copied Franco's illustrations.

The suggestion that the unknown artist of the Ellis Ovid copied Franco's illustrations and not vice versa explains a few unusual features of this manuscript. First, the Ellis Ovid's drawings are monochromatic and more reminiscent of engravings than most manuscript illustrations of the *Metamorphoses*. Second, the figures in the miniatures of the Ellis Ovid are labeled in Italian. This is noteworthy because the text of the Ellis Ovid is in Latin, so one would expect to find the illustrations captioned in the same language. The figures in the Venice edition of 1584, which was an Italian translation, are also labeled in Italian. The labels are also abbreviated in a manner similar to those in the Ellis Ovid. It seems reasonable to conclude that the artist of the Ellis Ovid copied Franco's frontispieces and that in so doing he did not bother to label the figures in Latin to correspond to the text.

Because the Ellis manuscript appears to be based on the 1584 printed Venetian edition, we have a new *terminus post quem* of 1584 for the date of the Ellis Ovid. Prior to this study, the manuscript was dated to c. 1550 based on the similarity between the Ellis Ovid's depiction of Phaethon's fall and an engraving made by Michelangelo in 1533.[16] This brief exploration shows that images could take many different paths. Although we usually assume that illustrations in manuscripts served as models for printed books, in this case, the images of a popular edition produced in Venice inspired the miniatures of the Ellis Ovid. [16] The miniatures of the Ellis Ovid show that in the early years of book production, printed images were so popular that they influenced manuscript decoration. Perhaps we can imagine, with Franco's edition having just come out and being extremely popular, some aristocrats in Northern Italy commissioning the Ellis Ovid for their son or daughter. Perhaps they hoped that a beautiful, handmade, highly-individualized edition of Ovid might encourage their child to do his or her Latin homework. If this is the case, it did not work, since the interlinear translation stops on folio 24v.

University of Missouri-Columbia

NOTES

1. I thank Anne Rudloff Stanton at the University of Missouri-Columbia for suggesting that I work on this manuscript and for being so supportive of this paper, and Norman Land (University of Missouri-Columbia) for reading a draft of this paper and providing helpful comments.
2. See Carla Lord, "Three Manuscripts of the *Ovide moralisé*," *Art Bulletin*, 57 (1975): 161-175.
3. Paule Demats, *Fabula: Trois études de mythographie antique et médiévale* (Geneva:

Droz, 1973).
4. Paul Barolsky, "As in Ovid, so in Renaissance Art," *Renaissance Quarterly*, 51 (1998): 451-474; Christopher Allen, "Ovid and Art," in Phillip Hardie, *The Cambridge Companion to Ovid* (Cambridge: Cambridge University Press, 2002), 336-367.
5. Barolsky 1998, 457-458; 452-453.
6. First published in Joan Stack, ed., *Art of the Book: Manuscripts and Early Printing 1000-1650* (Columbia, MO: University of Missouri, Board of Curators, 2003), item 27.
7. A. dell'Anguillara, trans., and Giacomo Franco, illus., *Le Metamorfosi* (Venice: B. Giunti, 1584).
8. I have not yet examined the Latin of the Ellis Ovid to determine the version of the *Metamorphoses* text.
9. Michelle P. Brown, *A Guide to Western Historical Scripts from Antiquity to 1600* (Toronto: University of Toronto Press, 1990), 126-134; Stack, *Art of the Book*, item 27.
10. This was noticed when examining the manuscript.
11. See C.M. Briquet, *Les filigranes* (Amsterdam: Paper Publications Society, 1968), vol. 3, item 3246.
12. L.M. Prindle, ed. *Mythology in Prints, Illustrations to the Metamorphoses of Ovid 1497-1824* (Burlington: the Editor, 1939), plate 1.
13. See Franco Munari, *Catalogue of the MSS of Ovid's Metamorphoses* (London: University of London Institute of Classical Studies, 1957). Munari catalogued 390 manuscripts of Ovid's *Metamorphoses* that date from the medieval through early modern periods. More recently several newly discovered manuscripts of the *Metamorphoses* have been published : see Frank Coulston, "New Manuscripts of the Medieval Interpretations of Ovid's *Metamorphoses*," *Scriptorium* 44 (1990): 272-275; Frank Coulston, "Newly Discovered Manuscripts of Ovid's *Metamorphoses* in the Libraries of Milan and Florence," *Scriptorium* 46 (1992): 285-288; Frank Coulston, "A Checklist of Newly Discovered Manuscripts of Pierre Bersuire's *Ouidius moralizatus*," *Scriptorium* 51 (1997): 164-186; Frank Coulston, "Two Newly Identified *Accessus* to Ovid's *Metamorphoses* in Oxford, Bodlean Library, MS Rawlinson B. 214, and London, British Library, MS Harley 2694," *Manuscripta* 42 (1998): 122-123. The Ellis Ovid is not included in his or any catalogue.
14. In 1889 Georges Duplessis catalogued the printed editions of the *Metamorphoses* that were illustrated between 1484 and 1619: see George Duplessis, *Essai bibliographique sur les différentes éditions de Oeuvre d'Ovide, ornées de planches publiées aux XV et XVIe siècle* (Paris: Vve L. Techener, 1889). Later in the early twentieth century, Henkel catalogued and classified the printed books of Ovid's *Metamorphoses* in M.D. Henkel, "Illustrierte Ausgaben von Ovids Metamorphosen im XV., XVI. Und XVII. Jahrhundert," *Vortäge der Bibliothek*

Warburg 6 (1926-27): 58-144. Lord provides a useful overview of printed editions of Ovid's *Metamorphoses* in Carla Lord, *Some Ovidian Themes in Italian Renaissance Art* (Ann Arbor: University Microfilms Inc., 1969), 61-83. Henkel's publication is the most comprehensive.
15. Horace Gregory, trans., *The Metamorphoses of Ovid* (New York: New American Library, 2001), 42.
16. Stack, *Art of the Book*, item 27
17. See Sandra Hindman and James Douglas Farquhar, *Pen to press : illustrated manuscripts and printed books in the first century of printing* (College Park: Art Dept., University of Maryland, 1977), pp. 104-113, for example.

Table 1: Scenes from each composite miniature of the Ellis Ovid

Book	Stories included	Stories excluded
Book 1	Creation, Gigantomachy, Pyrrha and Deucalion, Apollo and Daphne, Apollo and Python, Io, Argos, and Mercury	Ages of Man
Book 2	Phaeton, Jove and the Arcadian nymph, the Raven, Ocyrhoe, Mercury and Battus, and Jupiter and Europa	
Book 3	Cadmus, Acteon, Narcissus, Semele, Tiresias, Pentheus and Bacchus	
Book 4	Pyramus and Thisbe, the Sun and Leucothoe, Salmacis and Hermaphroditus, Ino, Metamorphosis of Cadmus, and Perseus	Mars and Venus
Book 5	Perseus's Battles, Arethusa, and Metamorphosis of the Pierides	Death of Proserpina
Book 6	Arachne and Minerva, Niobe and Latona, Marsyas, and Tereus, and Phocne and Philomela	Story of Pelops
Book 7	Jason and Medea, and Cephalus and Procis	Minos' War against Aegeus, and the Myrmidons
Book 8	Dionysus and Ariadne, Minos, Nisus, and Scylla, Daedalus, Meleager, and Baucis and Philomon	Story of Erysichthon

Book 9	Acheloüs's duel for Deianira, Some of the Labors of Hercules	Birth of Hercules, Byblis and Caunis, and Iphis and Ianthe
Book 10	Orpheus and Eurydice, Cyparissus, Jupiter and Ganymede, Venus and Adonis, Cinyras and Myrrha, Venus and Adonis, Pygmalion, and Atlanta and Hippomenes	Story of Apollo and Hyacinthus
Book 11	Death of Orpheus, Midas, Building of Troy, Peleus and Thetis, Metamorphosis of Alycone, Daedalion, and the Journey of Ceyx	Story of Sleep, and Aesacus and Hesperia
Book 12	Scenes from the beginning of the Trojan War	Death of Achilles, and Story of Caenis
Book 13	Dispute over Achilles' Arms, Fall of Troy, Aeneas, the Sacrifice of Polyxena, Hecuba's Grief, and Galatea and Polyphemus	Story of Glaucus
Book 14	Circe, Glaucus, and the Scylla, Aeneas visits Cumae, Picus and Canens, Pomona and Vertumnus, Iphis and Anaxarete, and Achaemides and Polyphemus	Conquests of Aeneas, Later Kings of Alba, and Other Kings of Italia
Book 15	Numa hears Myscelos' story, Pythagoras, Death of Numa, Cipus, Aesclepius, and Caesar	

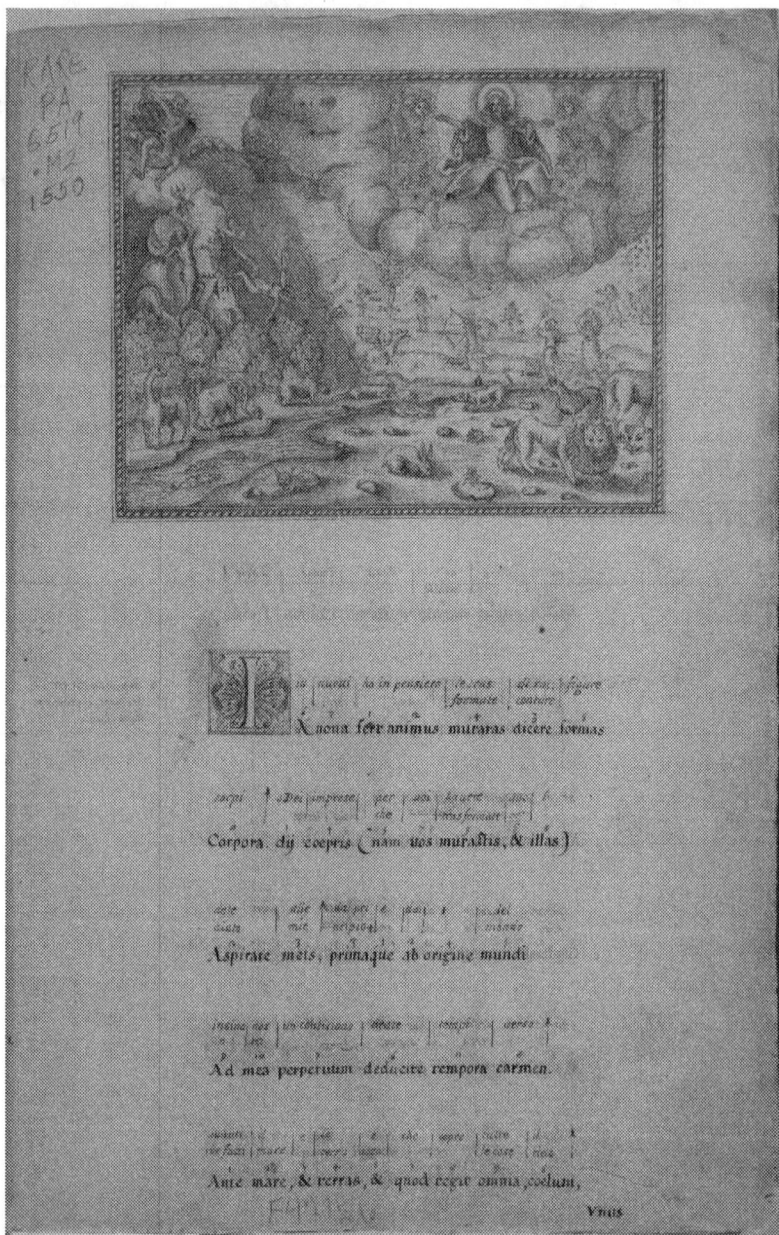

Figure 1, Ovid, *Metamorphoses*, Latin MS. Book I, fol. 1v. Courtesy of the Division of Special Collections and Rare Books, University of Missouri, Columbia.

Figure 2, Ovid, *Metamorphoses*, Latin MS. Book I, fol. 1v. Courtesy of the Division of Special Collections and Rare Books, University of Missouri, Columbia.

Figure 3, Ovid, *Metamorphoses*, Venice: 1584. Book I, frontispiece, fol. 8. Courtesy of the Division of Special Collections and Rare Books, University of Missouri, Columbia.

Figure 4, Ovid, *Metamorphoses*, Latin MS. Book II, fol. 43. Courtesy of the Division of Special Collections and Rare Books, University of Missouri, Columbia.

Figure 5, Ovid, *Metamorphoses*, Venice: 1584. Book II, fol. 28. Courtesy of the Division of Special Collections and Rare Books, University of Missouri, Columbia.

Figure 6, Ovid, *Metamorphoses*, Latin MS. Book V, fol. 164. Courtesy of the Division of Special Collections and Rare Books, University of Missouri, Columbia.

Figure 7, Ovid, *Metamorphoses*, Venice: 1584. Book V, frontispiece, fol. 154. Courtesy of the Division of Special Collections and Rare Books, University of Missouri, Columbia.

Figure 8, Ovid, *Metamorphoses*, Paris: 1617. Reproduced from Lester M. Prindle, *Mythology in Prints* (1939, plate 7).

A Note on a Hitherto Unpublished Life of St Margaret of Antioch from MS Eng. th. e 18: its Scribe and its Source

JULIANA DRESVINA

St Margaret of Antioch was one of the most popular female saints of the Middle Ages, along with St Katherine and St Mary Magdalene. Her legend was in many ways typical of an early Christian virgin martyr, including the elements of childhood conversion, a pagan suitor who persecutes the saint, gory tortures and finally death. Besides these typical elements, Margaret's story appealed to medieval Christians because it included such features as her confrontation with a hideous demonic dragon, which burst asunder after trying to swallow the saint; her violent subjection of the devil who came to tempt her in prison; and her *antemortem* prayer, in which she asked God that her devotees be blessed and especially that no disabled children be born in their households. These episodes not only captured the imagination of medieval people but became firmly established in iconography, making St Margaret one of the most frequently represented female saints between the ninth and sixteenth centuries.

The story of St Margaret was told throughout Europe both in verse and in prose, and over thirty versions — in Latin, Old and Middle English as well as in Anglo-Norman and French — circulated in medieval England.[1] Some of those texts were parts of cycles or collections, such as the *Legenda Aurea*,[2] *South English Legendary*,[3] *Gilte Legende*,[4] Osbern Bokenham's *Legendys of Hooly Wummen*[5] and the Sanctoral of the breviary.[6] Some versions existed as independent narratives. There are, for example, two Anglo-Saxon lives;[7] Lydgate's verse life of St Margaret written for Anne Mortimer, Countess of March;[8] or the poem known as *Maiden Margerete*[9] and its derivatives.[10] Although a few versions are extant in dozens of copies (such as the "G" Anglo-Norman life[11] or the one from the *South English Legendary*), most lives of St Margaret survive in one or two manuscripts, including such gems as the *Seinte Margarete* from the Katherine Group[12] and the less well-known life of the saint from the *Scottish Legendary*.[13] More unique versions of her life from lesser-known manuscripts are likely to be identified, shedding light on the development of the legend in medieval literature. The present paper describes one of them.

MS Eng. th. e. 18, in the Bodleian Library, Oxford (*olim* Phillipps 9227), is a late fifteenth-century manuscript, previously identified as containing a life of St Margaret only in *The Index of Middle English Prose* volume by Ralph Hanna.[14] It contains a unique prose life of St Margaret of Antioch in Middle English, incomplete at the beginning due to the missing leaf of the first quire. The total number of quires is three: a[8] (lacks 1), b[8] and c[4]. All of them are signed (but signatures cij and ciiij were cropped by a binder and are no longer visible). There are two catchwords, on folio 7v and on folio 15v. The text finishes on folio 19 recto, and the verso, now containing some early seventeenth-century notes, was initially blank.[15] This evidence indicates that the life was originally produced as a separate booklet. After production, however, it is very likely that this booklet was once bound up in a larger manuscript, another part of the same being MS Eng. th. e. 17 (*olim* Phillips 10106). This latter booklet contains a prose life of St Dorothy, also imperfect at the beginning, of the same size and copied by the same scribe. It consists of one quire in eight, wanting the first two folios; folios 1 and 2 (formerly 3 and 4) are both signed "+m." Its version of the St Dorothy legend is also found in another late fifteenth-century copy, Trinity College, Dublin MS 319 (fols. 2v-4v), and is known as "Dorothy 3" of the supplementary lives to the *Gilte Legende*.[16] The text of "Dorothy 3" in Eng. th. e. 17 finishes at the top of what is now folio 6v, and the rest of the page is blank,[17] thus suggesting that it also was originally produced as a booklet.

Although written by one scribe using spellings suggestive of the London metropolitan area,[18] the two lives vary slightly in their language and therefore were most likely copied from different exemplars. The dialect of MS Eng. th. e. 18 is similar (but not identical) to that of LALME Lp 4273

(Northamptonshire, Daventry, area), identified as that of Scribe D of the second part of British Library, MS Harley 1706.[19] The hand of Eng. th. e. 17 and 18 is that of the scribe who copied pages 3 to 15 of Bodleian Library, MS Douce 322 – or, perhaps even of the entire manuscript if Douce is written by a single scribe, as A. I. Doyle has suggested.[20] And to complete this circle of related manuscripts, the first part of British Library, Harley 1706 is a copy of Bodleian, Douce 322 (but Doyle doubts that Harley and Douce came from the same workshop on the grounds of the former's inferiority).[21] The linguistic profile of Douce 322 differs from that of MS Eng. th. e. 18 and from at least one part of the Harley manuscript: the dialect is of central Essex, which might suggest a metropolitan scribe. It is perhaps no coincidence that Eng. th. e. 18, copied by the Douce scribe, has linguistic parallels with the second part of Harley 1706, which, unlike its first part, apparently "never had any parallel … in Douce."[22] Even if Doyle is right in assigning Douce and Harley to two different scriptoria, the use of Douce 322 as an exemplar for copying Harley 1706 suggests some form of collaboration and mutual influence of independent workshops in London, connecting these manuscripts and the texts they contain.

The hand of Eng. th. e. 18 and Douce 322 is certainly the same: for instance, compare a page from Eng. th. e. 18, folio 18v, with the name of St Margaret in red and page 7 from the Douce manuscript, where this name also appears (see Figures 1 and 2), and the catchwords of the two manuscripts, characteristically framed in scrolls (Figures 3 and 4). The scribe of Eng. th. e. 17-18 and Douce 322 may also be the so-called "Trinity Anthologies scribe," responsible for copying most of the Trinity College, Cambridge, MSS R.3.19 and R.3.21, as argued by Linne Mooney.[23] Since the Trinity College anthologies may be connected with St Bartholomew's Priory in London, as argued by Fein,[24] it follows that Douce and Eng. th. e. 17-18 may also originate at St Bartholomew's. The difference in dialectal nuances among the three Bodleian manuscripts in question (Eng. th. e. 17, Eng. th. e. 18 and Douce 322) can be explained by the influence of their exemplars.

Another link connecting Bodleian, Douce 322, British Library, Harley 1706 and Cambridge, Trinity College R.3.21 is the penitential Middle English poems, *The Birds of Four Feathers* and *Pety Job*, which are contained in all three manuscripts.[25] It has been noticed elsewhere that both Douce 322 and Harley 1706 were in the possession of (predominantly female) members of noble families, who were closely associated with Dartford Priory and Barking Abbey, two metropolitan nunneries.[26] It has even been suggested that "the free renderings of the Nine Lessons in the vernacular" of the *Pety Job*, based on the liturgical commemoration of the dead, "could have supplied, for instance, nine days of the required readings in English during meals for nuns."[27] Although nothing in Eng. th. e. 17-18 points directly towards a monastic

owner, the inclusion of lives of female saints, especially such popular ones as
Margaret and Dorothy, points to a female audience, either nuns or pious laity.
For instance, lives of Saints Margaret and Dorothy appear together (along
with a Life of the Virgin Mary), in verse form, in Cambridge, University Library,
MS. Add. 4122, a fifteenth-century mass-produced pocket-sized book, copied
by a professional scribe for commercial purposes, apparently for a lay female
customer.[28]

Like the *Pety Job*, the Life of St Margaret in Eng. th. e. 18 was originally
divided into nine (unnumbered) chapters, preceded by short descriptive titles
in red; the beginning of the first chapter is now missing. The division could
have been used to provide the nine meal readings, as Karis Ann Crawford has
suggested for *Pety Job*,[29] but is more likely to reflect the liturgical nature of its
source(s): in most uses of England and Scotland, as well as in some continental ones, the feast of St Margaret was assigned nine lessons. Such corre-
lation with liturgical sources is not at all unusual for late-medieval
hagiography: another contemporary prose life of St Margaret, also extant in a
sole copy (in British Library, MS Harley 4012, fols 124r-130r), is a somewhat
peculiar translation of an entry for the feast of St Margaret from the Sarum
breviary.[30]

The choice of the main source for Eng. th. e. 18 is most unusual: the life
is a close translation of the Rebdorf version of *Passio Sanctae Margaritae* (BHL
5308), composed at some point between the eighth and eleventh centuries.[31]
The style and the language of Eng. th. e. 18 suggest that the translation was
executed not too long before the manuscript was produced, that is, in the fifteenth century.[32] This source is unusual in that, according to Mary Clayton
and Hugh Magennis, "[t]he Rebdorf version was not widely known or of major
literary influence in the early Middle Ages,"[33] and, one can add, in the central
and later Middle Ages either. Apart from the Rebdorf manuscript itself, the
Passio is found in nine manuscripts, all but one in Italian libraries, according
to a list prepared by the Bollandists[34] and repeated by Pietro D'Angelo.[35] One
more "ancient manuscript," once belonging to the church of Santa Maria ad
Martyres in Rome, was used by the Bollandists, along with the Rebdorf MS
itself, to prepare the *Acta Sanctorum* edition of the life.[36] A twelfth-century
Passio, British Library, MS Arundel 169 (folios 63v-67r), apparently produced in
England, can be added to the list of the extant copies of the BHL 5308. More
unidentified copies of the Rebdorf *Passio* are likely to exist in other reposito-
ries, since the Bollandists' listings are drawn mainly from libraries in Roman
Catholic countries. Overall, very little work has been done on the Rebdorf
Passio, except for the recent critical edition by D'Angelo, which does not mention the Arundel manuscript either. Such neglect is regrettable, as the text
merits "consideration as a highly thoughtful and accomplished piece of writ-

ing" with "much cultivation of rhetorical figures,"[37] especially when compared to better known and less complete versions of saints' lives.

Although one of the extant manuscripts of the Rebdorf version of the *Passio* is of English origin, the *Passio* must have had wider circulation on the continent than in England, at least by the late thirteenth century: I am not aware of any Old and Middle English or Anglo-Norman lives of St Margaret that demonstrate influence of the Rebdorf text,[38] nor do the Bollandists list any manuscripts with insular connections in their electronic Index to the BHL (although the Index is admittedly not comprehensive). It is possible that, if the version of the life of St Margaret in Eng. th. e. 18 was produced in cosmopolitan London, the source was of continental rather than English origin.

Let us now consider the relationship between MS. Eng. th. e. 18 and the Rebdorf version of *Passio Sanctae Margaritae*. Given the closeness of the translation, the missing first leaf of Eng. th. e. 18 could not possibly have contained both the *Prologus* and the beginning of the first chapter of the Rebdorf version. One leaf of Eng. th. e. 18 corresponds roughly with 2.5 sections from the Rebdorf version of the *Passio*. In the Rebdorf version, the first chapter begins at section 4 and continues to the middle of section 6, where the extant text of Eng. th. e. 18 begins (that is, on what is now its first folio); the top of folio 2r of Eng. th. e. 18 corresponds with the start of section 9 of the Rebdorf version; thus what is now folio 1r-v of Eng. th. e. 18 contains the equivalent text to sections 6 to 8 of the Rebdorf text, and the missing preceding folio would have contained the first chapter, sections 4 to 6 of the Rebdorf version. With this correspondence of text, it seems likely that the *Prologus* was not included in Eng. th. e. 18, nor probably in its source exemplar; that is, that the translation started from Chapter 1. Thus the beginning (the *Prologus*) of the "original" Rebdorf text was probably already absent from the source of Eng. th. e. 18.

To complicate matters, the final section of Eng. th. e. 18, which is chapter nine, is not taken from the Rebdorf version of the *Passio Sanctae Margaritae*, but in many ways is close to the version of the Life by Mombritius (BHL 5303), another version of St Margaret's Latin *Passio*, very popular throughout the Middle Ages and extant in over a hundred copies. The exemplar used for this last chapter of Eng. th. e. 18 must have been close to the text of BHL 5303.3, and hence British Library, MS Harley 5327, which is an eleventh-century pocket-book, again probably of English origin.[39] Compared to the historicizing and rhetorically-minded text of the Rebdorf version, the Mombritius version of the Life is more inclined to accept sensational elements such as demonic and angelic apparitions, the material presence of the dragon in Margaret's prison-cell, and the dragon's having actually swallowed the saint. The ending of the legend in the Rebdorf version is rather abrupt and unspectacular: there is, for example, no dramatic exchange between Margaret and her persecutor, Malchus, with his subsequent conversion. This version also includes no thunder or heavenly apparitions or speeches, and, even more importantly, no extended final prayer of the saint, in which Margaret catalogues all the good things she asks of God to grant to those who worship her, build a church in her name or copy or read her life. These good effects she prayed God to grant, especially that no disabled child be born in a house where St Margaret's name is called upon, were precisely those elements that made both the saint and her story so popular. These elements are all present in both the Mombritius version and in the last chapter of the version in Eng. th. e. 18.

Eng. th. e. 18, however, does not include the post-mortem section of the story, in which details of Margaret's burial are given, and the first-person address, identifying Theotimus as the author of the legend, is not recited. Instead it provides a concluding remark in the first person (but without a name), urging the audience to commemorate the saint and to worship God, only loosely corresponding to the latter's ending and ignoring the Mombritius version's point about the Last Judgement of Christ, concentrating instead on His "ioye and glory."

It is difficult to say whether these changes to the ending were already present in Eng. th. e 18's source (although none of the extant manuscripts of the *Passio* conforms to this pattern), or whether its author used several texts to compile his version of the legend. That neither the beginning nor the end of the original Rebdorf version are reflected in the Eng. th. e. 18 copy may argue in favor of the former: if the author of the English translation used a Latin text in booklet format, it is possible that the first and the last pages of the exemplar were damaged so he had to omit the *Prologus* and find another source for the ending. On the other hand, he could have found the unsensational ending of the Rebdorf version rather disappointing and replaced it with a more exciting and familiar ending of the saint's life — but that might already have been done by the copyist of his exemplar. The slight muddle concerning who exactly spoke to Margaret after her final prayer (Eng. th. e. 18 first names "an aungell with a crosse," but later turns him into a dove, "a coluer") suggests that the ending was changed by the scribe of Eng. th. e. 18 or by his translator source since this inconsistency is one of very few in the otherwise very high-quality composition.

As previously stated, the Rebdorf version of the *Passio Sanctae Margaritae* had almost no circulation in England, and, to the best of my present knowledge, was not utilized in breviaries of even very local, obscure use. The only known insular copy, British Library, Arundel 169, in some respects is similar to Eng. th. e. 18: it omits the *Prologus* and contains some material absent from the Bollandists' edition; on a number of occasions its wording is closer to that of the English version.[40] There are, at the same time, significant differences:

Arundel 169 is not divided into sections; it retains the "proper" Rebdorf ending; and it contains at least one passage not found in Eng. th. e. 18. This does not make Arundel 169 a viable possibility as an immediate source for Eng. th. e. 18. Instead, its source is very likely continental, although a possibility of an English copy, even a derivative of the Arundel version, cannot be ruled out altogether.

No established continental uses, e.g., Roman or Parisian, include St Margaret's day as a major feast, and therefore it is not ascribed as many as nine readings; however, many local uses do, as seen from existing pre-Trent missals and breviaries, some of which could have used the Rebdorf version as a source. The abundance of the uses and the scarcity of the extant evidence have made it difficult so far to establish the exact source-text for Eng. th. e. 18's life of St Margaret. Exemplars from France and Flanders appear to be most plausible candidates, not only due to their geographical proximity and close contacts with England in this period, but also because Latin lives of French origin sometimes compare St Margaret with Rachel: she humbly tended her nurse's sheep, just like Rachel did those of her father. This comparison is present in the Rebdorf version (and hence in Eng. th. e. 18) as well as the Paris version of St Margaret's *Passio*, more popular on the continent (especially in France) than the former, but is not made in any lives of Margaret of English origin.[41] If it is assumed that the translation to English was made shortly before the making of Eng. th. e. 18, there is a chance that the source originated in Italy, given the fair number of the manuscripts of the *Passio* in Italian libraries, datable from the eleventh to the early seventeenth centuries. On the other hand, at the moment it is not possible to establish the provenance of those manuscripts, and their location in Italian libraries does not necessarily prove Italian origin; besides, the intensification of cultural contacts between England and Italy in the late fifteenth century concerned mostly humanistic texts, although some examples of Italian hagiographic production for the English market are also known.[42]

Although the life of St Margaret in Eng. th. e. 18 does not repeat Latin syntax and demonstrates significant freedom in rendering of the original text, it was most probably translated directly from Latin and not from an earlier vernacular translation originating on the continent. The English version neither digresses from its source nor follows it slavishly. There are hardly any calques (only once *"inter manus"* is rendered rather awkwardly as "betwene the handys," fol. 3r) or obvious mistakes (on one occasion a quotation is missing, but it is not noticeable without looking into the corresponding text, and besides, the passage could have been already absent from the exemplar[43]).

The translator's additions are usually insignificant and designed to expand or emphasize points made in the original. Sometimes the translator shows off his competence in the Scriptures (unless these additions derived from his Latin original): when the Rebdorf version of Passio *Sanctae Margaritae* quotes as God's own words Psalm 90:13, "*Super aspidem & basiliscum ambulabis, & conculcabis leonem & draconem*" (col. 38A), Eng. th.e. 18 specifies, "thow seydest sometyme by the mouthe of the prophete dauid" (fol. 11v), and, later still, while referring to the three youths in the fiery furnace, Eng. th. e. 18 specifies, "somtyme in danyell dayes" (fol. 15r). Many versions of the life of St Margaret contain allusions and paraphrases of the Old and New Testaments, mostly of Psalms, but only the Rebdorf version and Eng. th. e. 18, as well as containing references to the Scriptures, mark these as quotations – perhaps with an intention to educate their audience.

The translator of Eng. th. e. 18 seems to be less gender-biased than the source text, tending instead to the other extreme: when Margaret is frightened by the approaching prefect and his men, the Rebdorf version says it is because of her "*femineæ fragilitatis*," which Eng. th. e. 18 translates, more neutrally, as "her oune freelte" (fol. 2v). On other occasions, "*viri*" used usually in the sense of "men" are often rendered more inclusively as "peple," "folke," or even "men and wemen." Such extended interpretation could have been conditioned by the intended audience of this particular text, predominantly female, or by the general tendency of the later Middle Ages to include women in their role as potential recipients of devotional literature as an influential group.

Although the literary merits of Eng. th. e. 18 derive mostly from its source, it nevertheless managed to reproduce in English that rhetorical sophistication, well-balanced composition and stylistic sobriety which makes the Rebdorf version stand out from other contemporary *Passiones*. The heated debates between St Margaret and her persecutor Olibrius, full of rhetorical subtleties, lie at the heart of both texts —gruesome tortures, divine and demonic apparitions, and spectacular conversions are secondary in significance. Perhaps on this occasion alone Margaret bests her match: soliloquies of the saint take one third of the life, those of her persecutor only fifteen percent. Olibrius is often less persuasive than Margaret, which makes her victory so impressive: his final argument is violence; his command to kill the invincible opponent is a silent acknowledgement of his own defeat in the verbal battle.

Eng. th. e. 18 was carefully proofread and corrected by the same scribe who copied it out, and then the manuscript was later annotated in the margins by a sixteenth-century hand, repeating those words of the main text that were smeared and hardly legible, which suggests that the life continued to be read at least several decades from the date of its production. It fits well into what we know of metropolitan professional book-production and its repertoire, and the unusual choice of the source — possibly of continental origin – may also be a consequence of its metropolitan making. The mixture of dialects in Eng. th. e. 18, its booklet form, as well as the existence of another manuscript containing "Dorothy 3" in addition to Eng. th. e. 17, suggest that Eng. th. e. 18 was not the only copy of that particular version of the life of St Margaret, and one would hope that such a quality literary production achieved wider dissemination.

Magdalene College, Cambridge

NOTES

1. See Charlotte D'Evelyn and Frances A. Foster, "Saints' Legends," in A *Manual of the Writings in Middle English*, gen. ed. J. Burke Severs, vol. II (New Haven: Connecticut Academy of Arts and Sciences, 1970), 410-439, 606-608. For a more up-to-date overview of the lives of St Margaret, see in my forthcoming thesis at the University of Cambridge: *The Cult of St Margaret of Antioch in Medieval England*.
2. Iacopo da Varazze, *Legenda Aurea*. Edizione critica a cura di Giovanni Paolo Maggioni, Seconda Edizione Revisita dall'Autore (Firenze: SISMEL, 1998), 616-220.
3. Charlotte D'Evelyn and Anna J. Mill, eds., *The South English Legendary*, EETS, o.s. 235 (London; Oxford University Press, 1956), 293-302.
4. Richard Hamer, ed., with Vida Russe, *Gilte Legende*, EETS, o.s. 327 (Oxford: Oxford University Press, 2006), 461-464.
5. Mary S. Serjeantson, ed., *Legendys of Hooly Wummen*, EETS, o.s. 206 (London: Oxford University Press 1938), 1-38.
6. F. Procter and Ch. Wordsworth, eds., *Breviarium ad Usum Insignis Ecclesiae Sarum* (Cambridge: C. J. Clay & Sons, 1886), vol. 2, cols. 502-506; S. W. Lawley, ed., *Breviarium ad Usum Insignis Ecclesiae Eboracensis* (Durham: Surtees Society, vol. LXXV, 1883), vol. 2, cols. 392-395; Walter Howard Frere and Langton E.G. Brown, eds., *The Hereford Breviary*, Henry Bradshaw Society, 40 (London: Harrison & Sons, 1911), vol. 2, 249-252.
7. M. Clayton and H. Magennis, eds., *The Old English Lives of St Margaret* (Cambridge: Cambridge University Press, 1994), 112-139, 152-171.
8. Sherry L. Reames, ed., with Martha G. Blalock and Wendy R. Larson, *Middle English Legends of Women Saints* (Kalamazoo, Michigan: TEAMS, 2003), 147-162.
9. The title is given to the poem by one of its editors, Oswald Cockayne, in *Seinte Marherete: the meiden ant martyr*, EETS, o.s. 13 (London: Oxford University Press, 1866), 34.
10. See Karl Reichl, *Religiöse Dichtung im Englischen Hochmittelalter* (München: Fink, 1973), 163-249.
11. See Birgitte Cazelles, *The Lady as Saint* (Philadelphia: University of Pennsylvania Press, 1991), 216-237.

12. Bella Millett and Jocelyn Wogan-Brown, eds., *Medieval English Prose for Women* (Oxford: Clarendon, 1990), 44-85.

13. Carl Horstmann, ed., *Altenglische Legenden, Neue Folge* (Heilbronn: Henninger, 1881), 3-12.

14. Ralph Hanna III, *The Index of Middle English Prose, Handlist* XI: *Smaller Bodleian Collections* (Cambridge: D.S. Brewer, 1997), 12.

15. See the notes on folio 19v: "James by the grace of god kinge of England Scotland france and Ireland defender of true faith and apostilere"; "Loue and wine in this agre:/ the elder better still the[r] bee;/so is our longe sute if it bee true/ change not a ould loue for a new"; and further, more appropriately, the following incomplete verse: "When god mad all hee made all good/ So woman was if she had stood/ Though woman was the cause of fall/ Yet Jesus christ mad amends for all/ When... all hee not."

16. Richard Hamer and Vida Russel, eds. *Supplementary Lives in Some Manuscripts of the Gilte Legende*, EETS, o.s. 315 (Oxford: Oxford University Press, 2000), xxiv, 243-249. This version is derived from a very similar life, extant in several manuscripts. See Hanna, *Index*, 12.

17. There is, however, a later pencil sketch of a bust of a man in distinctively Renaissance attire, enigmatically signed "Michael Angelo."

18. Ralph Hanna, "Middle English Books and Middle English Literary History," *Modern Philology* 102.2 (November 2004): 176-8.

19. Angus McIntosh, M. L. Samuels and Michael Benskin, eds., *A Linguistic Atlas of Late Medieval English. Volume Three: Linguistic Profiles* (Aberdeen: Aberdeen University Press, 1986), 378-9, Grid 454 261.

20. A. I. Doyle, "Books Connected with the Vere Family and Barking Abbey," *Transactions of the Essex Archaeological Society*, n.s. 25 (1958): 223.

21. *Ibid.*, 229.

22. *Ibid.*, 223.

23. Linne R. Mooney, "Scribes and Booklets of Trinity College, Cambridge, MSS R.3.19 and R.3.21," in *Middle English Poetry: Texts and Traditions: Essays in Honour of Derek Pearsall*, ed. by Alistair Minnis (Woodbridge, Suffolk: Boydell & Brewer, 2001), 241-66.

24. Susanna Greer Fein, ed., *Moral Love Songs and Laments* (Kalamazoo, Michigan: Medieval Institute Publications, 1998), 290.

25. See "The Birds with Four Feathers" and "Pety Job," in Fein, *Moral Love Songs and Laments*, 255-307. These are the only two texts in Trinity R.3.21 that are not copied by the main scribe of the manuscript, but by the so-called "Hammond Scribe"; see Mooney, "Scribes and Booklets," 241.

26. Doyle, "Books Connected with the Vere Family," 228, 232; Karis Ann Crawford, *The Middle English Pety Job: A Critical Edition with a Study of Its Place in Late Medieval Religious Literature* (unpublished Ph.D. Thesis, University of Toronto, 1977), cited in Fein, "Petty Job," 296.

27. Crawford, The Middle English Pety Job, 107-8, quoted in Fein, "Petty Job," 296.

28. Reichl, Religiöse Dichtung, 165.

29. See note 27.

30. For more information on the Life of St Margaret from MS Harley 4012 see my research into the Cult of St Margaret in Medieval England (PhD dissertation at the University of Cambridge, forthcoming).

31. Acta Sanctorum, Ed. novissima, curante J. Carnandet, et al. (Parisiis, 1863-75), Iulius, V, 33-39 (hereafter AASS); Bibliotheca hagiographica Latina, antiquae et mediae aetati (Bruxelles, Société des Bollandistes, 1898-99), no. 5308, vol. 1, 788. Terminus a quo is not possible to establish without seeing the original manuscript, presumably still in the library of the Augustinian monastery at Rebdorf, Bavaria; terminus ad quem is deduced from the date of the two second-earliest manuscripts, Biblioteca Apostolica Vaticana, Vat. Lat. 1195, fols 25r-31r, dated to 1075-1100 (M.-H. Laurent, Codices Vaticani Latini: Codices 1135-1266 ([Città del Vaticano]: Bybliotheca Vaticana, MCMLVIII), 104-105) and Biblioteca Neapolitana, Codex VIII. B. 3, fols. 291r-298v, dated the eleventh century (Albertus Poncelet, Catalogus codicum hagiographicorum Latinorum bibliothecarum Neapolitanarum, Analecta Bollandiana, 30 (Bruxelles, 1911), 154-156. The Vatican manuscript also contains St Jerome's Life of St Paul the Hermit, which the Rebdorf text refers to. Recently the Passio was tentatively ascribed to Peter, Subdeacon of Naples, a tenth-century hagiographer who translated several Greek lives into Latin (Pietro Suddiacono Napoletano L'opera agiografica, ed. Edoardo D'Angelo [Firenze: SISMEL, 2002], LXI-II, 239-242). For more information concerning the Rebdorf manuscript's literary qualities, see Mary Clayton and Hugh Magennis, The Old English Lives of St Margaret, 19-21, and Theodor Wolpers, Die englische Heiligenlegende des Mittelalters (Tübingen: Niemeyer, 1964), 101-106.

32. There are no distinctively archaic or dialectal forms that would facilitate more precise dating.

33. Clayton and Magennis, The Old English Lives of St Margaret, 9.

34. See the Bollandists' online index to their Bibliotheca Hagiographica Latina at <http://bhlms.fltr.ucl.ac.be >.

35. D'Angelo, Suddiacono Napoletano L'opera agiografica, 239. The only manuscript outside Italy in D'Angelo's or the Bollandists' lists is a twelfth-century copy in the Cape Town, South African Library, Grey Collection 48b4.

36. AASS, 33.

37. Clayton and Magennis, The Old English Lives of St Margaret, 20-21.

38. This conclusion is based on my research for my PhD dissertation.

39. Published by Bruno Assmann in his Angelsächsische Homilien und Heiligenleben (Kassel: Wigand, 1889), 208-20.

40. For example, on one occasion when AASS simply says "Margareta," Arundel 169 has "famula Christi" and Eng. th. e. 18 has "Crystes servaunt"; when

AASS says, *"quia terra et pulvis sumus,"* Arundel 169 has *"quia terra et pulvis sum,"* and Eng. th. e. 18 says, "for I am both erthe and duste."

41. The Paris version is not published in full. Excerpts can be found in Ingelore Orywall, *Die Alt- und Mittelfranzözischen Prosafassungen der Margaretenlegende* (Bonn, [no publisher], 1968), SS. 182-187. Reference to Margaret as Rachel begins a verse entry for St Margaret in a fifteenth-century chant-book, made for Dominican nuns in Poissy (Fitzwilliam Museum, MS McClean 63, fol. 192v).

42. On Anglo-Italian literary contacts in the late fifteenth century, see Lotte Hellinga and J. B. Trapp, eds., *The Cambridge History of the Book in Britain*, vol. III (1400-1557) (Cambridge: Cambridge University Press, 1999), chs. 2-5, 14-15: 47-147, 285-353; for an example of Italian hagiography in England, see a verse life of St Katherine in Latin dedicated by the Italian Pietro Carmeliano to Richard III (Richard's own copy does not survive; two others that do are Gonville and Caius College, Cambridge, MS 196/102 and Bodleian Library MS Laud. Misc. 501; see Anne F. Sutton and Livia Visser-Fuchs, "Richard III's Books XIV," *The Ricardian* 10:132 (March 1996): 346-386.

43. Eng. th. e. 18 says, "hys verrey dwellyng place ys in heuene and beholdeth all meke in herte as the prophete seyth" (fol. 8v). Compare the Rebdorf reading: *"quia in cælis habitat, & humilia respicit, atque secundum prophetam: Cælum illi sedes, terra autem scabellum pedum ejus"* (AASS, 37). The quotation is from Isaiah 66:1.

Lives of Sts Dorothy and Margaret (fragments), fifteenth century. Oxford, Bodleian Library, MS Eng. th. e. 18, fol. 18v. By permission of the Bodleian Library, Oxford.

Middle English Miscellany, fifteenth century. Oxford, Bodleian Library, MS Douce 322, page 7. By permission of the Bodleian Library, Oxford.

Lives of Sts Dorothy and Margaret (fragments), fifteenth century.
Oxford, BodleianLibrary, MS Eng. th. e. 18, fol. 7v (detail). By permission of the Bodleian Library, Oxford.

Middle English Miscellany, fifteenth century. Oxford, Bodleian
Library, MS Douce 322, fol. 33v (detail). By permission of the
Bodleian Library, Oxford.

Descriptive Reviews

Catalogue of Books Printed in the XVth Century now in the British
Library, BMC: Part XI: England.
The Netherlands: Hes & de Graaf, 2007.
Folio. x + 507 pp. + 89 plates (4 in color), 4 maps.

The *Catalogue of Books Printed in the XVth Century now in the British Museum* (BMC) began life in 1908. The present volume (Part XI) represents the culmination of nearly a century's scholarship during which the British Museum ceased to act as depository for books, manuscripts, and incunabula, and the British Library was born (1973). Parts I-X, XII, and XIII are already published, the latter (Hebrew incunabula) most recently, in 2004, by Hes & De Graaf of the Netherlands. The same publishers have now produced the long-awaited Part XI (English incunabula).

No editors are credited on the title page, but it is universally acknowledged that the major credit for this superb work must be given to Lotte Hellinga, with the seconded help from 1976 to 1984 of Paul Needham (then of the Pierpont Morgan Library, New York). Other colleagues, Margaret Nickson and Mirjam Foot, were also involved at this stage. It says much – more than should perhaps be said here – that after 1984 the work was put on hold until Lotte Hellinga's retirement in 1995 and the awarding of the Leverhulme grant which gave her the assistance of Caroline Cole and Lucy Lewis from 1996 to 1997. John Goldfinch, now in charge of incunabula at the British Library, contributed in enabling the work to come to fruition in 2006. During the period of gestation, publications by Needham and Hellinga have provided advance knowledge of the numerous new findings which are now available in this volume. I would personally single out, as invaluable to my own work, their respective *The Printer and the Pardoner* (Washington: Library of Congress, 1986) and "Tradition and Renewal: Establishing the Chronology of Wynkyn de Worde's Early Work," in *Incunabula and their* Readers (reviewed JEBS 7, 2004).

The introduction to the folio volume, which is simply bound and end-papered in dark green, covers eighty-four pages and is credited to Hellinga. It begins with an introduction to the series and the format of the entry descriptions and moves on through sections on "The Printers" (on whom, see Descriptions below); "Methods of Production" (a model of clarity and comprehensiveness); "Survival and Bibliometry" (with fascinating statistics, which, to take one of many possible examples, allow one to compare Caxton's devotional output of 35% with de Worde's of 47% and Pynson's of 17%);

"Books in English" (principally by Caxton, de Worde, and Pynson); "Books in Latin" and "Law French"; "Patronage and Commercial Independence"; and "Early Owners." It is impossible to stress the value of this material, which synthesizes, consolidates, and appraises the state of knowledge and scholarship in relation to these aspects of incunable printing. "The Formation of the Collection of English Incunabula in the British Library (formerly the British Museum) 1753-2006," by Margaret Nickson, John Goldfinch, and Lotte Hellinga, explains the incunable holdings of Sir Hans Sloane, the Old Royal Library, King George III's Library, the Grenville Library, and others. It is instructive to note the roughly equivalent number of English incunabula acquired from 1848 to 1900 with those acquired from 1900 to 2006 (in both cases between forty and fifty items). For a variety of reasons, only ten of these have been acquired since 1973, although it is heartening to note that four were acquired within the last few years.

The entries proper are preceded by chronologies, which list chronologically, in tabular format, the date, BMC number, Duff number, titles, as well as types, paper stocks, and other technical aspects, of the editions. The lack of a BMC XI number indicates that the British Library does not possess the edition and prepares the scholar for the absence of an entry. In all 323 copies of books are described in the *Catalogue* (221 editions) out of a total of 395 known to exist. Of course, the British Library cannot have everything (or everything printed in England between 1476 and 1500, anyway), but the entries themselves are so thorough and indeed indispensable (scholars will soon wonder how they ever managed without them) that these comparatively rare absences inevitably disappoint the scholar searching for the quick and authoritative description of an edition or print.

The entries ("Descriptions") deal with 323 copies of books (221 editions) by the English printers of this period: at Westminster, Caxton and de Worde; at London and Westminster, Julian Notary and associates; at Oxford, "printer of Rufinus," Theodoricus Rood, "printer of Mirk"; at London, Johannes Lettou (singly), with William Machlinia, and Machlinia (singly); at London or Westminster, "printer of Caorsin"; at London, Richard Pynson; at St Albans, "press of St Albans"; and at Paris (in an appendix), Guillaume Maynyal for Caxton. Each entry provides author, title, date; transcriptions of incipits, explicits, and colophons (most usefully, these are lengthier than in previous volumes); a bibliographical summary, including woodcut details; copy notes, on early owners, provenance, and bindings (by Margaret Nickson and Mirjam Foot); the pressmark (for an explanation of which, pages 4 to 5 are useful). The bibliographical summary departs from earlier practice in including a note that explains the dating of undated editions; an analysis of the contents; references to works such as the *Index of Middle English Verse*, the *Index of Printed Middle English Prose*, and the *Manual of the Writings in Middle English*, in order to link the edition with secondary literature; notes on the production of the book and on the woodcuts.

A few comments must suffice here in relation to my own use of the volume in recent research. The "Index of Authors and Anonymous Texts, Translators, Patrons, Dedicatees, and Printers" (undoubtedly comprehensive) must be searched first for the bold entries which indicate the pages where entries can be found. To take one example, the entries on the *Golden Legend*, printed by Caxton in 1483 and 1484 and by de Worde in 1493 and 1498/9, cover pages 144 to 149, 184 to 186, and 220 to 221. The first edition had two issues, and the British Library copy is a mixture of the two, as is usual. The difference in the contents of both issues is explained in the course of the lengthy description of the 1483-4 edition (pages 144 to 149), which is followed by a listing of each separate item in the BL copy. The entries for the next two editions (pages 184 to 186 and 220 to 221), where the Bible stories have been removed and other changes made, can then document any differences in content (as well, of course, as paper stock, quiring, etc.) in relation to the first entry. The first entry also records the state of scholarship in relation to the *Golden Legend* (immensely useful for anyone coming to a text for the first time) and exhaustive information on the technicalities of the edition.

It is hard to over-emphasize how valuable the contents material is. I have over the years spent some time attempting to come to grips with the different versions and contents of the printed *Golden Legend*, here laid out before me. At the time of publication of BMC XI, I was planning a visit to Lincoln in an attempt to make sense of the second issue of 1487 (as STC had described it). I am now reassured of the status and contents of that version and have no need to make the visit, and my old pencil notes on the *Golden Legend* can happily be consigned to recycling. In another example, both Caxton and de Worde frequently bulked out an edition with a few or more pages of an additional text or texts. I have recently been working on such material, painstakingly, since it requires trawling through the editions themselves (increasingly difficult in the British Library because of restrictions on incunables, but, thankfully, available, though less aesthetic and rather more cumbersome, on EEBO). Here I have the details before my eyes: I do not need to look at the edition itself to find that Caxton added the office for the feast of St Winifred to his Life of the saint, or to work my way through each page of Caxton's first edition of the *Festial* to find that there are texts on usury and indulgences in the middle of the book, or to look through the second edition to see that de Worde removed them and replaced them with three sermons and a tract, or to look through subsequent editions to check when these new sermons were first incorporated into the body of the *Festial* (in de Worde's first edition of 1493), or to trace the differences in other editions by Notary, Rood (or "printer of Mirk"), and Pynson.

In those areas which I can judge with some authority, the statements in the "Descriptions" are comprehensive, authoritative, and accurate. A great deal of thought, as well as research, has gone into compiling them. I understand the decision to ascribe the second edition of the *Festial* to the "printer of Mirk" rather than to Rood of Oxford (as has traditionally been the case) on the grounds that there is a gap of three years from Rood's last printing (which was anyway of Latin works) and that the paper stocks are different from those in earlier Oxford printing. The caution is typical of the scholarship of the volume, but the new inserted Latin in this edition (which Caxton used for his second edition, in preference to his own first edition) suggests a link with Rood's history of Latin works and perhaps offers an Oxford origin to the text (which is entirely new, not from any manuscript source). I note too that the entry for John Alcock's boy bishop sermon, on which I have been working recently, appears to assume that Alcock is writing in his own person, whereas it is clear that it is written for preaching by the boy bishop himself (who makes several comments and even jokes about school-life and schoolmasters). And why is the sermon ascribed to Alcock? This is traditional, but, if there is an explanation, it is not given here (nor elsewhere, as far as I know). After the "Descriptions," a section on materials deals with "The Paper of English Incunabula," "Printing Types and other Typographical Material" (where I note on page 339 that there is type evidence which links the second edition of the *Festial* to Rood), "Using Colour" (with figure illustrations and one plate in color, although there does not appear to be a list of figures in the volume), and then a description of the types arranged according to printer, clearly and fully described and explained, illustrated copiously by, in all, a further fifty-one plates. An "Appendix" supplies a table of English paper stocks. Thereafter follow "Abbreviations", "Bibliography", "Indices" (one of names and titles, as noted above; another of manuscripts mentioned in the introductions and "Descriptions"; the third an index of notes describing the copies, both very usefully names associated with early ownership and features, such as ownership annotation, or binding and bindings, as noted in the "Descriptions." The volume ends with "Synoptic Tables" providing a concordance of the main bibliographical references and catalogues.

The importance of BMC XI cannot be exaggerated. I have noted the strengths of the volume which have seemed most obvious and pertinent to me at this moment in relation to my own area of research, but I am well aware that the volume will yield up further insights as my research extends and my use of BMC XI develops. It is, after all, only two months old when I write this review. Lotte Hellinga and those who have worked with her over the years deserve (as they were accorded in a British Library conference one day in December of last year) congratulations, admiration and immense respect for

the completion of the volume. They, and it, will be held in esteem for generations, even centuries, to come.

Sue Powell, University of Salford

NICOLAS BARKER
and the CURATORIAL STAFF of THE BRITISH LIBRARY.
Treasures of the British Library.
London: The British Library, 2005. 280 pp.

Books are not single purpose items, and their reception depends as much on their audiences as on any innate qualities they may or may not possess. To me at least, the Early Book Society presents an audience comprising codicologists, paleographers, and medieval and Renaissance scholars as well as like-minded individuals, all of whom probably approach mass-market publications from a fundamentally different perspective than does the general public.

For many of us who teach, even with the advances offered by the Internet, large coffee-table books like the new edition of *Treasures of the British Library* function best as classroom aids, as handy ways to show our students a page from the Lindesfarne Gospels, or introduce them to a bit of *Beowulf*, Chaucer's portrait in Harley 4866, and so on. For classroom use, there are certain elements of book design that we simply expect to see, and chief among those, at least for pedagogical needs, is a list of plates. *Treasures of the British Library* lacks a list of plates.

Likewise, *Treasures of the British Library* might as well lack an index. It is impossible, for example, to find in the existing index any mention of either the Codex Sinaiticus or the Codex Alexandrinus—which are, quite arguably, two of the most important codices in the library's collection. As it turns out, the only way to discover an image of the Codex Alexandrinus is to look up the man who donated it, the Patriarch of Alexandria, Cyril Lucar—a name that is hardly on the tip of anyone's tongue even *in* the world of textual scholarship. The Codex Sinaiticus is also impossible to find even if one searches for Tischendorf, the Tsar, or the Soviet Union. When an image of Codex Sinaiticus and its accompanying text are finally discovered, it is a shock to discover that the compelling tale of the volume's cloak and dagger transit from Mount Sinai to London has been reduced to two sentences.

It is mystifying that such a valuable and significant manuscript as the Codex Sinaiticus—it is, after all, a book that the British Library has called "the world's oldest Bible and the most important Biblical manuscript" (http://www.bl.uk/news/2005/pressrelease20050311.html)—would be repro- duced in an exceedingly poor quality 2½" by 3½" black and white image, or that the reader is provided with its shelf mark and the image's folio number, but not with any indication of the meaning of the featured text. As unlikely as it seems, it actually appears that the plate itself is incorrectly labeled (the image of folio 260 in *Treasures of the British Library* is fundamentally different from the image of what purports to be same folio on the British Library's Images Online website, http://www.imagesonline.bl.uk/britishlibrary- store/Components/137/13752_2.jpg, and logically, both images cannot repre- sent the same folio).

Certainly, *Treasures of the British Library* presents a number of teachable moments though not precisely the ones that are expected. Instead, the volume provides the textual scholar with a good case study on how *not* to write, edit, design or print a book. For example, some connection between the text and the plates should have been made. There should have been more contextualizing photographs of the interior and exterior of the library's many incarnations. There should have been images of some of the more famous works referred to in the text—where is an illustration of the *Pearl* manuscript, for example, and why is the reproduction from *Beowulf* so tiny? There should have been some attention paid to quality control and detail—why are so many of the images either out of focus (see, for example, Stephen Bond's photograph of the new library across pages 4-5) or so poorly exposed as to be unrecognizable (*cf.* Thomas Banks' bust of Warren Hastings on page 76)?

Unfortunately, *Treasures of the British Library* is not a very useful book. At 25 dollars or so, it is not a complete waste of money, but its functionality for the purposes of pedagogy is extremely limited unless the class is studying editorial theory and the volume is used as a poor example of academic pub- lishing.

Carl James Grindley, Hostos Community College, The City University of New York

MICHELLE P. BROWN.
The World of the Luttrell Psalter.
London, British Library, 2006. 96 pp.

The Luttrell Psalter is an important illuminated manuscript in the British Library, originally produced in Lincolnshire, probably between 1330 and 1345, for Sir Geoffrey Luttrell. It is uniquely illustrated with a great many secular images of medieval life. This is a popular summary of commentary by the scholar who also worked on the full facsimile published by the British Library (£295 and 688 pages contrasting with these 96 pages at £9.95). It is an excellent introduction to the manuscript.

Despite its brevity, the text is slightly repetitive, many points being mentioned three times even in close proximity (e.g., the episode from Sir Geoffrey's early life, p. 45), and there is at least one howler: the preposterous myth that "Charing Cross" means "Dear Queen's Cross" (p. 17), a folk etymology for the Eleanor Cross seen off by the English Place-Name Society as far back as 1942, and since then frequently cited, so there is no excuse (and none for the British Library, either). Much of the codicological information of interest to members of the Early Book Society is consigned to an appendix, where we finally learn something of the overall contents of the manuscript, its script and its text. However, the book left me feeling well informed. Scholarly debates are frequently mentioned, with appropriate caution, and there is a good short bibliography.

The British Library employed an Italian fine-art printer, so the illustrations are printed to a sumptuous standard and on quality paper. Italian printers have Art (with a capital A), and they frequently put British printers to shame (the reviewer is a publisher). It is a disappointment to see many illustrations printed several times (the dinner scene from folio 208r appears on pages 8, 41, 58-9, 64 and on the back cover), when some are discussed without reproduction, and there are no cross-references for discussions that refer to a folio reproduced in another chapter. The publisher claims there are 90 illustrations, and this is correct, but many are unidentified fragments used for mere decoration.

My main criticism will be lost on most readers of the book but may appeal to members of this Society. The book has been "designed" by a London company in what I call the "Glossy Magazine School." Pictures are rarely printed with the scholarly need for context in mind but are subject to cruel guillotining and an ever-changing layout. There are far too many "bleeding chunks" for comfort. Where a whole leaf is reproduced without merciless hemorrhaging (p. 16), it is a revelation to see the margins and the relationship of the illustrations to the text (a point which is often made by the author but rarely respected by the designer). Each chapter begins with two wasted pages of "bleeding" detail, and the repetition of the opening lines which follow, and then, incomprehensibly, a page of text on a blue background which is difficult to read: why? The headings of captions and longer quotations are in a dot-matrix font not unlike that made by old computers in the early 1980s: why? I can think of no rational justification for these eccentricities. In sum: good text, superb printing, childish design. Should sell well.

Shaun Tyas, Paul Watkins Publishing

HELEN COOPER.
The English Romance in Time: Transforming Motifs from Geoffrey of Monmouth to the Death of Shakespeare.
Oxford: Oxford University Press, 2004. xvi + 542 pp.

In *The English Romance in Time*, Helen Cooper has produced the defini-
tive study of her topic. The reader who wants to know about the romance
genre and romance motifs from their first appearance in English (in texts produced in the decades following the composition of Monmouth's *History of the
Kings of Britain*) through the late Middle Ages and up to the Renaissance (in
the poems of Spenser and plays of Shakespeare, in particular) need read no
further.

The broad argument of the book is that while the characteristic narrative devices, locations, and situations of romance stay superficially the
same through the period of interest to Cooper, the uses and the meanings of
romance change. Cooper's study is of the romance "meme," a meme being
some thing or idea that replicates itself faithfully and adapts its forms readily. Cooper uses further analogy to describe her purpose: her book is a study
of the "historical semantics of the language of romance conventions" (4). As
both the scientific and linguistic metaphors suggest, her approach is taxo-
nomic: each chapter deals with a different convention. And yet Cooper is also
careful to ensure that the reader has a sense of how these conventions inter-
penetrate, overlap, inform and complicate one another. The quest, for
instance, forms the substance of the first chapter, a fascinating account of the
knight's adventures as a "substructure that is instinctive rather than learned"
(45). The quest may, especially when solitary, make sense to the reader in the
allegorical terms of medieval Christian spirituality, and yet it differs from the

pilgrimage in its routine insistence on the importance of the return to society. The knight will cycle back to, rather than seek a way out of, the world. This point enables Cooper to draw our attention to differences between the quest and the concern in her next chapter. Chapter 2 considers the journeys of the likes of Chaucer and Gower's Constance in rudderless boats. In romances where the matter is one of "Providence and the Sea," the journey, and its complicated relationship to the social world from which the hero or heroine has been set adrift, is a "crossing of the threshold out of human time" (124); it is this, and not reintegration of the traveler into the world, that is the stuff of meaning.

The remaining chapters of the book produce similarly striking insights. In chapter 3, magic is a defining characteristic of the romance genre because it "doesn't work." It is a point of deliberate confusion for the reader (a matter of wonder) and an obstacle to be overcome, or a breaking point for the hero and heroic ideals. In chapter 4, the fairy monarchs, and especially mistresses, familiar to us in their Renaissance garb (Titania and Gloriana), are written into a longer literary history, in which fairy and power, fairy and the privileged form of consciousness suggested by prophesy, are linked. Chapters 5 and 6 place female power, the romance heroine's capacity to name and choose the object of her desire, at the center of a study of both the concern with gender and interiority, and the tradition of misogyny (the trials of women) that are evident in romance. In chapter 7, magic is linked to political power: "when it comes to identifying the true heir, magic works" (324). Spenser is best able to wrestle with ideas about Elizabeth's lineage, future and past, in his epic romance, because "[t]he insistent concern of romance with identifying the rightful king is a reflection of the fact that rightfulness does not necessarily show in unequivocal ways" (324). Cooper ends with a chapter on "unhappy endings," focusing on those moments of uncertainty and incompletion which are inherent to each of the romance conventions she has described and which are best seen in quests unfulfilled and love affairs gone wrong – in that aspect of medieval romance that makes sense of the Renaissance concern with the tragic.

The particular relevance of Cooper's book to the readers of this *Journal* is its scope. It crosses the divide between medieval and early modern in the same way that romances did in manuscripts and in early printed books (as well as in new literary forms). Cooper goes a long way towards describing for us why it is, and why it is important, that we find romances in so many of the early books that we study.

Alexandra Gillespie, University of Toronto

ROBERT M. CORREALE and MARY HAMEL, EDS.
Sources and Analogues of The Canterbury Tales, vol. II.
Cambridge, D. S. Brewer, 2005. xvi + 824 pp.

This volume of the *Sources and Analogues* completes the two-volume set, the first volume having appeared in 2002. As a set, they replace the single-volume *Sources and Analogues of Chaucer's Canterbury Tales*, edited by W. F. Bryan and Germaine Dempster in 1941. As with the first volume of the pair, the aim has been to eliminate sources claimed in Bryan and Dempster that modern scholarship has discounted as not available to Chaucer (e.g., Sercambi's *Novelle*, formerly cited as a possible source for the frame but now known to have been written too late for Chaucer to have known it) or as of too distant relationship to the *Tales* for inclusion, and to add sources discovered or critically analyzed and adopted since 1941. There have been a number of new sources added, and more texts and partial texts of the sources given here, with—and this is new to the revision—full English translations of all non-English sources.

This second volume also adds two new chapters on sources and analogues to Chaucer's *General Prologue* and *Retraction*. The 1941 *Sources and Analogues* and the first volume of this set included a chapter on "The Frame," but no chapter discussing and citing the sources and analogues of the *General Prologue*: in this new chapter, the first of volume II, Robert R. Raymo draws on all the scholarship on the *Prologue* over the last 65 years. Raymo makes clear that our understanding of the sources for the *Prologue* has changed radically in this period partly because of Jill Mann's ground-breaking analysis of the elements of estates satire in the portraits (*Chaucer and Medieval Estates Satire*, Cambridge, 1973) and partly because of our greater acceptance of the influence of Boccaccio's *Decameron* on Chaucer's *Tales* and their *General Prologue*. The chapter on the *Prologue* breaks down its analysis into "springtime setting" followed by each of the pilgrims in order of their description in the *General Prologue*. Besides his principal debt to the *Decameron*, Chaucer was also heavily influenced by the *Roman de la Rose* and Guido del Colonne's *Historia Destructionis Troiae* for details of the *Prologue*—not surprising since he draws on all three in his other writings, especially on the *Decameron* for sources of some of the *Tales* themselves.

In the new chapter on the *Retraction*, Anita Obermeier discusses thirty-one sources and analogues for the *topoi* of the *Retraction* since, as she points out, no direct sources for it have been found. These are classed as influencing Chaucer's "authorial humility" (lines 1081-4), the "*Retractio* proper" (lines 1085-8) and the author's list of his own works.

The chapters included in this second volume deal with sources and analogues for the *General Prologue*, *Knight's Tale*, *Miller's Tale*, *Man of Law's Prologue and Tale*, *Wife of Bath's Prologue and Tale*, *Summoner's Prologue and Tale*, *Merchant's Tale*, *Physician's Tale*, *Shipman's Tale*, *Prioress's Prologue and Tale*, *Sir Thopas*, *Canon's Yeoman's Tale*, *Manciple's Tale* and the *Retraction*. In general, reading through this second volume, one is simply awed by the breadth of Chaucer's reading, not only of the medieval writings of Italy, France, and England, but of classical writings, commentaries that were standard university texts, writings from further afield, and not only literature but medicine, law, philosophy, and theology. I came away more convinced than I had been before by the arguments brought together here for the influence of Boccaccio's *Decameron* on the *Canterbury Tales*. Chaucer adopts not only details of the prologue and frame but story lines and details for several of the *Tales* as well, including two analogues for *The Merchant's Tale* and one for *The Shipman's Tale* added to the sources listed by Bryan and Dempster. If you own Bryan and Dempster's single volume, you should nevertheless obtain this new revised set, as it is a significant improvement on the former, not just adding the sources and analogues discovered since 1941 but discussing them in much greater depth and in light of current scholarly opinion about the *Tales*, and providing not only texts of the sources and analogues but English translations as well, so one does not have to be fluent in all of the languages Chaucer evidently could read in order to appreciate the sources from which he drew.

Linne R. Mooney, University of York

JANE COUCHMAN and ANN CRABB, EDS.
Women's Letters Across Europe, 1400-1700: Form and Persuasion.
Aldershot: Ashgate, 2005. xv + 336 pp.

Jane Couchman and Ann Crabb's collection of fifteen essays, which primarily focuses on the rhetorical structure of the letters of late medieval and early modern women, represents an excellent addition to the ever-increasing supply of scholarship on the complex literacies of women. The collection is divided into three large sections concerning private, public and religious letters, and the topics covered range from Susan Broomhall's work on French paupers' letters of the sixteenth century to Malcolm Richardson's essay on English women's letters of the late-fourteenth to mid-sixteenth centuries (using the example of Elizabeth Stonor, a cagey and engaging fifteenth-century Londoner) to Alison Weber's treatment of Saint Teresa of Avila's letters to her prioress. It is precisely this sort of flexibility and scope of offering that best highlights the collection's merits. By providing a broad European survey that transgresses social class, religion, time period and nationality, the collection is able to present a case for a certain consistency and coherency across the genre. Arguing that the background framework—however distantly removed—was the *ars dictaminis*, a number of the essays considerably increase our understanding of literacy in the past. Indeed, this volume serves to introduce several medieval literary theories to non-medievalists: it clarifies the complex interactions between scribe and "writer" and aptly represents the movement from the performance of dictation to an *amanuensis* to the performances of receipt and reading.

The volume is exceedingly well documented with an excellent bibliography, and the majority of the essays maintain a very high standard. There are few moments that are in any way problematic—a debatable point here and there is as serious as it gets, as when James Daybell, in his outstanding consideration of reading as a social act, argues that the typical letter writer's plea for a recipient to burn a letter could be explained as either evidence that these wishes were almost never carried out or evidence that the phrase was a code for something else. Both explanations ignore the more obvious solution: that the majority of letters with such *formulae* were, in fact, burned and that as a result, many letters written by women have not survived.

It is important, I think, for reviewer to occasionally defend a good book against a spurious charge. The full version of Ellen Moody's recent review in *The Renaissance Quarterly*, which was posted on her website (http://www.jimandellen.org/Reviewers.Couchman.html), says, in part, that: "There are linked troubling tendencies in this book. Important feminist and other political matters are replaced by unadventurous analysis of the characteristics of epistolarity and formal conventions" (*ibid*). Moody further complains that "The essayists are insufficiently frank about issues relating to women's bodies (like male violence) and too determined not to reinforce gender stereotypes and to remain objective and (above all) unsentimental." Couchman and Crabb's work, in reality, does a valuable service by opening a dialogue on authentically medieval and Renaissance literary theories and by presenting the paleographical and codicological artifacts of literary production. So what if Couchman and Crabb are "objective" and "unsentimental" (*ibid*) in their approach to this important material? Why the blazes should they not be? Is the study of epistolarity suddenly a second-class scholarly activity? It would be nice, if just once in a while, the long-standing and valid fields of scholarly inquiry represented by Couchman and Crabb and their writers were given the respect that medieval and Renaissance scholars typically give to other literary theories.

Carl James Grindley, Hostos Community College, The City University of New York

ANNE MARIE D'ARCY and ALAN J. FLETCHER, EDS.
*Studies in Late Medieval and Early Renaissance Texts in Honour of John
Scattergood.*
Dublin: Four Courts Press, 2005. 416 pp.

The twenty-four essays gathered here span literary criticism, manuscript studies, codicology, and intellectual, cultural, and political history. The
contributors combine detailed textual reading with historicism, continuing
the investigation of the interface of late medieval literary texts with their historical situation which has been the hallmark of Scattergood's own academic
oeuvre. The quality of festschrifts can be uneven, but it is hard to fault any of
these essays. Equally, their coverage of major texts ensures that this collection's value transcends the merely ornamental to constitute a creditable
library purchase for undergraduate reading lists.

The essays are organized alphabetically by contributor rather than
thematically or chronologically. There are a number of thoughtful readings of
aspects of central texts, such as John Burrow's discussion of courtesy in the
Book of the Duchess, Helen Conrad-O'Briain's analysis of *Sir Orfeo*, Angela Lucas's
account of *gentillesse* in the *Franklin's Tale*, and Alastair Minnis's re-evaluation of
the pardon scene in *Piers Plowman*. Less familiar texts and writers also receive
attention: Derek Pearsall revisits the *Flower and the Leaf* and the *Assembly of
Ladies*; Peter Lucas writes about John Capgrave; James Simpson investigates
the ethics of Caxton's *History of Reynard the Fox*; and Greg Walker interrogates
the textual integrity of *The Plowman's Tale*. Alongside these contributions are
historicizing accounts of both well-known and more obscure texts; these
include Alan Fletcher's discussion of baptismal theology and the importance
of both preaching and liturgical influences on *Pearl*; Anne Marie D'Arcy's

survey of leprosy, blasphemy, and heresy in Henryson's *Testament of Cresseid*; and Valerie Allen's essay on tournament and jousting which juxtaposes Chaucer's portrait of the Yeoman with Roger Ascham's 1545 treatise *Toxophilus*. This variety of different approaches is a fitting tribute to the extent and varied nature of John Scattergood's own interests and expertise.

All twenty-four contributions have their merits, but some will naturally be of greater interest to readers of JEBS, and it is these that I discuss in more detail. Richard Firth Green offers an edition of *The Hunting of the Hare*, a late medieval mock-heroic verse satire which survives uniquely in National Library of Scotland Advocates MS 19.3.1 (the Heege Manuscript). Green gives the text of the poem (previously printed only once in the early nineteenth century), with a commentary and discussion of its date and dialect, though he sensibly refrains from duplicating existing scholarship on Heege (particularly the work of Phillipa Hardman). His account of popular lore surrounding the hare draws on earlier medieval texts and visual sources including marginalia and images from cathedral misericords; some illustrations would have been appropriate here, but regrettably the volume has none at all, save the handsome frontispiece of its honoree. Other well known manuscripts make an appearance too: Wendy Scase writes about *Satires on the Retinues of the Great*, one of the neglected poems in British Library Harley 2253; Oliver Pickering discusses stanzaic verse in the Auchinleck manuscript; and Helen Cooper demonstrates that the date of Auchinleck cannot precede 1331.

Julia Boffey's essay, "Chaucer's *Fortune* in the 1530s: Some Sixteenth-Century Recycling," flags some similarities between Chaucer's poem and "A dyalogue bitwene the playntife and the defendaunt," a poem printed by Thomas Godfray in the 1530s. This work is attributed to William Calverley, who might have been a member of the Yorkshire gentry or alternatively (and more intriguingly), a thief and a pirate. One would like to know more about this interesting figure, but Boffey eschews further detective work to discuss the poem's indebtedness to Lydgate and to consider its part in the sixteenth-century's reappropriation of an earlier generation of literature. John Thompson's analysis of the assembly of the Chaucer canon in early modern London discusses the activities of John Stow and Thomas Speght, and focuses in particular on Chaucer's only-known Marian poem, *An ABC to the Virgin*, a text not greatly to the taste of sixteenth-century post-Reformation readers. Noting that the poem was only admitted to the Chaucer canon through the back door of Speght's 1602 edition and that even then it was discreetly packaged as a private prayer beloved of the wife of John of Gaunt, Thompson demonstrates that Stow must have known about the poem for at least forty years from his documented handling of various fifteenth-century manuscripts in which it occurs. Thomson's account of the latter is compact and slightly misleading. He refers to "the collection owned by the fifteenth-century London bibliophile John Shirley, now British Library, Harley 2251" (p. 355), which elides the fact that this manuscript was copied by the Hammond scribe partly from a Shirley exemplar, Cambridge Trinity College R.3.20. We can also be more certain than Thompson's discussion suggests that all three parts of the latter codex (now disassembled as Sion Arc.L.40.2/E.44, British Library Harley 78, and Trinity College R.3.20) passed through Stow's hands. A slightly later early book preserver and bibliophile features in A.S.G. Edwards's contribution which reminds us that Elias Ashmole, the seventeenth-century antiquarian, made transcripts of Chaucer's *Cook's Tale* and *Gamelyn* in Oxford Bodleian Library MS Ashmole 45. This copy of the *Cook's Tale* seems to have been mostly ignored by modern bibliographers and editors, even though collation with other surviving manuscripts shows that its text preserves the unique testimony of an otherwise lost witness. Edwards provides a transcription and thereby justifies entitling his piece "A New Text of *The Canterbury Tales*?"

If Tony Edwards's title might be regarded as rather headline-grabbing, Ralph Hanna's could scarcely be more prosaic ("Notes on some Trinity College Dublin Manuscripts"), but for members of the Early Book Society such a title is instantly alluring. Here are brief accounts (modestly described by Hanna as "notes on a few oddments," p. 171) of five manuscripts in the Trinity College library, nos. 69, 75, 271, 423, and 432. These are notes on points of interest rather than full descriptions, with a good measure of information about paper stocks where applicable, linguistic analysis, and scribal hands. For example, the note on MS 69 expands the account of this manuscript given in Hanna's *London Literature* 1300-1380 (Cambridge University Press, 2005), connecting the material copied by the first scribe with texts circulating among London book-producers of *c*.1330-1400 and drawing attention to the fact that the manuscript's second scribe, responsible for the Early English Prose Psalter, also copies that text in Princeton, Scheide Library, MS 143. Hanna's contribution is a service to scholarship since modern catalogue entries on the medieval English manuscripts at TCD are not yet available; as he comments, this is because John Scattergood is the person charged with preparing them. Hanna sees his brief, therefore, as one that goes beyond the usual laudatory rhetoric of the festschrift with its congratulation for the honoree's lifetime of scholarly achievement. Instead he chooses "to talk about work John hasn't published and offer a few gleanings that may encourage him to use his retirement to get back to it" (p. 171); one can only concur with this exhortation.

Margaret Connolly, University of St Andrews

EAMON DUFFY AND DAVID LOADES, eds.
The Church of Mary Tudor: Catholic Christendom, 1300-1700.
Aldershot, UK, Burlington, US: Ashgate, 2006. xxxi + 348 pp.

This important book extends Eamon Duffy's groundbreaking revision of the Whig view of the Reformation in *The Stripping of the Altars* into the brief reign of Mary Tudor (1553-8). Unlike many books of this sort, the sum of the parts makes up a highly satisfying whole, indeed an exemplary and comprehensive account by the leading scholars in the period and subject. The introduction by David Loades is an impressive long chapter on "The personal religion of Mary I," in which, with humanity and careful judgment, he analyzes the Queen as Catholic, monarch, and woman, reaching the convincing conclusion that "for all her humanist education, Mary was a woman whose convictions were stronger than her reason." While this might sound chauvinistic, in context it is not, and ample evidence is provided for Mary's lack of political acumen (although, given what she had gone through, it would have taken a tougher woman than she clearly was to act more politically).

Elizabeth, of course, was that tougher woman, and as Loades says at the end of the second essay, "The Marian Episcopate" (which he again authors, taking the reader through the details of who was in and who was out): "Elizabeth was able to do in 1559 what Mary had felt herself unable to do – make a clean sweep and start a new task with a new team." Next in this section ("The Process"), Claire Cross looks at how Mary set about re-Catholicizing England through "The English Universities, 1553-8," a fascinating chapter which stresses the magnitude of the task (particularly in Cambridge), after all the unpicking of the previous decades. The tactics might have been successful, had Mary lived (and the whole of the book, inevitably, raises the question: what if Mary had lived?). They were certainly sufficiently ruthless, in terms of visitations, burnings, sanctions, bribes, and there is perhaps a touch of naiveté, after such a sustained campaign, in Cross's conclusion that by 1558 "the allure of Catholic humanism" was once more being felt in the colleges. C. S. Knighton next looks at "Westminster Abbey Restored." Loades has already pointed out that Mary did not reconstruct the regular orders but that could not be done overnight. It took a few years, up to late 1556, to restore Westminster as a Benedictine abbey, and it was to remain the only restored monastic foundation. When Elizabeth was crowned there in January, 1559, it was a monastic foundation, but by June it had been returned to a secular chapter and the old business of selling off assets had been undertaken all over again. After Knighton's careful unpicking of the intricacies of this brief period of monastic restoration, Ralph Houlbrooke provides a case-study of "The Clergy, the Church Courts and the Marian Restoration in Norwich," remarkable for "the capitulation or flight of her leading Marian clergy." John Barret, Norwich's longest-serving evangelical minister, was one of those who capitulated, to the bewilderment of his old friend, Robert Watson, who in the end fled abroad. There was really little choice, unless one was prepared to die, as five layfolk did in Norwich in the spring and summer of 1557. The enforcers were John Hopton and his notorious chancellor, Michael Dunning, and John Barret himself, who managed to keep his prebend in Norwich Cathedral even in Elizabeth's reign.

Part II ("Cardinal Pole") contains three essays on Reginald Pole, who, reluctantly, returned to England in 1554, was ordained priest in 1557, and two days later was instituted as England's last Roman Catholic Archbishop of Canterbury. Thomas F. Mayer asserts the success of Pole's campaign: "That England did not remain a Catholic country must be accounted much more of an accident than we have been readily prepared to admit." Whether the Spanish thought Pole was doing enough is another matter: certainly the Spanish ambassador accused him of being "very lukewarm," and opinion today varies on whether the Jesuits should have been brought over to help further the re-conversion. Undoubtedly, that would have met greater popular resistance than Spanish presence in England did anyway, where the Spanish Dominicans presided over the burning of 280 English men and women. However, John Edwards's focus in "Spanish Religious Influence in Marian England" is not on burning but on the advances made in restoring Catholic liturgy by Bartolomé Carranza, the friar charged with re-establishing the English Province of the Dominicans (who was thanked by arrest, imprisonment, and trial on his return to Spain after Mary's death). Again, one cannot escape the persecution of Mary's reign, in the context of which being lukewarm, like Pole, seems a highly desirable characteristic. In the same section, Eamon Duffy's contribution provides him with an opportunity to correct a misreading of Pole's letter to Carranza and to demonstrate that Pole is not fundamentally critical of preaching and in fact sees its value as propaganda, especially in conjunction with the press. Indeed, Pole instituted an annual sermon on St Andrew's Day (celebrated as the anniversary of England's return to the Papacy): Harpsfield preached the first, at St Paul's, in 1557, and Pole himself preached one at Whitehall in the next year, which Duffy discusses as an example of Pole's "tough and specific analysis of the problems confronting the Church in London."

Finally, Part III looks at "The Culture" of the Marian period, including chapters on "The Marian Restoration and the Mass," "The Theology and Spirituality of a Marian Bishop: the Pastoral and Polemical Sermons of Thomas Watson," and "The Persecution in Kent." The first two contributions, "The Marian Restoration and the Mass" by Lucy Wooding and "The Theology and Spirituality of a Marian Bishop: the Pastoral and Polemical Sermons of Thomas Watson" by William Wizeman SJ, are very text-based and so, like Duffy's, of potential interest to JEBS readers in their analysis of printed propaganda in the Marian period. Wooding demonstrates, with an abundance of textual evidence, the central role of the Mass in the Marian period, arguing convincingly, that, although in this respect no different from pre-Reformation attitudes, "the sermons, treatises, ballads and polemics from the 1550s, as well as the official decrees of Mary I's government, speak a very different language to that of 100, or even 50 years before" and that "Protestant rhetoric had served to recalibrate Catholic thought." Wizeman concentrates on the sermons of Thomas Watson, in Mary's reign, master of St John's College, Cambridge, dean of Durham, and then bishop of Lincoln. Wizeman's discussion of Watson's defence of the authority of the Councils of the Church and his preaching on the Eucharist and the other sacraments, as well as his analysis of Watson's Catholicism as compared to pre-Reformation Catholicism, complement and expand on the material in the previous essay. In "Marking the Days: Henry Machyn's Manuscript and the Mid-Tudor Era," Gary G. Gibbs claims that Machyn's "diary" is better seen not as a personal and private text but as a chronicle, a convincing argument on the basis of the bland but very useful quotations Gibbs supplies. This essay needs some tight editing, however, and Gibbs' venture into Machyn's dialect was a mistake (as he himself seems to have realized), especially since he is clearly not familiar with the material or the discipline (the great work of Alexander Ellis is described as "a nineteenth-century text by R. J. Ellis" and the English academic R. M. Wilson becomes R. N. Wilson): "So was Henry Machyn from south-east Yorkshire or anywhere else besides London? In some ways it hardly matters. In his writing, Machyn never longed for the countryside." Finally, although the editors have tried to stave off the burnings as long as possible, they cannot be ignored. Patrick Collinson, in "The Persecution of Kent," says: "It will not do to shove them into an embarrassed corner." Did he know his contribution would be last? More heretics were burnt in Kent than anywhere else except London, and most in Canterbury itself. Of the 61 martyrs, half came from the villages and cloth towns of the Weald, all but two were layfolk, one in three were women, several held heterodox opinions which meant that they were not "orthodox Protestants" but Freewillers and others who had picked up a bit of this and a bit of that. Although such people "could not stand accused of any whopping great heresies" (Collinson enjoys a demotic style), they nevertheless were fitted into the drop-down charges needed by the central administration, as Collinson demonstrates by very effective use of Foxe's various editions of Acts and Monuments. This is an important article by an elder statesman of the historical period who knows the material like the back of his hand. It fittingly concludes an important volume that has clearly been compiled with the (successful) intention of correcting the statement in The Stripping of the Altars of its co-editor, Eamon Duffy, that "a convincing account of the religious history of Mary's reign has yet to be written."

Sue Powell, University of Salford

RUTH EVANS, HELEN FULTON and DAVID MATTHEWS, EDS.
Medieval Cultural Studies: Essays in Honour of Stephen Knight.
Cardiff: University of Wales Press, 2006. xi + 286 pp.

This collection of eighteen essays pays tribute to the work of Stephen Knight in creating and shaping the emergent field of medieval cultural studies. The volume is arranged in five sections, though there is naturally some overlap between these. After a brief introduction by the editors, the first section offers three essays which set out to define the field of medieval cultural studies. This brief is perhaps best achieved by David Matthews who gives a lucid account of the distinctions between medievalism, medieval studies, and cultural studies, acknowledging that while the representation of the former has often been negative, "it is clearly in the interests of medieval studies to draw into its orbit pseudo-medievalist phenomena, in order to benefit from recent modernity's extraordinary love affair with the middle ages" (p. 20). The two other essays adopt less generalized approaches: Larry Scanlon addresses one particular aspect of contemporary culture, the obscene, focusing on the French fabliau *Le chevalier qui fist les cons parler*; and Thomas Hahn charts the academic investigation of Robin Hood and outlawry by historians during the 1950s-1980s.

Knight's own work on Robin Hood is well-known, so it is not surprising to find the first of the volume's three thematic sections devoted to this figure. W.M. Ormrod gives an interesting account of the authority of writing in the medieval outlaw tradition, identifying and discussing in turn four types of written documentation which feature in the Robin Hood ballads. These are: letters endowing individuals with the king's authority; letters of summons to justice; letters written by subjects to the king; and charters of pardon.

Ormrod's analysis of these reveals a great deal about the social, political and legal context from which the Robin Hood tradition emerged and reminds us that the study of historical documentation may usefully extend our understanding of medieval literature; we are also given an incidental but interesting insight into the information processing of the medieval era. Helen Cooper's contribution is also concerned with authoritative writing, offering a mini-edition of the strange eclogue A *Tale of Robin Hood, dialogue-wise between Watt and Jeffrey* which is otherwise available only in two increasingly hard-to-come-by nineteenth-century printed editions. Cooper discusses the poem's unique survival in British Library MS Harley 367, a composite volume of miscellaneous papers partly associated with John Stow; she also attempts to identify and date the poem by considering its unusual seven-syllable trochaic metre and by linking its occasion to the Marprelate controversy of the late 1580s. Thomas H. Ohlgren gives a compelling and insightful account of the two earliest surviving Robin Hood poems, *Robin Hood and the Potter* and *Robin Hood and the Monk*, which survive respectively in Cambridge University Library Ee.4.35 and Ff.5.48. Ohlgren has published fuller accounts of these manuscripts in *Nottingham Medieval Studies*; here he reprises his findings to argue that both these poems were collected and copied by the manuscripts' original owners because their subject matter of grievance and protest had personal resonance for them. Finally, in this Robin Hood section, Martha Driver considers the idea of the hero in late medieval texts, modern film and popular culture by examining specific uses of persuasive speech; a series of appendices to her essay helpfully gives the texts of the speeches discussed.

The irrepressible Robin Hood also spills over into the second of the volume's thematic sections, officially dedicated to "Historical Chaucer." The four essays here offer a range of detailed accounts of aspects of the cultural context of Chaucer's work, which in practice, as in so much modern criticism, means mostly the *Canterbury Tales*. Helen Phillips considers how far the *Friar's Tale* seems to draw on the Robin Hood tradition; Helen Fulton (who, to be fair, also discusses the *House of Fame*) describes late fourteenth-century Cheapside; and Stephanie Trigg examines how Chaucer conceptualizes "the people," one of the most contentious issues in cultural studies, as the subjects of the Pardoner's preaching, focusing on the simple parish priest who is supposedly duped by the Pardoner and asking whether the "lewed peple" (p. 169) of the Pardoner's audience are deceived as easily as he claims. The resolutely Anglocentric focus of these essays is expanded by Henry Kelly's account of the culture of war and Henry Bolingbroke's participation in the campaigns in Lithuania in the 1390s. Similarly, in the volume's third thematic section which is devoted to romance, Sheila Delany considers the metamorphosis of *Sir Bevis of Hampton* into an early sixteenth-century Yiddish version, *Bovo-bukh*, which was composed by the German Elias Levita in Padua. Ruth Evans gives a reading of *Sir Orfeo* which depends on the motif of *homo sacer* and which is informed by the work of the Italian philosopher Giorgio Agamben. The most notable contribution here is Diane Speed's account of chivalric perspectives in the Middle English Otuel romances which contains a good deal of information about the various Otuel texts which circulated in medieval England. Speed's detailed reading of one of these, *Roland and Otuel*, demonstrates the particular differences of this retelling of the story and offers some light on its unique survival in the context of the Thornton manuscript.

The volume's fifth section, entitled "Cultural Politics/The Politics of Culture," seems rather more miscellaneous than the others, beginning as it does with a resolutely medieval contribution from Margaret Clunies Ross on the skaldic ekphrasis poem in medieval Norway and Iceland, and ending with the obligatory bibliography of the honoree's work, compiled by Lucy Sussex. In between are two essays which combine medieval and modern material in the context of crime fiction. The first, by Geraldine Barnes, takes the topic of medieval murder and modern crime fiction and focuses on London, ranging, elegantly enough, from Chaucer and *Athelston* to Josephine Tey. The second, by Margaret Rogerson, examines a number of modern mystery texts that include reference to medieval mystery plays, treating two novels, Geraldine McCaughrean's *A Little Lower than the Angels* and Barry Unsworth's *Morality Play*, most extensively. These attempts to combine the medieval with modern crime fiction are suitable final offerings since they recall yet another aspect of Stephen Knight's career. His happy free-ranging through worlds as disconnected as Arthurian literature and Australian crime fiction, and his deft engagement in both academic criticism, medieval and modern, and journalism, demonstrate his consummate ease and achievement in very different spheres, more typical of earlier medievalists, such as the manuscript scholar and ghost story writer, Montague Rhodes James. As a celebration of Knight's work, this multi-focused collection succeeds in hitting all of its targets.

Margaret Connolly, University of St Andrews

CONSTANCE B. HIEATT and the late TERRY NUTTER with JOHNNA H. HOLLOWAY. *Concordance of English Recipes: Thirteenth through Fifteenth Centuries.* Tempe, Arizona: ACMRS, 2006. xvii + 135 pp.

This concordance of edited Middle English recipes will be very useful for scholars researching this area or working on descriptions of manuscripts containing recipes. The body of the work is arranged into four columns: "Recipe" (e.g., "Canabens with bacon"), "Lemmatized," i.e., Lemmatized Recipe Name (e.g., "Beans, Dried, with Bacon"), "Source" (e.g., "OP4(36)," i.e., item 36 in Hieatt's edition of *An Ordinance of Pottage* from New Haven, Yale University MS Beinecke 163), "Ca." (somewhat obscure and not explained in the Introduction, but seemingly *circa* since this column gives an indication of date, e.g., "1460"). It is the lemmas that are arranged alphabetically rather than the Middle English names, so that a number of entries with the lemma "Blancmanger," for example, are arranged in alphabetical order of source abbreviations, and the Middle English spellings are not arranged alphabetically. There is a Glossary of Recipe Titles used as Lemmas and Cross-Index of Variant Titles (obscure titles only are dealt with) which make one's mouth water ("**Pokerounce** spiced clarified honey spread on bread slices"), or rather more often, not ("**Bruce** pork organ meat cooked with leeks," "**Garbage** chicken giblets and odds and ends"). The effect of fasting on recipes is indicated by entries such as "**Tart for Lent** a tart filled with fruit and fish, **Tart of Fish out of Lent** tart of eels in a custard base of eggs and creams" and the medieval fondness for decoration by entries such as "**Hats** small fried pastries shaped like hats," "**Potwise** forcemeat made to resemble flower pots." There is also an Appendix of Renaissance Versions of Medieval English Recipes.

Sue Powell, University of Salford

KATHRYN KERBY-FULTON.
Books Under Suspicion: Censorship and Tolerance of Revelatory Writing in Late Medieval England.
Notre Dame: University of Notre Dame, 2006. 488 pp.

What would it mean for a book to be "under suspicion"? The appositive "censorship" in the title of Kathryn Kerby-Fulton's new book conjures for a reader visions of inquisitional flames consuming agonized bodies, whether of books or their authors. This is an image of the western Middle Ages familiar enough to contemporary readers and in any case suggests a logical progression from suspicion: a suspect book – one judged dangerous or wrong, with or without good reason – would make a likely candidate for censorship. "Tolerance," Kerby-Fulton's second appositive for "books under suspicion," may provoke some consternation, however. To make sense of it, we must reach for an expansive sense of the word "suspicion," one that includes not only "apprehension of guilt or fault" but also discernment of innocence or virtue, an "imagination of something (not necessarily evil) as possible or likely" (OED). More importantly, we are invited to acquire an image of the Middle Ages that is somewhat less familiar than the one featuring banned and burning books: in that picture, medieval society is surprisingly solicitous toward heterodox texts, ingenious and resourceful in giving them shelter and aiding their passage to additional readers. In *Books Under Suspicion* Kerby-Fulton brings this second image of medieval culture brilliantly to life in the specific instance of attitudes toward revelatory writing in England from 1329 to 1437, a period of robust tolerance, and on the whole, as she puts it, "an age of *failed* censorship" (16).

In the foreword and introductory chapter, Kerby-Fulton defines the scope, methodologies, and core intellectual stakes of this immensely learned, ambitious, and "revelatory" book. The cultural phenomenon at the heart of her study is revelatory theology, which she defines as "novel theological perspectives arrived at via a claim to visionary or mystical experience" (14). These novel perspectives give rise to the revelatory writing that comprises Kerby-Fulton's primary material; that writing survives in a wide variety of genres, including "prophecy, inspired exegesis, visions from prison, mysticism, dream vision, miracles, inquisitional testimonies" (2). But, as Kerby-Fulton makes clear, this book is not an exploration of revelatory writing as such; instead, it is "a study of the circumstances in which this literature comes under suspicion" (20). In order to recognize a text as one that is "under suspicion," Kerby-Fulton applies a number of tests: records of institutionally promulgated censorship or confiscation; texts' reception histories legible in marginal responses, codicological contexts, ownership, and provenance; imitations of polemical works; stylistic clues, such as a "rhetoric of constraint" and "functional ambiguity"; and, finally, ideological traits, in the form of allusions to any of a number of "hot-button" issues of the day, from disendowment to anti-mendicantism to the proliferation in Europe and England of fanatical "reformist" sects (18-19).

And it is Kerby-Fulton's elucidation of those conditions that yields this book's major break-throughs for scholarly appreciation of the religious climate of this period. First, she establishes the inaccuracy and, what is worse, the poverty, of a scholarly tendency to equate the history of censorship in late-medieval England with the history of Wycliffism. Against this "too lonely" (3) narrative, Kerby-Fulton posits a vanguard of "Ricardian and Lancastrian radicalisms [that] were both more pluralist and more adventurous (and Wycliffism often more conservative) than we have so far imagined" (14). In recuperating Wycliffism's companion radicalisms, Kerby-Fulton also brings into view a spacious territory of tolerance and intellectual freedom in late-medieval English culture, especially with respect to visionary experience and mystical and apocalyptic theologies. Moreover, in the course of her analyses of works as aesthetically and chronologically far-flung as Chaucer's translation of the *Roman de la Rose*, the Latin pro-Wycliffite broadside "*Heu quanta desolacio*," and Margery Kempe's *Book*, Kerby-Fulton shows that this province of free-thinking was inhabited by Latin and vernacular authors and audiences from a broad spectrum of English society. Finally, these analyses also demonstrate the particular instrumentality of a manuscript culture in protecting intellectual liberty.

The book's ten chapters fall into three main sections: the first five take up alternative salvation histories; the next three consider the mostly quickening influence of continental revelatory writing on female mysticism in

England; and the last two examine alternative salvation theology in relation to the work of Chaucer and Langland in particular. In each of these three main sections, Kerby-Fulton first presents, in thorough and always engaging detail, the historical contexts that gave rise to the suspicion in which the movement under consideration was held, moving thence to illuminating examinations of literary and codicological traces of that suspicion. In what follows I sketch a sampling of Kerby-Fulton's studies in the latter category in order to illustrate the particular rewards this work offers to scholars of book history.

Following an opening chapter that chronicles the evolution and devolution of alternative salvation histories as they were propounded in the apocalyptic prophecies of Hildegard of Bingen and Joachim of Fiore, chapter two is devoted to codicological evidence of the censorship of Joachite Franciscanism in England before and after Wyclif. A core section of that chapter discusses a series of intriguing examples of what Kerby-Fulton's titular "books under suspicion" actually look like as physical objects. Here she examines extant copies of works by Joachim, Peter Olivi, and Henry of Costesy, explicating their missing pages, marginalia – and excised marginalia – "nota" marks, erroneous attributions of authorship, and instructions of bequest (a copy of Olivi's *Postilla* on Matthew was to be chained in Merton College) as canny suppressions of text, authorship and ownership. This is an especially insightful and fascinating discussion and reveals with concrete elegance the genius of Kerby-Fulton's capacious governing term, "suspicion." Her analyses of these "suspect" books counter the specter of ruthless, monolithic institutional censorship with the possibility of multiple agents and objects of suspicion and, paradoxically, make room for censorship's opposite, tolerance. For here, alongside evidence of the machinations of censorship, we also see traces of tolerant owners and readers altering books in order to protect them from the suspicious eyes of institutional censors, even as they make them available to suspicious readers of another sort altogether: readers sympathetic to these suspect texts and with eyes to see through their protective disguises.

In subsequent chapters in this first section, Kerby-Fulton continues to develop a portrait of a rich and variegated spectrum of attitudes in England towards works linked to "optimistic" (50) heterodox salvation histories: chapter three explores the fourteenth-century revival of interest in the banned books of Gerard of Borgo San Donnino and William of St. Amour; chapter four considers the "vogue" (188) of Hildegardiana; and chapter five takes up the visionary prison writing of Walter Brut and the author of *Opus arduum*. These first five chapters are also punctuated by a trilogy of case studies entitled "Dangerous Reading among Early *Piers* Audiences," which approach the question of whether and to what degree *Piers Plowman* was "under suspicion" as a work of revelatory writing specifically. Together these crystalline case studies chart whole new territories of the textual and codicological network of the "Piers Plowman Tradition" and, perhaps even more importantly, provide a magisterial demonstration of the interpretive power of the very category of the "suspect" book. This hermeneutics is particularly clear in Case Study 2, which sketches a mutually illuminating interface between Piers and a cluster of poems in a booklet in London, British Library MS Cotton Cleopatra B.ii, one that shows the influence of Piers on later works even as it sheds new light on certain local moments in Piers.

In sections two and three of Books Under Suspicion, Kerby-Fulton goes on to develop this new, specifically non-Foucauldian "hermeneutics of suspicion" – that is, the identification and deployment of marks of suspicion as a tool for close-reading – that she demonstrates so powerfully and economically in these case studies. Focusing on writings in Middle English, including The Chastising of God's Children, The Book of Margery Kempe, M. N.'s translation and glosses of Marguerite Porete's The Mirror of Simple Souls, Julian of Norwich's Revelation, Langland's Piers Plowman, and Chaucer's House of Fame and "Retraction," these chapters reveal again and again the truly astonishing, and heartening and inspiring, currency and diversity of non-Wycliffite revelatory theology in England over the hundred-some year period Kerby-Fulton examines.

Books Under Suspicion is bound to mark a turning point in scholars' understanding of the pervasive cultural awareness and tolerance of heterodox theology in late-medieval England. That turning point will be evident not only in scholars' use of the wealth of information and insight that Kerby-Fulton makes available in this book but also in the new research it will stimulate. As if to aid us both in compassing the current project and in initiating that new research, Kerby-Fulton prefaces Books Under Suspicion with a detailed chronology of non-Wycliffite incidents of heresy and related events. Beginning with an entry for 1161-66, during which time the "Patarini" or "Cathari" first appeared in England and ending with the 1457 trial before Bishop Grey of Ely of a case of "mixcd Free Spirit and Wycliffite beliefs" (lii), this chronology marks out the broader scope of Kerby-Fulton's study and the even broader horizon for further research that her work enables.

Martha Dana Rust, New York University

JULIAN M. LUXFORD
The Art and Architecture of English *Benedictine Monasteries,*
1300-1540: A *Patronage History,* Studies in the History of
Medieval Religion XXV.
Woodbridge: Boydell, 2005. xxii + 281 pp.

This is a wide-ranging book with a great deal of material which has
been handled and organized admirably. It deals with the most populous and
influential medieval religious order. It covers a long period and a broad geographical area (south-west England), and in its remit of "art and architecture"
and "patronage history," it inevitably treats of very many different items of gift
or bequest: buildings, sculpture, illuminated manuscripts, stained glass, tap-
estries, and so on. The book arises from Luxford's doctoral thesis (most
clearly in the careful setting up of the research model and structure in Part I,
which covers "Materials for a History," "Documentary Sources," and "Surviving
Art and Architecture"). Broadly, the volume is based on internal and external
patronage, the subjects of Parts II and III respectively. Appendix 1 lists the
Benedictine houses in the south-west, and Appendix 2 "Motives and
Misconceptions in the Patronage of Superiors." There is a list of the many
manuscripts cited (many, but not all, rolls, registers, and chronicles), and
there are forty-five illustrations, over half of manuscripts. JEBS readers will
perhaps be most interested in those which were the gifts of patronage, such
as the Sherborne Missal, which is well discussed and illustrated (notably in
the brilliant dust jacket, almost making up for the fact that this is the only colored illustration in the volume).

The illustrations of manuscripts are very well chosen and well reproduced. These include the ownership inscription of Alice Champnys in her Shaftesbury book of hours, mouth-watering details from the Sherborne Missal, cute calendar illustrations from a Wherwell nun's psalter, an illuminated initial and ownership inscription in a historical compendium belonging to a Glastonbury monk, an illustration and ownership inscription from a *Legenda Aurea* owned by a Winchester monk, and a great deal more. The index is serviceable but slightly exiguous, and manuscripts are not found as such, although "decorated manuscripts" directs one to look for entries for individual houses (a map and list of the forty-five houses covered in the study, fewer than those that were in existence which are listed in Appendix 1, is provided just before the introduction). These entries turn out to be copious and fully discussed, to be expected in the case of "the greatest of all late medieval Benedictine books," the Sherborne Missal, but similarly thorough and detailed in describing a book of hours from Gloucester now in the Pierpont Morgan Library or the cartulary from Glastonbury now in the Bodleian Library. Footnotes are particularly strong, so that even manuscripts from lesser houses, such as Romsey, are well described and have copious secondary references in the footnotes. (Appendix 1 usefully gives the approximate income of *c.* 1535 to indicate the rich and poor houses, Glastonbury at £3,311 being the richest by far and Ellingham in Hampshire the poorest at £14, with no evidence of patronage.)

Luxford has a relaxed style: royal visits to Benedictine houses must have "stung," ignoring private ownership of goods by monks may have been because the bishops "had larger fish to fry," and the conclusion is titled "Five Things We Would Like to Know." The relaxed style, together with the intense engagement with history as well as art history throughout this book, makes it very readable (it has been highly commended in the Longman-*History Today* Book of the Year Prize for 2007). Despite its far-ranging and copious material, it is not dry and not simply a book for reference. Luxford's volume is highly commended by this *Journal* too.

Sue Powell, University of Salford

JULIA MARVIN, ED. and TRANS.
The Oldest Anglo-Norman Prose Brut Chronicle: An Edition and
Translation
Medieval Chronicles, 4.
Woodbridge: The Boydell Press, 2006. x + 442 pp. 1 b&w plate.

Recent years have seen the emergence of a broad interest in the
medieval prose *Brut*. This is entirely justified and indeed long overdue in the
light of the evidence that the surviving manuscripts provide of the way the
English Middle Ages took to its heart this vernacular narrative of British history from the foundation of Britain to various points from the thirteenth to
the fifteenth century. The *Brut* appears in Anglo-Norman and Middle English,
as well as in a small number of Latin versions translated from Middle English.
The Anglo-Norman and Middle English manuscripts survive in formidable
numbers and reveal through their evidence of revisions and continuations as
well as marginalia how medieval readers engaged with the text. The great
watershed in the study of the *Brut* is Lister Matheson's *The Prose Brut: The
Development of a Middle English Chronicle*, published in 1998. The prominence of
Middle English in the title reflects the main focus of the book but it takes into
account as well the Anglo-Norman and Latin manuscripts. The main problem
that those interested in the *Brut* face is the lack of modern printings. Only
Friedrich Brie's two-volume edition for the Early English Text Society aims to
present a comprehensive picture of the *Brut's* narrative in Middle English.
This was published in 1906 and 1908, and approaches to editing have developed significantly since then. There is no declared editor for the Latin versions. In Britain and North America the study of medieval literature is

dominated by Middle English, and there was always a danger that emerging *Brut* studies would ignore or give short shrift to the versions that form the foundation of its vast textual tradition, namely the Anglo-Norman texts. Julia Marvin's edition heads off that possibility in grand style and forces those already engaged in or about to embark on projects connected with this network of texts to confront the "oldest Anglo-Norman prose *Brut*," that is, the earliest surviving form of the text.

Julia Marvin's achievement with this edition is considerable. Working in what must at times have seemed like almost a scholarly vacuum, she has presented a substantial, highly informed and well judged edition and translation of the earliest version of the *Brut* along with introduction, explanatory notes, textual notes, and index. The narrative extends from the legendary foundation of Britain by Brutus to 1272 (the death of Henry III). In this edition the Anglo-Norman text and the modern English translation run to a total of 223 pages. Julia Marvin makes a compelling case that this narrative is the work of a single author who judged his audience well and used a style that was clear, concise, and not ornamented with extensive vocabulary and imagery. The most complex language concerns land tenure and law which is suggestive of the audience to which the text was directed. She argues that it is the very plainness of the style that gives authority to the narrative; the author was consciously imitating the style and narrative structure of the Bible as it was understood in the Middle Ages. The intellectual framework is the typological: episodes in the legendary history of Britain are like episodes in the Old Testament and function as types to give significance to the events of recent history. A central argument of the Introduction is that the overriding purpose of the work is to present a narrative that takes account of British and Anglo-Saxon history and at the same time shows the consolidation of the national identity under Norman authority.

Marvin is particularly astute in her discussions of the Arthurian narrative in the *Brut* and how the compiler modified in radical ways the emphases of his sources, producing a distinctive account that presents Arthur as more diplomat than warrior and as an idealized version of Edward I. It is important to be reminded that the *Brut* contains the version of the Arthur story that was most widely distributed in the Middle Ages, and this edition will force some major reassessments of interpretations of medieval perceptions of Arthur which frequently are based on romance literature alone.

One of the most intriguing questions concerning the *Brut* is why this vernacular text was such a success. Marvin characterizes this first version as "secular, pragmatic, and above all baronial" (p. 4) and argues that these features, which are carried over into most later versions in all three languages, account in no small way for its enduring popularity. The text owed no obvious allegiance to any one institution – the church or the government – and therefore was able to provide a broader view of British history and the British realm.

The Introduction is comprehensive and addresses some difficult issues, the most problematic of which concern the sources (pp. 20–40) and dating and authorship (pp. 40–47). There is no shying away from opening up to thorough investigation these problems that have lain dormant for so long, and the Introduction pushes to the very edge of what can be gleaned from the available evidence and invites others to enter the debate. The Explanatory Notes (pp. 297–346) follow the text. These are concise and well focused, and will support any reader who is not wholly familiar with the sweep of history that the narrative takes in. The general editors of the Medieval Chronicles series have followed the more recent practice of placing the textual apparatus or, as here, the Textual Notes (pp. 347–410) separate from the text, in this case following the Explanatory Notes. There is much here to explore not only for textual critics but for scholars of reception and language.

In one part of the Introduction Marvin presents the best account I have read of the history of scholarship on the *Brut*, and – if there are any doubters left – the best case for concerted work on the whole of the textual tradition of the *Brut*. It is the textual tradition that most demands attention. This volume is a major contribution to *Brut* studies, Anglo-Norman studies and medieval studies in general, and Julia Marvin is to be commended for producing an edition that will no doubt be in use for many generations to come.

William Marx, University of Wales, Lampeter

WILLIAM MARX AND RALUCA RADULESCU, EDS.
Readers and Writers of the Prose Brut. Trivium 36.
University of Wales, Lampeter, 2006.

It is a pleasure to review an important collection of essays which could only have been assembled after Lister Matheson's 1998 study of English prose *Brut* manuscripts. Matheson categorizes the diverse groups of this much-rewritten historiographical text, thus enabling a variety of specific endeavors and approaches. William Marx and Raluca Radulescu's introduction to the nine essays arranges them into three themes, namely the prose *Brut*'s origins and development, the evidence of marginalia for readership and reception, and late medieval and early modern reception. These categories overlap, necessarily, in that the marginalia in question date to the sixteenth and seventeenth centuries and reflect significant uses to which several manuscripts were put. As a whole, the volume's contents bear interest in their consideration of prose *Brut* texts and their manuscripts as any other late medieval materials might be approached: this special issue of *Trivium* represents a significant achievement in drawing the *Brut* further within the pale of medieval literary, historical, and textual studies. One key to (re)invigorating a neglected text is to end its treatment as an oddity *sui generis* and essentially to perform its participation in concerns shared by other practitioners in the field.

Opening *Trivium* 36 is Julia Marvin's groundbreaking inquiry into the antecedent texts underlying the earliest version of the Anglo-Norman prose *Brut*. Though essentially an excerpt from the introduction to her edition (Boydell, 2006) of the *Brut* text in London, British Library, MS Additional 35092,[1] the essay's strength is its discussion of the *Brut*'s many intertextual relations, including not only Wace's *Roman de Brut*, Gaimar's *Estoire des Engleis*, and the *Havelok* texts, but several "house" chronicles whose influence beyond monasteries has been difficult to trace hitherto. The Barlings chronicle (Oxford, Magdalen College, MS lat. 199) emerges as a crucial link between the prose *Brut* and material shared with the *Annals of Waverley* in London, British Library, MS Cotton Vespasian A.xvi. Though Friedrich Brie acknowledged similarities with *Waverley* in 1905, Marvin's work is the first in a century to provide evidence for refocusing Brie's dismissive comment, a much-needed move given that many medieval chronicles hold parts of their content in common with *Waverley*.

The work of another important edition underlies William Marx's discussion of the text known as the *Davies Chronicle*, part of which he has reedited as *An English Chronicle, 1377-1461: A New Edition* (Boydell, 2003).[2] Here, Marx successfully refutes Paul Strohm's assertion that insufficient evidence of textual reception exists during the later Middle Ages. As Marx observes, several other essays in the current collection belie this claim; his own examines the tension between a Lancastrian continuation (1377-1437) to the prose *Brut*, and the Yorkist continuation (1440-61) that follows it. Though the second and third examples of kingship, betrayal, and rebellion occurring towards the current article's end are echoed from Marx's introduction to his edition—see, for example, pp. 67-68 alongside the edition's pp. lii-liv—the elaboration is very welcome for offering an alternative view of such moments within a complex narrative.

In complementary ways, Tamar Drukker and Elizabeth Bryan's respective essays examine writing as a tool for processing thought as one reads. Drukker's study attends to marginal repetitions, sometimes in more than one language, of textual content. She finds that while perusing the *Brut*, readers often flagged similar features, such as kings' lives and certain provocative themes; reasonably enough, they chose at times to expand marginally upon a narrative moment that the main text glosses over. As an appendix, Drukker catalogues the heading-like annotations in two manuscripts (London, British Library, MS Additional 12030; Cambridge, University Library, MS Ee.4.32) and classifies them by type. Bryan investigates marginal repetitions and dilations as well, with an impressively detailed discussion of the sixteenth- and seventeenth-century readers of Oxford, Bodleian Library, MS Hatton 50. For Bryan, the three noting readers can be seen clearly to interact: for example, Reader 1's hotly anticlerical comments sometimes receive a temperate reply or correction from the more neutral Reader 3. Bryan appends useful transcriptions of these readers' dialogue as well as a list of narrative events that received marginal comments from multiple readers; the latter bears an intriguing resemblance in choice of topic to the short, *précis*-sized historiographical texts that preceded the prose *Brut*.

John Scattergood investigates another means of processing the conventions of genealogical and historiographical *mise-en-page*, a refiguration undertaken before the manuscript he discusses (Dublin, Trinity College Library, MS 505) was set for release. His essay includes several plates of the prefatory material that precedes TCD 505's *Brut*, namely an illustrated *précis* deriving ultimately from Geoffrey of Monmouth, which the codex presents in two columns that have been bisected by genealogical roundels. Scattergood's discussion seeks to contextualize the codex in several useful ways, from Gabrielle Spiegel's study of French genealogies to fifteenth-century antiquarian activity in England. What may be the nearest analogue, however, is the set of interrelated thirteenth- and fourteenth-century rolls on which Olivier de Laborderie has published several articles,[3] and it would be exciting to see TCD 505 placed in dialogue with its formal antecedents.

Carole Weinberg uses Edward III's interest in chivalry to focus her comparison of one prose *Brut* text's continuation (in Cambridge, Corpus Christi College, MS 174) with Ranulf Higden's *Polychronicon* and material attributed to Adam Murimuth. Though she warns readers that the results highlighted by the key passages she has found are "tentative and speculative," the essay demonstrates some very persuasive connections; this confluence of texts would support further inquiry and discussion, whether by Weinberg herself or others. Raluca Radulescu revisits a favored topic, fifteenth-century gentry readers, and draws attention here to the tendency of codices these readers owned to contain both prose *Brut* texts and family genealogies, thus binding together national and personal histories. Amy Noelle Vines, too, addresses the personal ties several owners had with prose *Brut* manuscripts. She provides useful evidence that women as well as men inscribed their presence into the margins of prose *Brut* texts—though surely we can be secure by now in the awareness that women participated in these textual communities. Like Drukker and Bryan, Vines appends a transcription of one marginal annotator's work (in San Marino, Calif., Huntington Library, MS HM 136).

To close the collection, Christy Desmet's discussion of the prose *Brut*'s afterlives follows Albina and her sisters through John Hardyng's *Chronicle*, printed by Richard Grafton in 1543, and through William Caxton's 1480 printing of the English prose *Brut* (though she cites Wynkyn de Worde's 1515 publication of the latter). For early modern readers of these printed texts, Albina comes to displace Brutus as the rightful original settler of the island, whether dubbed Albion or Britain. Desmet suggests that though sixteenth-century humanists sought to eradicate both foundational figures as non-historical, antiquarian imperatives enabled their restoration within literary productions instead—Edmund Spenser's *Faerie Queene* as well as late Elizabethan and early Jacobean tales of Lear / Leir—to supply a suitably legendary backdrop for contemporary political concerns.

Though occasional errors occur in several essays, they are superficial (e.g., "Hidgen" for "Higden," p. 41; "Beinicke" for "Beinecke," p. 197). The volume's Index of Manuscripts demonstrates how widely the essays range and offers a final, quiet gesture towards the relevance of prose *Brut* studies to other aspects of late medieval literature, history, and commentary.

Sharon K. Goetz, University of California, Berkeley

NOTES

1. It appears that *Trivium* 36 was originally to be published in 2005, in which case Marvin's essay would have served as advance notice of the edition's significant findings.

2. Reviewed in JEBS 9 (2006): 186-8.

3. See also Chapters Three and Four of my unpublished dissertation, "Textual Portability and Its Uses in England, *ca.* 1250-1330" (Univ. of California–Berkeley, 2006), which (respectively) analyze similar prefatory material accompanying *Li Rei de Engletere* and discuss *Li Rei*'s transformation from codex to roll form.

KARI ANNE RAND, ED.

The Index of Middle English Prose: Handlist XVIII: Manuscripts in the Library of Pembroke College, Cambridge, and the Fitzwilliam Museum.
Cambridge: Brewer, 2006.

Kari Anne Rand continues her excellent work with the volumes of IMEP, this time covering Pembroke College, Cambridge, and the Fitzwilliam Museum (where her research was interrupted by the new Courtyard development). The Pembroke medieval collection consists either of books from the medieval working library, or most interestingly, from William Smart's 1599 donation of (opinions vary) around a hundred manuscripts from the Benedictine abbey of Bury St Edmunds. Sadly, there are very few vernacular items, and the provenance is unknown of the only three manuscripts which contain Middle English material of any length, MS 215 (Chaucer's *Boece*), MS 237 (the Wycliffite sermon cycle, the principles of indexing somewhat abbreviated, as explained on page xxi), and MS 285, here called "Sacerdos Parochialis" texts.

More rewarding is the collection of medieval manuscripts at the Fitzwilliam Museum, the bequest in 1816 of Richard Fitzwilliam, seventh Viscount Fitzwilliam of Merrion (together with the money to build the Museum). The bequest included 130 illuminated medieval manuscripts, three-quarters of them Books of Hours, exhibited in 2004 and 2005 but mainly to be viewed surrogately in the fine *Cambridge Illuminations* (2005), edited by Paul Binski and Stella Panayotova. In particular, the Macclesfield Psalter was a star of the exhibition (there is a small but well illustrated book of that name also published by the Fitzwilliam Museum). Thanks to M. R. James, Assistant Director and then Director from the 1880s to 1890s, by the time of his catalogue in 1895, the Museum owned 239 medieval manuscripts and fragments. In the first half of the twentieth century, especially the first decades, further medieval manuscripts arrived, most significant for this volume the McClean bequest of 203 medieval manuscripts in 1904.

The volume provides numerous items of interest, even where the Middle English content appears to be non-existent (e.g., Fitzwilliam 2-1957, the Shaftesbury Hours made for Elizabeth Shelford, abbess of Shaftesbury, 1505 to 28), or the prayer to the Virgin and measure of the Cross in the Carew Poyntz-Hours (MS Fitzwilliam 48). The longest texts are found in the religious material of McClean MS 127 (Nicholas Love), MS 129 (*The Life of St Katherine of Alexandria*), and MS 132 ("The Doctrine of the Heart," and the two texts which were to make up the much later publication of *The Tree and xii. Frutes of the Holy Goost* (STC 13608), and McClean MS 181 (*Canterbury Tales*), MS 182 (Lydgate's *The Serpent of Division*), and MS 186 (the *Brut*). Of interest to the present reviewer is Fitzwilliam MS 261, the volume of plague tracts which (from the heraldry) seems to have belonged to Lady Margaret Beaufort (but not purchased by the Museum until 1902). MS Fitzwilliam 41-1950 is also intriguing. It was probably made for Margaret Beauchamp, and has notes on the Syon and Sheen pardons and various prayers in English, but it was in the abbey of Echternach in Luxemburg in 1610. (Margaret's first husband, John Talbot, first Earl of Shrewsbury, had died in the last battle of the Hundred Years' War in 1453.) This IMEP volume provides an excellent reference tool, but it is also a fascinating book to dip into and find the unexpected fact or association. While not so comfortable for browsing, it would be a tremendous boon to have IMEP available on-line, and we must assume that day will come, if not in our own lifetimes!

Sue Powell, University of Salford

JANE ROBERTS.
Guide to Scripts used in English Writings up to 1500.
London: British Library, 2005. xv + 294 pp.

This book is set to become the only tool for teachers and learners of English medieval palaeography. Jane Roberts provides a brief but clear and concise general introduction to the subject, covering the scope of the work, an overview of the scripts of the period, the fate of manuscripts in the post-medieval period, some general points on describing scripts, how the book is organized, and notes on the transcriptions (but the first letter fifteen lines up on p. 8, <w>, should surely be "wynn" instead?) and on Latin abbreviations. All this is easy to take in and tells the beginner everything (s)he needs to know.

The book is then divided into eight further parts: insular background, Anglo-Saxon minuscule, English Caroline minuscule, proto-Gothic, Gothic *textualis*, anglicana, and secretary, with a brief afterword. The format of each of the sections on scripts is the same: a comprehensive but concise explanation of the script and its context and manuscripts, followed by plates (a magnificent 58 in all) on the recto of the pages, and *en face*, the manuscript and hand details, followed by a transcription, a careful and immensely helpful description of the features of the hand as shown in the plate, and notes on contexts for the manuscript, its size, and a bibliography. Forty supplementary plates are interspersed through the volume, as addenda to each transcribed and discussed plate, to illustrate or complement aspects of the main plate. There is a section too of eight color plates (from the Lindisfarne Gospels to the York Plays) which replicate plates in the main body of the text to give a fuller picture of the effect of color on decoration and layout. As a teaching/learning tool, it is invaluable, but even for those of us who are not palaeographers or learners, the book offers a number of uses (not to mention mere pleasures). The plates have been chosen from the most representative, but also the best known, of medieval texts, so that there are facsimiles of pages from (for our period) *Piers Plowman* (two different manuscripts), *The House of Fame*, *The Canterbury Tales*, *Troilus and Criseyde* (three different manuscripts, with one reproduced too in color), Gower, Hoccleve (Chaucer's portrait page), Lydgate, and others. There are also lesser texts which are rarely seen in facsimile: *The Cloud of Unknowing* with a continuous marginal Latin gloss (in color as well as in black and white), Lavynham's *Little Treatise on the Seven Deadly Sins* (two interestingly different manuscripts), and pages from the York Plays and the rather scrubby Digby Plays. Several plates are of historic and social relevance, as well as serving as examples of their scripts, for example, the inscription that records a common profit book, the scribe's signature at the end of the unique copy of Margery of Kempe's autobiography, and a page from the unique copy of the *Morte Darthur* that shows two scribal hands. There is a full bibliography and indexes cite people and places in the plates, people in the commentaries to the plates, manuscript pages discussed, and other manuscript pages reproduced.

Jane Roberts has dedicated the book to her former teachers and friends at the University of London, Julian Brown and Albinia de la Mare. These are great names, and the work is a worthy tribute to them.

Sue Powell, University of Salford

JOHN SCAHILL with MARGARET ROGERSON.
Middle English Saints' Legends, Annotated Bibliographies
of Old and Middle English Literature VIII.
Cambridge: Brewer, 2005. vii + 209pp.

Readers will already be familiar with these very useful Annotated
Bibliographies of Old and Middle English Literature. This, the eighth volume,
deals with medieval saints' lives in thirteen separate sections, including an
overview of general works, *South English Legendary*, *Smaller Vernon Legend
Collection*, *Northern Homily Collection*, *Scottish Legendary*, John Mirk's *Festial*,
Speculum Sacerdotale, The Sermon Collection in Bodleian MS. Hatton 96,
Osbern Bokenham's *Legends of Holy Women*, *Gilte Legende* and William Caxton,
John Capgrave's Saints' Legends, *St Erkenwald*, and independent legends. Each
section begins with a summary of the state of research, with cross-references
to the bibliographic items which follow. Each item in the bibliography is fol-
lowed by a description (the annotation) of greater or lesser length, depending on the entry, since some entries are obscure (but nonetheless welcome).
See, for example, item 352: seven pages on "The *Golden Legend* as Treated by
Jacobus de Voragine, William Caxton, and Henry Wadsworth Longfellow,"
published in *The Dublin University Magazine* in 1852, and others of greater significance, such as, for example, item 396: Manfred Görlach's *The South English
Legendary: Gilte Legende and Golden Legend*. The annotations include details of
reviews of the bibliographic item. There is an index of scholars and critics
responsible for the bibliographic items, an index of the Middle English texts,
and a manuscript index. The standard of accuracy appears to be very high.
John Mirk's *Festial* is very well known to me, but I found a few items I had been
unaware of. They were minor but to find even minor items after nearly forty

years of working with the *Festial* indicates the thoroughness of the bibliography. The excellent index (which lists individual sermons and legends as well as titles or authors) notes all references to a work in the bibliography as a whole.

Sue Powell, University of Salford

EDITH SNOOK.
Women, Reading and the Cultural Politics of Early Modern England.
Aldershot: Ashgate Publishing, 2005. 188 pp.

Edith Snook's book is a study of representations of reading in women's writing between 1540 and 1640. Anne Askew, Katherine Parr, Dorothy Leigh, Elizabeth Grymeston, Amelia Lanyer and Mary Wroth create images of themselves as readers and discuss reading practices through a generically diverse range of texts. Snook argues that for them all "being a reader provides a way of speaking, a technique for authoritative self-invention." She draws on Kate Flint's observation in *The Woman Reader* 1837-1914 that reading is "a fulcrum: the meeting-place of discourses of subjectivity and socialization" and argues that previous studies of early modern women's reading have focused on the subjectivity – the private aspirations of the woman reader – and neglected the woman reader's potential social and political significance. Snook sets out to redress this balance, and she makes a persuasive case for the social importance of early-modern women's reading: it politicizes the family and gives women a direct relationship to the state.

In each chapter, material is organized around a particular woman or pair of women who exemplify different aspects of the female reader – Askew and Parr and Protestant polemic; Grymeston and the Catholic reader; Leigh and the maternal voice. Through this framework Snook achieves a neat balance: her authors clearly lead her discussion, which is always well rooted in their texts; at the same time, Snook maintains her own focused line of enquiry. Theories of women reading and writing sensitively illuminate and never overwhelm the selected texts. Thus the book's structure gains an advantage which outweighs its attendant disadvantage – while the argument within each chapter is clear, the reader must sometimes work hard to connect the argument across chapters, and, occasionally, important theoretical discussion seems unhelpfully delayed. For example, it is eighty-one pages into the book that Snook discusses the generation of a history of gender through a fusion of political history, traditionally told as a history of men, with social history, the more usual venue for discussing women's history. She cites Joan Wallach Scott's observation that through such an approach "women's history critically confronts the politics of existing histories and inevitably begins the rewriting of history." Snook's exposition of a history of gender occurs during her discussion of Dorothy Leigh and Puritan discourses of vernacular reading: applicable as it seems to Snook's entire project, it might perhaps have come in the introduction, alongside Snook's helpful discussions of early modern education and the female reader.

Although the majority of texts considered by Snook circulated in print, a number of texts surviving in manuscript form are also included, and there is generous discussion of the special circumstances relating to manuscript as opposed to print circulation. For Lady Mary Wroth, the ability of a reader to undermine a writer, particularly a woman writer, is threatening, and coterie publication in manuscript facilitates authorial control. For Elizabeth Grymeston, the manuscript practice of compiling commonplace books offers a method by which every reader becomes a potential writer. "With her allusive and citational mode, she writes as a reader," and ultimately makes it into print. For early modern women, commonplace books and manuscript compilations were common reading material as they had been for their medieval predecessors, and Elizabeth Grymeston's reading and writing methods may have much in common with those of Julian of Norwich, for example. [1]

David Wallace has recently urged the questioning of "periodization paradigms" as applied to English women: the experiences and texts of premodern women may be misaligned with narratives of development built on an overwhelmingly male canon. [2] It is a strength of Snook's book that it includes brief but significant allusions to medieval women as vital antecedents of her subjects. In particular, Snook indicates continuities between Amelia Lanyer's *Salve Deus Rex Judaeorum* and medieval women's devotional readings of Passion narratives. As is clear in premodern literature, Passion narratives required exemplary, affective readings, readings which can now be understood only through a historicized understanding of their local social, cultural, political contexts. Scholars of early modern literature must recognize the same reading model at play in Lanyer's work in order that Lanyer's represented readers may illuminate the dynamics of gender, class, and race in seventeenth-century England. As Snook's work indicates, the English milieu which emerges from a study of the *Salve Deus Rex Judaeorum* may be very different from that which emerges from *The Book of Margery Kempe*, say, but for Kempe and Lanyer there may be striking similarities in the function of the Passion narrative in the creation of their books.

Elisabeth Dutton, Worcester College, University of Oxford

NOTES

1. In my forthcoming book, *Compiling Julian: The Revelation of Love and Late-Medieval Devotional Compilation* (Woodbridge: Boydell and Brewer, 2008), I argue that Julian of Norwich's text is influenced structurally by the form of compilation, which also validates the voice of the author-compiler. Snook indicates that similar influences are at play in Grymeston's work.
2. David Wallace, "Periodizing Women: Mary Ward (1585-1645) and the Premodern Canon," *Journal of Medieval and Early Modern Studies* 36:2 (Spring 2006): 397-453.

MICHAEL STAUNTON.
Thomas Becket and his Biographers.
Woodbridge: Boydell, 2006. viii + 246pp.

Interest in Thomas Becket has extended from his dramatic death in his own Cathedral on December 29, 1170, for over three and a half centuries until the comparably dramatic end to his cult with the Henrician dismantling of his shrine. Phyllis Roberts' inventory of sermons, *Thomas Becket in the Medieval Latin Preaching Tradition: An Inventory of Sermons about St. Thomas Becket c. 1170-c.* 1400, Instrumenta Patristica, 25 (The Hague: Martinus Nijhoff, 1992), found 184 separate manifestations of the saint in sermon form. The source (unusually in sermon lives) was not primarily the *Legenda Aurea*. Instead, and appropriately, the principal sources were home-grown, those works (mostly Lives) which appeared in England almost immediately, as a direct reaction to, and record of, his martyrdom.

Michael Staunton's book deals with ten works, seven completed within four years of 1170, two within six years, and the other a decade later. Nearly all the memorials were written by men who had known Becket personally; four had been present at his murder (John of Salisbury, Benedict of Peterborough, William of Canterbury, and Edward Grim), and John of Salisbury and William Fitzstephen had served in Becket's household for many years. But others, such as Guernes, the French cleric, barely knew him (certainly not to speak to) and yet felt emboldened to record his life. Some works were by what might be called professional writers and scholars: John of Salisbury, Herbert of Bosham, Alan of Tewkesbury, and Benedict of Peterborough, but clearly others were not. Edward Grim was just a clerical visitor to Canterbury on the day of the murder and nearly lost an arm defending

Becket. These were men who had known Becket in some small or great way and wanted to memorialize so remarkable and controversial a man and his death.

Staunton organizes his book so as to bring out the differences between these men and their accounts, and then to take the reader through the saint's life as it appears in the different manifestations. After a concise and clear introduction, six chapters deal with the biographers themselves, followed by a further five chapters which study crucial periods of Becket's Life: conversion, conflict, trial, exile, and martyrdom. In these five chapters, Staunton constructs a life of Becket based on the twelfth-century material and other contemporary sources, looking at these crucial episodes in order to see how, with the benefit of hindsight, the biographers interpreted Becket hagiographically, seeing now the sanctity displayed in his throwing off his worldly life, his conflicts with the King, his encounters with his other opponents, his flight to France in 1164, and his return to an embraced martyrdom in 1170. This is an original, highly readable book, well rooted in its sources, but widely accessible to anyone interested (and what medievalist cannot be?) in England's most famous saint.

Sue Powell, University of Salford

ANNE F. SUTTON.
The Mercery of London: Trade, Goods and People, 1130-1578.
Aldershot and Burlington, Vermont: Ashgate, 2005. xvii +
670pp.

EBS conferees and JEBS readers will be familiar with Anne Sutton's
meticulous and often ground-breaking use of the archives at her disposal as
Historian Emeritus to the Mercers' Company of London. In this weighty and
important volume, she has charted the rise and fall of the London mercery
(broadly, haberdashery) in seventeen packed chapters, from "Definition and
Location: The London Mercery 1130s-1230s" to "A New Company?" The brief
conclusion and summary characterize the 1578 Mercers' Company as by then
"an endowed 'institution' with charitable responsibilities, and no longer a
body of traders concerned to protect and facilitate their particular mistery."
  The fifteenth and sixteenth centuries are likely to be of particular
interest to readers of this *Journal*. Chapter 7, "Success on All Sides: The
Mercers in Fifteenth-Century London," considers in its first section the role of
books and education in the piety of the late medieval mercers, the famous
Dick Whittington among them, and assesses the relationship of mercers to
literacy, heresy, book ownership, and pious outreach. In tracing and identifying mercers, the reader is considerably aided by three of the five appendices,
which give the names and (for benefactors) the biographies of mercers who
were benefactors, wardens, and mayors of London up to 1578. Chapter 8, "The
Mercery Trade in London: Prosperity and Conflict," looks at the roles of
women, apprentices, and others in the trade, and (for there is much practical
business information here, very ably handled) protectionism at home and
abroad. Chapter 9 has a very useful final section on "The Mercer Governorship

of Caxton, Pickering and Wendy, 1462-85," which puts Caxton in pre-printing business context. Chapter 13, "Religious Change, Wealth and Faith," looks at the mercers after the Reformation: the conservatives (and here there is interesting material on the Guild of the Holy Name of Jesus at St Paul's), the book traffic from the Netherlands which brought evangelical texts to London, the role of the English house in Antwerp, the various persuasions of the mercers and their families, the profits made from the dissolution of the monasteries, and the effects of the religious changes of the sixteenth century on the mercers' great church, its furnishings, liturgy, clergy, and preaching.

Anne Sutton has demonstrated in her many publications the importance of the London companies in understanding medieval London in all its aspects. This book will be invaluable to those who wish to know more about one of the most influential London trades and as a reference book (it has an excellent index) will offer new discoveries to any scholars interested in medieval London and its inhabitants and life. It is not to deflate the book that I note two typos only – an omitted letter on page 405 and the impish running head "The Mercenary of London" on page xvii.

Sue Powell, University of Salford

Notes on Libraries and Collections

Rare Books and Special Collections, University of Montreal / Livres rares et collections spéciales de Université de Montréal
Samuel Bronfman Building
Bibliothèque des lettres et sciences humaines
3000 Jean-Brillant St, 4th Floor
Montréal, Québec, Canada
Telephone: (514) 343-6111, extension 3832
http://www.bib.umontreal.ca/CS/
Hours: M, T, H, F 9am-5pm, W 9am-7pm. Hours may be reduced outside of term-time.

Steadily growing since its foundation in 1985, the Rare Books and Special Collections library comprises more than 120 000 books, documents and artifacts. The collection is particularly strong in the history of Quebec and Canada and in the related fields of travel and exploration. It has equally impressive holdings in the history of medicine, theology, education, and literature, much of which would be of interest to members of the Early Book Society. The collection is especially worthy of attention because it is not indexed in the major catalogues, such as the various STCs. Only 15 of the 35 incunables are in the ISTC, and even fewer appear in Goff's Incunabula in American Libraries. (When Goff lists the volumes, he provides the location of Bibliothèque de St-Sulpice, Montreal, whence these volumes originated.) Most of the collection is recorded in the computerized library catalogue (ATRIUM), but other treasures may be uncovered in the old card catalogue. Latin books dominate, but the volumes' publication locations and provenances range across Europe. The collection contains one medieval manuscript, several manuscript fragments dating from the late eleventh or early twelfth century and from the fourteenth century, 35 incunables, and about 300 sixteenth-century printed books. The holdings increase yearly: acquisitions since June 2006 include volume five of Galen's Opera omnia (Basel, 1538) and Simon Goulart's French translation of Seneca, Les Oeuvres morales et meslées de Sénecque (Paris, 1595).

The library's complete manuscript is a fourteenth-century vellum copy of Raymundus de Pennaforte's (1175?-1275?) selections from the

Decretales of Gregory IX, the *Summa de poenitentia et matrimonio*. The text, which measures 146x100mm, is presented in two columns of 46 to 53 lines per page and contains rubrication and several decorated initials in blue and red ink. It is written in one hand—a small Gothic book hand—with the exception of annotations in English and Latin. These annotations are written in English hands dating from the fourteenth through the seventeenth century. They cover the first four pages of the volume, which were left blank, and are also found in the margins of the text itself. The manuscript is thought to be of English origin.[1]

Eight manuscript fragments, consisting of 8 full sheets (400 x 280mm), were found in the binding of the library's copy of volume four of Antonius de Florentius's *Summa Theologica* (Venice, 1481). The fragments, which contain incipits and decorated initials, form part of an Italian legendary dating from the late eleventh or early twelfth century. The second set of fragments was recovered from the bindings of the library's copy of the 1493 reprint of the four-volume German Bible, glossed by Nicolaus de Lyra. The fragments represent three separate works: the first set of fragments consists of three folios of text and musical notation from a late fifteenth-century German hymnal; the second, a folio of a fifteenth-century German Gradual; and, finally, four folios of a commentary on canon law, written in Latin in the fourteenth century.

Of the 35 incunables, about a third are in their original bindings and many contain illuminations and hand-colored woodcuts and initials. For instance; all of the woodcuts in volume four of the 1493 German Bible, already noted for its manuscript fragments, have been hand-colored; Thomas Aquinas's *Catena aurea seu continuum in quatuor evangelistas* (1475) contains miniatures of Matthew and Luke, and a miniature of Aquinas himself adorns his *In omnes S. Pauli apostoli epistolas* (1495). The oldest of the incunables, the *Expositio super canonem missae* and Guillaume Durant's *Rationale divinorum officiorum*, both date from 1470. Other incunables of note include: Ulricus Ulmer's *Fraternitas Cleri* (c. 1483) and Pietro di Piasi Cremonse's 1491 edition of Dante's *Commedia* with Landino's commentary. The 1491 Dante is the first edition of the *Commedia* to contain some of Pietro Mazzanti da Figline's emendations to Landino's commentary, and it is the first to follow the *Commedia* with a selection of the poet's *canzoni*. A useful companion piece to the latter is a first edition of Aldus Manutius's *Le terze rime di Dante* (Venice, 1502). This was the first edition of the *Commedia* to be based on a newly available manuscript, edited by Pietro Bembo, as well as the first to be printed in a small format. Also noteworthy is a copy of the fourth and final volume of the Bible glossed by Nicolaus de Lyra, with his *Contra perfidiam Iudaeorum* appended (1481). It is in a contemporary binding, with underlings and hand-painted initials and rubrication in red, blue, and gold. On the front and back outer leaves of the volume are secular and sacred English songs with musical notation written in a late fifteenth- or early sixteenth-century English hand. One complete leaf, with recto and verso inscriptions, and one torn leaf is found at each end of the book.

The collection includes sixteenth-century prints of works by authors such as Aristotle, Plato, Boethius, Plautus, Ovid, Erasmus, Maimonides, Peter Lombard, Augustine, Ptolomy, Pico della Mirandola, Machiavelli, Petrarch, Robert Estienne, Henri Estienne, Guillaume Budé, Leon Battustra Alberti, Aquinus, Avicenna, Reginald Pole, Antonio de Guevara, and Justus Lipsius. Early texts of travel and exploration abound: there are works by Jacques Cartier, Hernán Cortés, Francisco Alvares, Arrien, Odoardo Barbosa, Piero Quirino, Giosafat Barbaro, Alberto Campense, Paolo Iovio da Como, Ambrogio Contarini, Giovanni Battista Ramusio, Fernando de Alcaron, Jerónimo Osório, André Thévet, and many others, all printed prior to 1600. A second important strength is medical texts: sixteenth-century editions of works by Galen, Hippocrates, Ambroise Paré, Pierre Franco, Francisco López de Villalobos, Aulus Cornelius Celsus, Girolamo Fracastoro, Jean Fernel, Jean de Gorris, and Charles Estienne are held at the library.

While rich in Latin publications, the earliest English books in the collection date to the seventeenth century. Four out of these five English volumes reflect the library's strength in travel narratives. They are: a copy of the third edition of Samuel Purchas's *Purchas his Pilgrimage* (1617); Edward Grimeston's translations of Jean de Serres's *A General Inventory of the History of France* (1607) and of José de Acosta's *The Natural and Moral History of the East and West Indies* (1604); and, the English translation of Martino Martini's *Bellum tartaricum, or, The Conquest of the Great and Most Renowned Empire of China* (1654). The fifth early English print is Richard Baker's 1642 English translation from Italian, *Discourses upon Cornelius Tacitus*. The copy of Purchas is not indexed in L.E. Pennington's *The Purchas Handbook*, and none of these five volumes appears in the STC.

The Rare Books and Special Collections library is on the fourth floor of the "Bibliothèque des lettres et sciences humaines," situated in the main university campus. The university is centrally located, easily accessible by public transport, and, as is to be expected from a large, urban campus, a wide variety of amenities—cafés, restaurants, shops, ATMs—and tourist attractions can be found within walking distance. The library is open to the general public. Upon entry to the rare books room, readers will be asked to show a piece of valid photo identification. In addition, readers can obtain temporary access to the computer catalogue and to the internet, as well as borrowing privileges from the library's main collection. In order to do so, scholars based outside of Canada should provide a letter of introduction from their department chair. Academics from other Canadian universities have borrowing and computer privileges through the various national and provincial agreements in place; they must show the presentation card distributed by the library at their home institution. Wireless internet service is provided, and ethernet ports are available at all desks in the reading room. The library is a lovely place to work: it is modern, bright, quiet, and comfortable, and the staff is extremely helpful. I hope to see some of you here in the future.[2]

Joyce Boro, Université de Montréal

NOTES

1. This manuscript is described in Bruno Roy, "*Spicilegium Montis Regii*: Description de quelques manuscrits conservés à Montréal," *Memini. Travaux et documents publiés par la Société des études médiévales du Québec* 3 (1999): 171-194.
2. I would like to extend a special thanks to Geneviève Bazin, the director of the library, for her assistance with this project.

University Archives
Université de Montréal
Roger-Gaudry Building
2900 Édouard-Montpetit St, room E-615
Montréal, Québec, Canada

Telephone: (514) 343-2251

http://www.archiv.umontreal.ca/

Hours: M-H 9 am - 12 pm and 1:30 pm – 5 pm. They prefer visitors to call in advance to make an appointment.

A second medieval manuscript is housed in the archives of University of Montreal. Also located on the main campus, the archives are a short walk up the hill from the Rare Books library. The archives are open to the public, but scholars should make an appointment prior to visiting the center.

This manuscript volume consists of six separate manuscripts on paper, originating in Vienna or nearby in Central Europe and bound in the early fifteenth century. In the fifteenth century, it belonged to the Viennese intellectual and rector of the University of Vienna, Jean Harrer de Heilbronn (d. 1495), as is suggested by his ownership mark on folio 1r: "Liber domini Iohannis de Haylprunna. Contenta in eo require in principio libri." The first of the six manuscripts is Hugues Ripelin's *Compendium theologicae veritatis* (f. 1r-118v). The second includes three texts, possibly gathered by Marsile of Padua: Marsile of Padua's *Parviflores philosophorum* (f. 119r-146r); Nicolas de Dinkelsbühl's *De perceptione sacramenti in die Parasceves* (f.146v-148r); and, *Sermo de Assumpcione* (148r-149r). This is followed by de Dinkelsbühl's *De communione sub utroque* (f.150r-161r); Erhard de Pölan's *Commune aureum de sanctis* (f. 162r-239v); Leonard Haydel's *De philosophia christiana* (f. 240r-256v); and, the sixth manuscript is Theobaldus de Sexania's *De erroribus Iudeorum in Talmut* (f. 257r-272v).[1]

Joyce Boro, Université de Montréal

NOTES

1. This manuscript is described in Bruno Roy, "*Spicilegium Montis Regii*: Description de quelques mansucrits conservés à Montréal," *Memini. Travaux et documents publiés par la société des études médiévales du Québec* 3 (1999): 171-194.

About the Authors

Joyce Boro is Assistant Professor of English at the Université de Montréal. Her edition of *The Castell of Love: A Critical Edition of Lord Berners's Romance* will be published in 2007 in the Medieval and Renaissance Texts and Studies series by the University of Arizona. She is also the author of further articles on Berners, *Huon of Burdeux*, and romance as well as of reviews for this journal.

Alexandra Barratt is Professor of English in the Department of Humanities, at the University of Waikato, New Zealand. She has recently published *The Knowing of Woman's Kind in Childing: A Middle English Version of Material Derived from the Trotula and Other Sources* and is currently at work on *Anne Bulkeley and Her Book in Early Tudor England*, a detailed study of London, British Library MS Harley 494, for the Texts and Transitions series published by EBS and Brepols.

Margaret Connolly was Senior Lecturer in Medieval and Renaissance English at University College Cork until 2005; she currently teaches part-time at the University of St. Andrews and is a general editor of the Middle English Texts series. Her publications include *Contemplations of the Dread and Love of God* (EETS o.s. 303, 1994); *John Shirley: Book Production and the Noble Household in Fifteenth-Century England* (1998); and (with Thomas G. Duncan) *The Middle English Mirror: Sermons from Advent to Sexagesima* (MET 34, 2003) She is currently preparing *Index of Middle English Prose Handlist 19: The Manuscripts of Cambridge University Library, Main Collection Dd-Oo*.

Juliana Dresvina is currently pursuing graduate work at Magdalene College, Cambridge. For her Master's degree from Moscow State University (History Faculty), she focused on the writings of Julian of Norwich. Her doctoral project is an interdisciplinary study of the cult of St Margaret of Antioch in medieval England, due to be finished later this year. She has recently produced a new catalogue of St Radegund's Priory charters (available online). Her new edition of Julian of Norwich's *Revelations of Divine Love*, with a preface by Rowan Williams, is currently being prepared; for this edition, she is also supplying the first-ever Russian translation of Julian's writings.

Martha Driver is Distinguished Professor of English and Women's and Gender Studies at Pace University in New York. A co-founder of the Early Book Society for the study of manuscripts and printing history, she writes about illustration from MS to print, book production, and the early history of publishing. In addition to publishing some 40 articles in these areas, she has edited thirteen journals in ten years, including *Film & History: Medieval Period in*

Film. Her books about pictures (from woodcuts to film) include *The Image in Print: Book Illustration in Late Medieval England* (British Library Publications and University of Toronto) and *The Medieval Hero on Screen: Representations from Beowulf to Buffy*, edited with Sid Ray (McFarland).

Elisabeth Dutton is Research Fellow of Worcester College, University of Oxford. She has published on the late medieval mystics, compilation and miscellany manuscripts, and medieval and Renaissance theater.

Alexandra Gillespie is an Assistant Professor in the Department of English at the University of Toronto. She works on late medieval literary culture and manuscripts and early printed books: she has recently published *Print Culture and the Medieval Author* (Oxford University Press, 2006).

Sharon K. Goetz is Associate Editor at the Mark Twain Papers & Project at the University of California-Berkeley. She recently completed her dissertation, "Textual Portability and Its Uses in England, *c.* 1250-1330," and several entries for the *Encyclopedia of the Medieval Chronicle* (Brill, forthcoming). Her day job involves textual criticism in both codicological and electronic contexts; her current research investigates successive layers of revision in several late-thirteenth century manuscripts.

Carrie Griffin is a temporary Lecturer in medieval and Renaissance English at University College Cork. She teaches courses on medieval and early modern drama, outlaw literature, and the reception and treatment of medieval literature in the Romantic and Victorian periods. Her research interests lie in manuscripts and early printed books, palaeography, materiality and book history, and in transmission and reception theories and medieval literary theory. She is co-director of the *Making Books, Shaping Readers* research project at the English Department, UCC (http://www.ucc.ie/en/mbsr), and she is currently preparing an edition of the Middle English *Wise Book of Philosophy and Astronomy*.

Carl James Grindley is an Assistant Professor in the English Department of Hostos College, City University of New York. His recent works include: "The Elementary Middle Ages," in *Mass Market Medieval*, edited by David Marshall (McFarland, 2007):140-153, and "Arms and the Man: The Curious Inaccuracy of Arms and Armor in Contemporary Film," *Film & History* 36.1 (May 2006): 14-19. Four chapters of his novel *The Fear of Contagion* will appear this spring in Miles Clark's upcoming *Red Anthology* (No Record Press).

Maidie Hilmo is Adjunct Assistant Professor at the University of Victoria and is currently working with Kathryn Kerby-Fulton on A *Guide to Middle English Manuscript Studies: Medieval Book Culture and Reading Practices*, funded by the University of Notre Dame. She is the author of *Medieval Images, Icons, and Illustrated English Literary Texts: From the Ruthwell Cross to the Ellesmere Chaucer* (Aldershot: Ashgate, 2004). She is also co-editor of *The Medieval Professional Reader at Work: Evidence from the Manuscripts of Chaucer, Langland, Kempe, and Gower* (Victoria: University of Victoria, English Literary Studies, 2001) and of *The Medieval Reader: Reception and Cultural History in the Late Medieval Manuscript* (New York: AMS Press, 2001).

Sanae Ikeda is a PhD student in the English Department at Keio University in Tokyo and has been working on printed books and studying the printing process. She is currently working on a project to research the Philip Gaskell Collection at the Keio University Library.

William Marx is Reader in Medieval Literature at the University of Wales, Lampeter. His most recent publication is a collection of essays edited with Raluca Radulescu, *Readers and Writers of the Prose Brut*, published as volume 36 of *Trivium* (reviewed in this issue of JEBS).

Linne R. Mooney is Professor in Medieval English Palaeography at the Centre for Medieval Studies, University of York. Her current research centers on late-medieval English scribes, and she is the author of many articles on scribes and book production in late-medieval England. She is currently working on a book about scribes of Middle English literary manuscripts in late fourteenth- and fifteenth-century England. As the editor of "*Nota Bene*: Brief Notes on Manuscripts and Early Printed Books," she is a regular contributor to JEBS.

Daniel W. Mosser is Professor of English at Virginia Tech, where he also directs the Center for Applied Technologies in the Humanities. He is co-editor and co-creator of the Thomas L. Gravell Watermark Archive (www.gravell.org), author of the "Witness Descriptions" on the *Canterbury Tales* Project's digital editions, co-editor of *Puzzles in Paper*, and the author of articles on Middle English manuscripts, fifteenth-century paper stocks, and Chaucer incunabula. He is currently completing A *Digital Catalogue of the Manuscripts and Pre-1500 Editions of the Canterbury Tales*, to appear on CD and the Web. He will be the Leverhulme Visiting Professor at the Centre for Medieval Studies at the University of York in fall 2007 and fall 2008.

Niamh Pattwell is Lecturer in Middle English Literature at the School of English and Drama, University College Dublin. She is currently editing an edition of *Exornatorium Curatorum* for the Middle English Text Series and working on the Index of Middle English Prose for Trinity College, Dublin, with V.J. Scattergood. Among other projects in progess is an article on a fourteenth-century book-list. Her recent publications include articles on The Sentence of Cursing and on simony in the "Pardoner's Tale."

Sue Powell is Senior Lecturer in English Language and Literature at the University of Salford, where she teaches the history of the English language, Chaucer and medieval Arthurian literature. As review editor for JEBS, she regularly contributes several reviews to each issue. Her essay "What Caxton Did to the *Festial*" appeared in JEBS 1 (1997). Her research interests are in manuscripts and early printed books, with particular relation to late medieval and Tudor preaching and devotional texts.

Stephanie Pryor is a Ph.D. candidate in Art History and Archaeology at the University of Missouri-Columbia and is expected to complete her degree in the spring of 2009. She specializes in Roman, late antique, Byzantine and medieval art. Her dissertation focuses on the visual programs of female rulers from the Hellenistic to late antique periods. She has worked on archaeological projects in Italy, including Rome and Pompeii, as well as in Israel.

Nicole Rice is Assistant Professor of English at Yale University. She has recently completed a book manuscript entitled *Spiritual Ambition and Religious Discipline in Late Middle English Literature*. This study of vernacular literary responses to lay spiritual aspirations in late-fourteenth-century England considers prose guides together with poetry and reformist texts. She is currently working on the surprising afterlives of fourteenth-century spiritual guides in fifteenth-century manuscripts: an article entitled "Walter Hilton's *Mixed Life* and the Transformation of Clerical Discipline" is forthcoming in *Leeds Studies in English* 2007. Other work in progress includes a collaborative article on light-bearing and civic controversy in the York and Chester play cycles.

Martha Dana Rust is Assistant Professor of English at New York University. Her first book, *Imaginary Worlds in Medieval Books: Exploring the Manuscript Matrix*, is forthcoming from Palgrave Macmillan in May 2007. Her current projects include a book on lists in late-medieval England and an electronic edition of Chaucer's *Clerk's Tale* for the Canterbury Tales Project.

Shaun Tyas is an independent publisher of academic history with a personal interest in the Middle Ages, bibliography and medievalism.

www.ingramcontent.com/pod-product-compliance
Lightning Source LLC
Chambersburg PA
CBHW061003280326
41935CB00009B/810